Gendered anthropology

During the last three decades a remarkable degree of progress has occurred in the study of gender within anthropology. *Gendered Anthropology* offers a thought-provoking, lively examination of current debates focusing on sex and gender, race, ethnicity and politics, and provides insights which are still too often lacking in mainstream anthropology.

The acceptance of gender as a new analytical category implies the acceptance of a knowledge that has formerly been considered marginal and on the periphery. Clearly, the reason for the absence of gender studies from mainstream anthropology does not reside in its lack of relevance to theoretical, methodological and ethnographical advances and the chapters in this volume show its capacity to bring new understanding to current controversial problems. Demonstrating this relevance, the contributors consider critically both advances in gender studies and contemporary controversial issues concerning gender and its interrelations with other areas including the effects of new reproductive technologies, rights to sexual variance, controversy over the nature of marriage, and the relationship between gender, class, ethnicity and race.

Gendered Anthropology will be of particular value to undergraduates and lecturers in social anthropology and gender studies.

Teresa del Valle is Professor of Anthropology at the Universidad del Pais Vasco/Euskal Herriko Unibertsitatea.

European Association of Social Anthropologists

The European Association of Social Anthropologists (EASA) was inaugurated in January 1989, in response to a widely felt need for a professional association which would represent social anthropologists in Europe and foster co-operation and interchange in teaching and research. As Europe transforms itself in the nineties, the EASA in dedicated to the renewal of the distinctive European tradition in social anthropology.

Other titles in the series

Conceptualizing Society
Adam Kuper

Revitalizing European Rituals
Jeremy Boissevain

Other Histories
Kirsten Hastrup

Alcohol, Gender and Culture
Dimitra Gefou-Madianou

Understanding Rituals
Daniel de Coppet

Gendered anthropology

Edited by Teresa del Valle

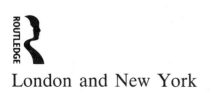

London and New York

First published 1993
by Routledge
11 New Fetter Lane, London EC4P 4EE

Simultaneously published in the USA and Canada
by Routledge
29 West 35th Street, New York, NY 10001

Reprinted in 1996

Phototypeset in Times by Intype, London
Printed and bound by Biddles Ltd, Guildford and King's Lynn

British Library Cataloguing in Publication Data
A catalogue record for this book is available from the British Library.

Library of Congress Cataloguing in Publication Data

Gendered anthropology/edited by Teresa del Valle.
    p.   cm. – (European Association of Social Anthropologists)
    Includes bibliographical references and index.
    1. Sex role – Cross-cultural studies.   2. Sex – Cross-cultural
    studies.   I. Series: European Association of Social Anthropologists
    (Series)
    GN479.65.G49   1993
    305.3–dc20   92-40487
                                                          CIP

ISBN 0–415–06126–1 (hbk)
ISBN 0–415–06127–X (pbk)

Contents

Illustrations

Contributors

Teresa del Valle, Professor of Social Anthropology and Head of the Seminario de Estudios de la Mujer, Universidad del Pais Vasco. She trained in both History and Anthropology and has taught at the University of Guam, was a researcher at the Micronesian Area Research Center, and was a grantee at the East–West Center of Honolulu, Hawaii. The result of fieldwork among the Chamorros of Guam (1975–6) was published as *Social and Cultural Change in the Village of Umatac Southern Guam* and *Culturas oceànicas, Micronesia* (1987). She was the first EASA vice-president (1988–90). Publications on Basque culture include: *Mujer vasca. Imagen y realidad* (1985) and *Korrika, rituales de la lengua en el espacio* (1988).

Hildegard Diemberger received her training in both social anthropology and Tibetan studies at Vienna University. Since 1982 she has been doing research in eastern Nepal and more recently in southern Tibet. Besides gender, her main topics are history, religious traditions and the conceptualization of landscape among Tibetan marginal groups, and she is currently working as a researcher of the 'Arbeitsgruppe für Ethnologische Studien Tibets', University of Vienna.

Marianne Gullestad, Research Professor of Anthropology at the Norwegian Centre for Child Research at the University of Trondheim, Norway. She has spent 3 years as a visiting research associate at the University of Chicago. Her fieldwork interests have led her to the study of Norwegian gender systems, family relations and the cultural practices of everyday life. Her many publications include: *Kitchen Table Society. A Case Study of the Family Life and Friendships of Young Working Mothers in Urban Norway* (1984) and *The*

Art of Social Relations. Essays on Culture, Social Action and Everyday Life in Modern Norway (1992).

Signe Howell, Professor in the Department and Museum of Anthropology at the University of Oslo, Norway. Fieldwork in the Malay peninsula led to *Chewong Myths and Legends* (1982) and *Society and Cosmos: Chewon of Peninsular Malaysia*. The applied dimension of her work is evident both from time spent in Kathmandu, Nepal at the International Centre for Integrated Mountain Development and from her report on *Women and Development in Nepal*.

Ruth Kronsteiner, University of Vienna, is working on her PhD thesis, 'Processes of "Hausfrauisierung" in a Black Sea village in Turkey in consideration of migration'. From 1985 to 1990 she worked in a women's association for Turkish migrants. She is co-founder of the Coordination Office of the Educational and Advisory Institutions for Women from Foreign Countries in Vienna and is currently training in analytical psychotherapy.

Marit Melhuus is Senior Lecturer and Head of Department at the Department and Museum of Anthropology, University of Oslo. She has worked for many years with Latin-American peasantries, including doing fieldwork in Argentina, which resulted in the publication *Peasants, Surplus, and Appropriation: An Analysis of Tobacco Growers in Corrientes, Argentina* (1987). Her last fieldwork was conducted in Mexico. She was formerly a researcher at the Work Research Institute, Oslo, heading a project on Norwegian seamen's families. Author of numerous articles focusing on gender, modernity and change, she is currently completing a manuscript based on a Mexican mestizo community.

Henrietta Moore, Lecturer in Social Anthropology, London School of Economics. Her published works include: *Space, Text and Gender: An Anthropological Study of the Marakwet of Kenya* (1986) and *Feminism and Anthropology* (1988).

Verena Stolcke, Associated Professor of Social Anthropology, Universidad Autónoma of Barcelona, Catalunya. She studied at the University of Oxford and subsequently taught at the University of Campinas in Sao Paulo, where she was head of the Department of Anthropology. She is the author of *Marriage, Class and Colour in Nineteenth-Century Cuba* (1974) and *Coffee Planters, Workers and Wives. Class Conflict and Gender Relations on Sao Paulo Plantations, 1850–1989* (1988). She communicates her knowledge in many different settings, including to feminist groups, university students, and at international conferences.

Sabine Strasser, University of Vienna, is working on her PhD thesis, 'Violence and consent. Gender relations in a village in Eastern Turkey'. She is a co-founder of a women's association for Turkish migrant women and is currently working in the Coordination Office of the Educational and Advisory Institutions for Women from Foreign Countries in Vienna.

Serge Tcherkezoff, Maître de Conférences of the Ecole des Hautes Etudes en Sciences Sociales (Paris). After teaching in Africa (Burundi), he began to analyse extensive archival material on the Nyamwezi-Sukuma (Tanzania) sacred kingship and ritual system (PhD, EHESS, Paris 1981, various published papers, book in process). Another study, of the classification system of this society, led to a comparative analysis of data and of methods in anthropology (*Dual Classification Reconsidered*, Cambridge University Press, 1987, original edition in French, 1983). After a field study in 1981–2, and others since 1987, in Western Samoa, he is studying Polynesian cultures (hierarchies, gender categories, ethos, political and cultural change), together with a reappraisal of the relevance of holistic models in anthropology.

Preface

This volume grew out of the panel 'Constructing Genders' at the first EASA conference (European Association for Social Anthropologists) held in Coimbra, Portugal, in 1990 and of which I acted as convenor. Five of the present chapters were presented as papers at the panel, while Chapter 6 by Sabine Strasser and Ruth Kronsteiner has been added subsequently. Henrietta L. Moore was the commentator at the panel.

Teresa del Valle

Acknowledgements

I first want to thank all the contributors and other people who participated in the panel 'Constructing Genders' at the Coimbra conference, as well as those who have written about the panel in the EASA bulletin and in other publications. The different opinions voiced were a proof that the issue of gender is neither an easy one nor one that can be obviated. Second, thanks to Hildegard Diemberger and Andre Gingrich for making the contacts with Sabine Strasser and Ruth Kronsteiner. Finally, I want to thank the members of the present Executive Committee, especially Kirsten Hastrup, Verena Stolcke and Marilyn Strathern, for their support in various ways, and Adam Kuper for his initial editorial help.

Introduction

Teresa del Valle

UNCOMFORTABLE FIELDS OF KNOWLEDGE

The study of gender is the field within anthropology where, objectively speaking, the widest set of advances have occurred in the last three decades. The case has been argued by Moore (1988); it is put forward by Howell and Melhuus, included here in Chapter 2; and it stood at the heart of the debate at the symposium 'Constructing Genders' at the Coimbra conference, as McDonald (1990) commented after the event. Through the presentation of the seven chapters that comprise this volume, I delve into the argument that the knowledge of gender, and gender systems, affect, question and contribute significantly to the discipline of anthropology as a whole.

A DIVIDED POPULATION: WHAT IS GOOD FOR SOME IS IRRELEVANT FOR OTHERS

Different theoretical periods can be recognized by systematic dominant characteristics (Moore 1988; Morgen 1989: 9). A review of the literature carried out by Quinn (1977) and Lamphere (1977) has proved most helpful in this respect, allowing one to see developments in the way studies have been conducted across different cultures. I stress the value of establishing an agreement on the points of departure. This allows for evaluations of what has been said, of the way it has been expressed and, concurrently, the identification of its ideological constructions. Indeed, the historical contextualization of developments in the field is relevant for apprehending the connection between the feminist movement and scientific advancements. There are examples of cumulative knowledge, of progress as a result of criticism and of divergent views. For feminist anthropology, it is too soon to look back unless it is to obtain a vision of its short but productive history in order to move ahead.

Gender studies are imbued with a critical approach and a certain amount of urgency in the manner concepts are presented, tested and revised, as the sequence of theoretical periods shows. The debate over the validity of the differences between sex and gender is once more posed by Moore in Chapter 7 as she gathers the thought of other female anthropologists. However, the use of the term 'gender', which has been constructed by English speakers, runs into considerable difficulties when it is used in other linguistic contexts. Di Coiri (1990: 134–6) points this out for the case of Italian and Spanish. In Spanish, 'género' is primarily understood as a category to differentiate names, adjectives, pronouns and articles; initially its anthropological usage leads more to confusion than to clarification, and people often use 'gender' as a substitute for 'sex'. It will take some imagination to construct a term that will not only account for the meaning attributed to gender in English, but will also be a more encompassing universal concept with the capacity to express the variety that is constantly being discovered about women and men cross-culturally. For this enterprise, the joint efforts of scholars from different cultural and linguistic backgrounds are necessary. Concurrently, the need for new concepts indicates that we are moving into new dimensions and that the old categories are a restraint on how the results of novel approaches to human experience can be expressed. In the meantime, we are faced with a discrepancy between the meaning/meanings attributed to the concept, and the need to expand and/or to transform it.

Stolcke (Chapter 1) stresses some of the fluidity of terminology. Sex, gender, and sexuality are shown as the products of the emergence of different trends in anthropology as well as in other fields. She continues on the path of wishing to make an entity out of gender but without recurrent reference to biological sex, an effort which represents a further step in the search for new knowledge concerning processes of social differentiation. As it turns out, the traditional division between cultural and scientific knowledge of biological phenomena as two separate realms has proved short-sighted. Gender scholars are posing questions that more and more will show the bias and the ideological constructs underlying advances in demography, genetics and new reproductive technologies.

This point surfaces in the fine critique of Dumont by Melhuus (1990), where she expresses her surprise at Dumont's problem concerning the acceptance of hierarchy underlying modern society. 'Had Dumont been interested in gender relations he might have seen that his idea of hierarchy is not as radical and difficult to grasp as he himself claims!' (1990: 153). Gender views and gender interpretations produce knowledge which affects the understanding of power and the elaboration of hierarchical differences. It contributes to the understanding of how processes of inequality are formulated and developed. Morgen (1989: 2–3) stresses the critical contributions to mainstream anthropology of the works of Ortner, Reiter, Slocum, Rubin, Leacock and others. The chapter here by Howell and Melhuus shows in detail how gender has affected the study of kinship and of personhood, even though this has not been openly acknowledged. Furthermore, Tcherkezoff's insightful critiques of previous interpretations of binarism and hierarchy in Samoan culture (Chapter 3) show the dynamism of gender studies: theory advances insofar as criticism is based on new reflections and new fieldwork. In fact, the recognition of different trends with identifiable positions will be a sign of reflective maturity.

However, frequently such contributions have been ignored, as Morgen stresses when talking about the centrality which Marcus and Fisher give to the self-conscious reflection on the writing of ethnography: 'while there are a number of references to gender in the book, and the index claims two references to "feminism", at no time do the authors credit feminist anthropology for its pioneering work on the issue of *representation* (primarily the representation of women)' (1989: 7).

The study of gender may make at times tangential contributions to ethnography yet poses the problem of an incomplete ethnography when it is ignored. Nash shows how research that has considered women 'has brought a multidimensional analysis to the study of Latin American society' (1989: 239). It has become clear, as Warren and Bourque indicate (1989: 398), that when we apply gender to the analysis of technology, and the impact of technological change, it no longer appears the neutral category that it has often been presented as. The consideration of women's lives reveals dimensions that have been overlooked. Poverty considered in general is different from poverty studied in relationship to the female population. The concept of the 'Feminization of poverty' draws attention to characteristics related to conditions produced by and about women; it questions the validity of an understanding of social inequalities and of economic analysis of contemporary societies which ignores gender. This embraces the recognition of emerging new situations for women, especially those of monoparental families as well as those of traditional circumstances of poverty that had been kept in the dark (Fernández Viguera 1990: 105). One would like to see the results of studies conducted by feminist anthropologists in Latin American, Western European and African countries, reflected in the general literature of economic anthropology. In turn, this knowledge should lead to questioning male policy-making of male-biased development and approaches to demographic control.

Female anthropologists who have studied different societies claim that 'we cannot describe institutions as if they were gender neutral when they are not' (Potash 1989: 189). And can we consider a social reality that is not genderized in Collier and Yanagisako's (1987b) phrase? The bias sometimes attributed to gender studies loses ground in view of the gaps presented by studies where society is described in a general way or where gender is silenced. Such studies cannot stand the test regarding knowledge of power distribution; criteria for distribution of wealth and labour; the inequalities that result from the application of indiscriminate technological development; and ideological constructions. The wealth of possibilities that Stolcke opens for us (Chapter 1) when she considers sex, gender, ethnicity and race, forces us to think in terms of what is missing when we address one of the four without having the others in mind. In the following chapter, Howell and Melhuus point out the possibilities contained in the fact that kinship systems are inherently gendered, and the consequences of this for theoretical and methodological considerations. It should lead, for instance, to a revision of the existing discrepancy between the sex categories of kinship diagrams, and the scarce information ethnographies give about sex and gender. The symbols of conventional kinship diagrams in anthropology present men and women as fathers, mothers, brothers, sisters. This structuring is rarely accompanied by concrete references to the significances and meanings contained by the terms and in the framework of gender relations they represent.

A difference between the early period of women's studies, which was concerned with origins and universalities, and the present one is that we are more aware of the complexity of the issues, and of the short-sightedness brought about by the ignorance of gender in the whole orientation of the discipline. This concern in turn acts as a springboard for new directions.

In considering how thought and action resulting from social movements interrelate with scholarly production, gender studies has been more innovative than any other field within the discipline in the same period of time. The influence of the feminist movement is acknowledged by scholars across disciplines: feminist theory offers redefinitions of the history of culture, of the concept of culture itself, of relations with nature, and of ranking systems and communication systems, as the philosopher Valcárcel says (1991: 69). Gender contributions within anthropology afford a good case through which to apprehend the dynamism created by scholars building up their knowledge on an awareness of outside influences on their fields of interest. As Strathern (1987) shows, agreements in objectives between anthropology and feminism lead both to conflicts of recognition and to acknowledgement of mutual contributions. Indeed, a genderized anthropology presents an excellent case study of the elaboration of orthodox academic knowledge over time, and of the difficulties many scholars encounter when they want to open new paths of enquiry. This is demonstrated by Strasser and Kronsteiner in the first part of Chapter 6.

Yet even within gender studies, and I fear this can be generalized to anthropology as a whole, knowledge is elaborated on the basis of the analysis of sources published mainly in English. Hopefully, in as much as indigenous people present their views and channel studies that are not generally known to the public eye, we can count on alternative sources of data and analysis. Without denying the existing dominion of English in scientific discourse, institutional policies of translation should help to incorporate knowledge from the periphery. This volume is a contribution to such an endeavour, as the papers incorporate thoughts and references from various languages and cultural settings. People have criss-crossed multiple frontiers. New names appear in their bibliographies and I assume they respond to the scope of each contributor's intellectual tradition.

Genealogical knowledge

What the philosopher Amorós has observed of the negative influence that women's lack of genealogical recognition has on the development of a strong identity for women as a category,[1] can also be applied to mainstream anthropology. The review of the literature on gender studies, however, points to just such a genealogy. There are references to key studies or to review articles representing an appraisal of seminal contributions. Even though it represents not a Eurocentric bias, as Morgen states (1989: 1), but an Anglo-Saxon one, an intellectual genealogy has indeed emerged.

Both Morgen and Moore (1988) give names, identify issues, state trends and rescue ethnographic examples. The result is a coherent body of knowledge which moves between the United States and Great Britain (in some instances a few French names are included), and can be contextualized within the social concerns of women and their struggles for social and cultural recognition.

Simone de Beauvoir and Margaret Mead are two solid ancestresses in this intellectual genealogy, and there already exists a sort of consensus about key influences and how different tendencies have developed their own lineages. The challenge at this point is to see how that genealogical reality, and what it represents and signifies, becomes integrated into the intellectual genealogy of the discipline. As McDonald has said:

> there are still some of us, however, who feel that the more self-consciously 'feminist' critiques of mainstream domains have largely left the old domains, their categories and assumptions, intact, that there is a far more daring theoreticality to be pursued, and that a self-delimiting 'feminist industry of critiques' risks becoming, in spite of itself, no more than the epistemological petticoats of the world it claims to challenge.
>
> (1990: 12)

The strategy is clear: if the genealogy is left as a separate category, the advancements gained towards a general theory of how inequality is created, transmitted and validated, will remain on the periphery. The genealogy will remain for the most part like a matrilineal system with uxorilocal residence and the few males entering the chart will have to acknowledge female ancestresses and a 'mother's brother's role' for themselves if they want to obtain a place. Concurrently, new initiatives for studying what has already been investigated might start from a male angle outside of the matrilineal system, under a different category – as if nothing had been done previously. If so, a process of 'stealing' women's accumulated intellectual wisdom might entail trying to introduce changes in 'residence rules' and thus developing some bias toward virilocality. Such a process has been studied in the Basque ethnographic context (del Valle 1991); it is alluded to by Morgen when she refers to the appropriation of gender contributions to what is identified as 'the reflexive movement in anthropology' (1989: 7); and is stated very forcefully by Marcia-Lees *et al.* (1989). However, there will be moments whan a name will be included in the general genealogy as has occurred with Strathern; the recognition of her contributions at the Coimbra

conference are stressed (Eriksen 1991: 76). Those of us who have
followed her contributions since the times when first women and
later gender were marginal categories, know Strathern has occupied
a central place in other matrilineal genealogies. Thus, main questions arise concerning not only the process of construction of knowledge, but that of its identification, validation and full incorporation.
How does the process of validation of knowledge occur within
anthropology? What are the mechanisms and how do they affect
women and men differently? This is a topic in need of further
research.

ADDRESSING ISSUES OF RELEVANCE TO CONTEMPORARY SOCIETY

More than any other field within the discipline, feminist anthropology is deeply connected to changes in society and the demand
for change emanating from diverse interest groups. Concurrently,
the degree of this connection gives a special element to the study
of gender, namely questions about the many situations in which
women live, and the many variations in what it takes to be a woman
or man.

We do not find the same interrelatedness in other fields such as
ecological anthropology and the ecological movement, or political
anthropology and minority movements, to mention a few. In our
contemporary society, at a time (1990–1) when in a very short
period we have been faced with contradictory discourses about the
right to engage in destructive war under the proclamation of its
sanctity,[2] and when nations have proclaimed the right to assume
the salvation of mankind without the consent of those who had to
be saved, it is difficult to find any kind of inspiration within contemporary anthropology, to situate the various affirmations and actions
critically.

There are numerous contemporary examples of racism and discrimination: the marginalization and horror of the Kurdish population; the horrors of natural disasters in overpopulated areas of
Asia such as Bangladesh; famine in African societies; the restrictions upon immigration. These do not fit into overall concerns of
the discipline, even though anthropology has data of populations
all over the earth, and the conceptual and methodological tools to
approach them. I am not arguing in terms of pure versus applied
anthropology. My position is geared towards the capability of
anthropologists (not of anthropology) to address issues which

transcend space, time, national alliances and academic intellectual traditions, in order to illuminate present-day world-wide pressing problems. They are difficult to address insofar as they are related to different levels of power structures. This is the point about the naturalization of social inequalities which Stolcke addresses in Chapter 1. She has sought to uncover their intellectual basis: the naturalization of social realities has the strength of making them immutable and is linked to different kinds of power. It poses and uses the strategy of interpreting cultural differences as an expression of fixed physical characteristics.

The 'fixing' of reality is a complex issue in that it is related to political processes and ideological justifications, as Stolcke says. She presents a good case for criticizing symbolic approaches where political contextualization is missing. For her, symbolic meanings 'structure inequalities between women and men as social agents'. She thus raises significant issues with respect to understanding the process of naturalization. And to those raised by other scholars (Moore 1988; del Valle 1991), she adds questions about the social dimension regarding demographic arguments and racial policies that are increasingly present in Europe. Thus she makes a case in favour of the capacity of anthropology to address constructively present-day problems. The key to it is the need to uncover how ethnic, racial and gender discrimination are based on interpretations of biological linkages.

When we consider critically both advances in gender studies and contemporary controversial issues concerning gender and its inter-relations to other areas of experience, we find that gender studies can help place the latter issues in a proper context. I refer to: (a) the effects of new reproductive technologies; (b) rights to sexual variance; (c) controversies over the nature of marriage and its linkage to heterosexuality and procreation; (d) relationships between gender, class, ethnicity and race; (e) the development of new domestic groups; and (f) construction of discriminatory discourses on the basis of its linkage to natural phenomena or religious transcendence. All these issues can be integrated into the framework of developing gender studies, for I believe it has the capacity to address them as general issues.

Strasser and Kronsteiner (Chapter 6) enter a greatly problematic field: the displacement and placement of populations and the mingling of culture and politics. At the present time, immigration constitutes a problem emanating from artificial constructions such as the concepts of a First and Third World; North and South; East and

West, and of Europe as a central area. Based on the knowledge I have of the 'guardian role' of boundaries assigned to the Spanish State by the European Community, I cannot but evoke those many other extreme situations concerning people from African countries in search of new economic opportunities in Europe which appear in the central pages of the newspapers ('Temas de nuestra época', *El Pais*, 1991: 1–8). The problems, questions and answers move, in Chapter 6, across boundaries from Vienna to Eastern Turkey, and are powerful precisely because they reveal current European trends of rendering certain non-geographic boundaries fixed: those boundaries which separate people on the basis of wealth, opportunities and power. Issues raised by Stolcke about the intellectual sources of racism are ethnographic realities in Strasser and Kronsteiner's chapter.

The shortcomings of fixed categories have a strong advocate in Moore's approach to the variability and fluidity of gender identities (Chapter 7). Her chapter intertwines the point with data from the other papers. Female as well as male identities are fluid and subject to change; as creations, they are products of specific social groupings acting in accord with particular value systems. Close attention to marginal situations may well give us new insights into the differences Moore posits, insofar as creative changes tend to emerge more from the margins than from circumstances regarded as normal (del Valle 1989: 145).

THE PROBLEM OF DISTANCES

The chapters in this volume contribute methodological insights in addressing the problem of distances. Even though gender scholars have often been criticized for choosing a subject embedded in their own experiences, they are the ones who face in a very creative manner the insider–outsider dilemma.

From the studies of gender, we see new integrative views arising. The approach which focuses on how women and men as social actors are conscious of their possibilities and limitations, and act pragmatically to achieve their ends once it is made clear that neither are mere pawns of political and economic manoeuvering (Potash 1989: 191), leaves no room for women's assumed passivity. Nevertheless, other studies show realities where, no matter how much women want to change their lives and make economic, legal and sexual decisions, they are restricted by the power of the State, the Church and/or the family. These studies lead us to recognize the relevance of seeing things through the perspective of time, and of deploying some type of systematic approach which allows for contextualization. An important perspective raised by anthropology lies in the concept of distance. Postmodernists have stressed the 'other' as a central category in anthropology, but whether we focus on the 'other', or on culture, or on systems as the object of our enquiry, the ability to play with distances is implied in all. Gender scholars have shown numerous examples of moving in their theorizing and research from 'woman' as a unifying category, to the identification of the variety the concept contains. Thus, gender scholars are well suited to face problems of shifting delimitation and categorization.

Inner boundaries

The concept of inner distance is well developed in the study by Gullestad about Norwegian homes (Chapter 5). The short distance that exists when one is studying women in one's own culture, as Gullestad does, reveals the depth which the closeness provides. She proposes three contributions to existing assumptions: (a) to the dimensions of power and prestige that had been of general concern in gender studies, she stresses those of love, sexuality, spiritual communion and dependency; and, she implies, the analyst should constantly be open to new experiences and new research questions to ask; (b) to a dynamic approach, she brings the balance between the study of the differences and the sameness between the genders; and (c) to a holistic view, she places particular stress on the interaction between gender and other kinds of social differentiation, concentrating on gender and class for her study. The discussion about the position of gender in relation to the other sources of differentiation mentioned – age, generation, kinship, race, ethnicity, region and social class – remains open.

Powerfully, the idea of equality and sameness emerges from the general framework of dominant ideologies, and constitutes the centre of social values among urban working-class families in Norway. Thus, Norway presents a strong case of a society with a dominant value also found in traditional feminism. And yet the existence of boundaries that differentiate outside from inside, and some of the symbols devised, are similar to those found in Mediterranean cultures which lack that ideology of equality and sameness. This makes the selection of the home as the object of study a good comparative strategy. The richness of the differences appears in the meanings attributed to each one of the inside–outside boundaries.

A valuable contribution lies in the way Gullestad focuses on the interrelations between the household's inhabitants. With this, she gives an equal place to both women and men in her account. Gullestad explores how the sense of the couple searching for an equilibrium in their contribution to improve their shared setting, is differentiated by class differences. This leads us to think in terms of possible conflicts in a household where the man and woman come from different socio-economic backgrounds. Would the ideology of equality and sameness in their own project of life be stronger than the different expectations about equality and sameness within their expected class orientations? Following Gullestad's discussion, one tends to think positively, that home improvement, as she puts it, is 'culturally central'.

Chapter 5 contributes to our understanding of how social and cultural values are expressed in an ordinary context. One comes to understand how aesthetic and moral values can have separate universes and be combined in the symbol of the house. It is a good example of the way shared strategies deal with diversity and complexity from the outside through working with a perceived unity and simplicity on the inside.

Highly relevant to this is the discussion of how the new trends within the home are intertwined with changes in the status of women outside. The strongest criticisms which feminist studies have made of women in the house are here given an answer through a new symbolic definition of the home by women. The central issue of negotiation entails strong communication between the couple. Given the fact that divorce remains high, home decoration appears as a strategy to bring more equality into the relations in the home. Without knowing the statistics for initiating divorce on the part of females or males, one can imagine that in those cases where women are the initiators, the strong drive for equality and sameness may be the reason. In this manner, Gullestad's chapter presents strategies which both focus on the household and are simultaneously compatible with the struggle by women to improve their social condition at a wide level.

Gullestad has given insights for the study of the home in relationship to other encompassing spaces. The home is not an isolated space but an expression of the way people navigate between family and friends; work and leisure; openness and closeness, to mention some of the spheres of action. Thus the home in this context appears as an active concept (del Valle 1991).

Across boundaries

In the search for new ways of understanding how gender is constructed and expressed, Diemberger (Chapter 4) and Tcherkezoff (Chapter 3) distance themselves from their own cultures and enter Nepalese and Samoan worlds. Some of the theoretical questions raised by Howell and Melhuus (Chapter 2) find an answer in both chapters as they show the interrelationship between gender and other aspects of social structure.

Diemberger's chapter presents a beautiful example of the construction of sexuality and reproduction where the female body attains particular importance for the social construction and interpretation of gender identity. We enter into the development of personhood and its cultural basis. A metaphoric richness emerges which links up with studies done by Godelier (1982) and Martin (1987). The conceptualization of kinship, it becomes clear, cannot be understood if gender is obviated. The female body as a central organizing principle has its context in history, religion, politics, ecology and economy, as links are established between the body, the surrounding space and the sacred. Symbols of the female body become vehicles for presenting kin relations.

The last part of Chapter 4 which refers to unusual women is highly interesting. Within the understanding of the predominance of male rule and male references as ultimate values, women emerge as sources of change and of power. It is true that they are marginal and unusual women, and this in turn confirms their power. However, they exist as models incarnating change. This creates an open path which shows the changing nature of the female's position. More knowledge of these women could be put in a cross-cultural comparison with women who in other cultures are considered marginal to their society.

Tcherkezoff applies Dumont's holistic methodology to the understanding of Samoans' views of their society, as he aims to dismantle binary interpretations of culture, and especially those related to gender and kinship categories (Chapter 3). He considers binarism as a foreign classification which does not allow native categorization to emerge. Through his knowledge of Samoan culture, he deciphers the intricacy of native terminology, and the situational usage of language, in an attempt to get at native views. Emphasis is placed on the contextualization of roles and categories within the framework of the entire cultural system. Instead of binary oppositions as other authors have advanced them, he identifies relations as a basic organizational principle. Relations are oppositions not in the binary sense but in the sense that each relation has two culturally recognized different elements, one of which embraces the other. The key to identifying which is dominant in each relation results from applying the most encompassing relation to the other. The outcome is a hierarchy of relations.

Instead of the binarism male–female, Tcherkezoff finds that the most encompassing relation is that of sister–brother; it is the source of all the others. And within that relation, the sister is the one that encompasses the other. The unequal distribution of male–female power, which Tcherkezoff acknowledges exists in Samoa, springs from a sister-oriented organization. In its broader sense, consanguinity rather than gender would be a higher-level principle; other categories, such as that of spouse, will be defined in relationship to men. Marriage places women in a rather dependent situation, while the sister always encompasses the brother. Rights and obligations defining the role of sister do not conform with meanings attributed to female, as the relation of pastor to village shows. The pastor (a male) has characteristics of the sister (a female). Furthermore, in this relation, the village is encompassed by the sister. Thus, in Tcherkezoff's view, not gender but consanguinity is the determining general principle.

SEARCHING FOR INTERPRETATIONS: WHY THE CONTRIBUTION OF GENDER STUDIES IS IGNORED

Concurrent with the opinion voiced, that gender studies have little effect on mainstream anthropology, there is a need to search for the reasons that would illuminate the issue.

It has been pointed out that resistance to incorporating the contributions of feminist anthropology within mainstream anthropology is related to the fact that the study of gender has been, and still is, the concern of women (McDonald 1990: 12). I have gathered abundant data from female anthropologists cross-culturally, and from professionals in other fields engaged in gender studies, to back this point. Male anthropologists, for the most part, claim that they cannot study gender because they do not understand it; it is women's concern. One interpretation would be that they have considered it a secondary field. Should they show an interest in this field, they will have to acknowledge previous work, and thus have to review previous accomplishments that ignored gender. One can admit innovations coming from a new school of thought, but to admit that a whole category of analysis has been left out historically is to recognize that something is incomplete.

However, the issue is much more complex than that. There are multiple reasons, ranging from the status of scholars to conceptual limitations and to cultural interpretations, that account for academic ignorance of feminist anthropology. Strathern (1987), after dismantling the argument about how the existence of different paradigms accounts for the separation of anthropology and feminism, argues that it is not the discrepancy between the fields but their very closeness that sets them apart. A further reason results from the interconnectedness between academic life and socio-cultural forces.

Academic life is not constructed in isolation, even though we might have to struggle to make our field relevant to non-academic people. Anthropologists are part of an integrated system of thought and action; they are influenced by the times they live in, and by general approvals and disapprovals about what is relevant or irrelevant in society. The interplay of various influences appears in the construction, validation and dissemination of knowledge. While in other areas within anthropology – economic, political or symbolic anthropology or kinship studies – the discipline's value is weighted in terms of consistency, clarity, creativity, explanatory and interpretative value, contributions to the field of gender are measured by other parameters set by a strong cultural and scientific bias. The identification of intellectual genealogies from within the field of gender, by internal recognition of contributions to the field of anthropology, are kept silent for the most part, as if they were isolated lineages. A few daring male anthropologists have recognized the chain of contributions. Those who have brought their findings into interaction with the accumulated knowledge coming from feminist anthropology, talk about fears of marginality, of feeling like strangers in a foreign world – while their female counterparts feel right at home. This is received as a new and uncomfortable experience and leads to the consideration that the search for explanations and interpretations of discrimination of knowledge has to be pursued in a framework wider than the strictly academic world.

The importance I attribute to the identification of this wide setting springs from my own experience as a female Basque anthropologist interested in the study of gender in a situation where, for the most part, contributions to Basque anthropology have been divided along the lines of sex. Studies of the *baserri* (rural total institution), if done by male anthropologists, do not incorporate critical studies done by their female counterparts. In this line, the creation, activities and research of the Women Studies Seminar of the University of the Basque Country are regarded as peripheral. Yet while the study of real women is set aside, Basque mythology about feminine identities may be the subject of intellectual endeavours.

In 1981, female researchers were faced with a strong male enthusiasm concerning the existence of a Basque 'matriarchy'. The issue was the subject of great debate in academic and non-academic circles during the 1970s and early 1980s; a time when, as far as I am aware, no other society or people was targeted with such a concern. The team study that we conducted over a period of three years and in seventeen communities dismantled the arguments about real female power. But this did not influence the convictions of the believers in matriarchy (del Valle *et al.* 1985). Thus the search for interpretations had to move from the phenomenon itself to the analysis of the strong emphasis placed upon ethnicity. It was found that the elaboration of the myth of Basque matriarchy constituted a gendered tool which had been used in the development of an ideology related to both historical and revolutionary nationalism. Basque matriarchy provided a powerful ethnic marker. It could not be dismantled by academic discourse because it affected key issues of Basque identity (del Valle *et al.* 1985: 44–54). The recognition of advancements in feminist anthropology questioned established beliefs about women's roles.

In summary, the acceptance of gender as a new analytical category implies the acceptance of a knowledge that has already been considered marginal and on the periphery; it is a way to understand society and culture that has been constructed, developed and expanded by those who are not placed at the centre where recognized knowledge develops and expands. In the final analyses, we are not faced with a purely academic issue about the production of knowledge. It is clear that the absence of gender study from mainstream anthropology does not reside in its lack of relevance to theoretical, methodological and ethnographical advances. The chapters in this volume show its capacity to bring new understanding to current controversial problems. It is rather a political issue which embraces a variety of items. In some social analyses, as in the Basque case, absence might be related to ethnicity, in others to the control of sexuality and reproduction, and in academia, to the control and validation of knowledge.

Thus the resistance gender scholars may face in having the results of their studies integrated and their contributions recognized should itself be deconstructed from a framework which considers the production of knowledge within the discipline. The issue concerns the areas where gender studies question basic assumptions and established findings; how the intellectual genealogy would be affected by internal contributions being recognized outside of this genealogy; and the process by which anthropological knowledge as such obtains validation.

There is a long way to go and I tend to think that the integration of knowledge will be, for the most part, something feminist anthropologists have to do. As Strathern says, the uncomfortable bond between anthropology and feminism 'is lived most dramatically in the tension experienced by those who practice feminist anthropology' (1987: 286). As we navigate between two fields, we have to search, to identify, to contextualize and to integrate questions and answers, names and baggage coming from both directions. It lies within our task, as some of the chapters in this volume show, to identify the linkages with mainstream thought, to deconstruct what has been affected by gender studies, and to place gender scholars in the general intellectual genealogy.

NOTES

1 Ideas expressed at sessions of the Seminars held in Madrid and Donostia San Sebastian between 1988 and 1990 related to the interdisciplinary study 'Mujer y Poder' [Woman and Power], sponsored by the DGICYT, the Institute of Philosophy and the CSIC and directed by Celia Amorós.
2 The reference here is to the Gulf War.

1 Is sex to gender as race is to ethnicity?

Verena Stolcke

La coustume est une seconde nature qui destruit la première.
Mais qu'est que nature, pourquoy la coustume n'est elle pas
naturelle? J'ai grand peur que cette nature ne suit elle-mêsme
qu'une première coustume, comme la coustume est une seconde
nature.

(Pascal, *Pensée*, 1670, quoted by Lévi-Strauss, 1985: 1)

The uterus is to the Race what the heart is to the individual: it
is the organ of circulation to the species.

(W. Tyler Smith, *Manual of Obstetrics*, 1847,
quoted by Poovey, 1986: 145)

Western common sense distinguishes nature from culture as two
self-evidently distinct aspects of human experience. This chapter
challenges such a dualist perspective. My aim is two-fold. As long
as they are not endowed with social meaning, nature and culture
might be conceived as two distinct realms. Often, however, social
orders are presented as natural facts. Here I want to explore how,
in class society, social inequalities tend to be marked and legit-
imated by construing them as rooted in natural differences. This is
not a one-way conceptual procedure. In addition, I want to pick
up Pascal's point that these 'natural facts' may themselves turn out
to be cultural constructs.

The image of women reflected in Dr Smith's assertion quoted
above is a case in point. It is exemplary of the way in which the
nineteenth-century medical profession conceptualized women on the
basis of a very particular notion of their nature. A few decades
later, another medical man elaborated further on this view of
women: it was, he argued, 'as if the Almighty, in creating the
female sex, had taken the uterus and built up a woman around it'
(Poovey 1986: 145). Women's essence resided in their womb. Yet,

perhaps inadvertently, Dr Smith added yet another idea. Not only did their womb define womanhood. The uterus and hence its bearer had a specific function, namely that of reproducing the race. In this chapter I propose to provide an explanation for this biologist's natural notion of women's role in Western culture and to suggest what 'race' has to do with it. The aim is to develop a theory of inequality in class society which will account for the relatedness of both phenomena.

Hitherto, feminist theory has envisaged women largely as an undifferentiated social category. In recent years, black women's dissatisfaction with what they felt to be white feminists' lack of sensibility for their specific forms of oppression has added, however, a new issue to the feminist agenda, namely how to address the way gender, class *and* race intersect in creating commonalities but also differences in the experience of women. As Moore insists, it is high time that we pay special attention to the differences among women:

> This phase will involve the building of theoretical constructs which deal with difference, and will be crucially concerned with looking at how racial difference is constructed through gender, how racism divides gender identity and experience, and how class is shaped by gender and race.
>
> (Moore, 1988: 11)

I want to go a step further and ask *why* there are these intersections between gender, race and class.

There is also another reason that adds urgency to this inquiry, namely certain demographic arguments and policies that accompany the building of the European Community. Widespread alarm among European politicians over declining birth rates and their alleged consequences for the future financing of the Welfare state, and a pro-natalist offensive to curtail the often limited gains made by women with regard to free abortion, go hand in hand with an increasingly explicit racism directed against so-called non-Europeans.

I do not pretend, however, to formulate a universal theory that accounts for cross-cultural variations in gender inequalities. To begin with, I only hope to elucidate the political processes and ideological justifications which, in an interdependent and dynamic manner, structure gender and 'racial' inequalities in bourgeois class society. The crucial phenomenon in this connection is the tendency in class society to ideologically 'naturalize' social inequalities. The central question is why, beside class, it is especially 'sexual' and

'racial' differences that stand out among other available characteristics of human beings (for example, body height) as significant
markers of social inequality, and how these interact in reproducing
women's oppression in general and the particular differences
between them in class society.

Initially, I survey the diverse ways in which feminist theory has
addressed the social construction of gender hierarchies. The human
species reproduces itself bi-sexually; I focus especially on the controversial causal nexus between the natural fact of biological sexual
differences between human males and females and the engendered
symbolic meanings which structure inequalities between women and
men as social agents. As a next step, I discuss some of the vast
literature on race and ethnic relations of the past three decades.
Here, my focus will be mainly on British and some North American
studies of race relations. I deal with notions of ethnicity and ethnic
group only insofar as the terminological disagreements and the
uneasy conceptual shifts in these studies between the terms 'race'
and 'ethnicity' exhibit specific theoretical problems similar to those
entailed in the analysis of gender relations. The main question
refers to the very 'nature' of the supposedly natural differences
which are endowed with social meaning to mark relations of
inequality. Note, however, that my approach is neither constructivist nor relativist but anthropological-historical. As I argue, gender
inequality in class society results from a historically specific tendency
to ideologically 'naturalize' prevailing socio-economic inequalities.
As I see it, this 'naturalization' is an ideological subterfuge intended
to reconcile the irreconcilable, namely a pervasisve ethos of equality
of opportunity of all human beings born equal and free with really
existing socio-economic inequality in the interest of the latter's
beneficiaries. It is this ideological 'naturalization' of social condition, which plays such a fundamental role in the reproduction of
class society, that accounts for the specific importance attached to
sexual differences.

FROM SEX TO GENDER

The term 'gender' as a category of analysis was introduced into
feminist studies in the 1970s. Feminist research had demonstrated
that what were then called sexual roles varied widely cross-culturally
(Moore 1988: especially Chapter 2). Hence, these could not be
simply reduced to the inevitable natural and universal fact of sex
differences.

The analytic concept of 'gender' is meant to challenge the essentialist and universalist dictum that 'biology is destiny'. It transcends biological reductionism by intepreting the relationships between women and men as cultural constructs which result from imposing social, cultural and psychological meanings upon biological sexual identities. As a consequence, it became necessary to distinguish between 'gender' as a symbolic creation, 'sex' which refers to the biological fact of being female or male, and 'sexuality' which has to do with sexual preferences and behaviour (Caplan 1987; Showalter 1989). In order to explain these cross-cultural variations in the relationships between women and men, the historical and social roots of these variations needed to be sought.

Upon the introduction of the concept of 'gender' followed the development of gender theory. It is not devoid of disagreements. Although the theorization of gender as a social creation has gained ground progressively, as yet feminist theory neither provides an undisputed model for its analysis nor is there consensus about the concept of gender itself (e.g. Jaggar 1983; Moore 1988). Gender has become a kind of academic shorthand that stands for socially defined relationships between women and men, but its political meaning and implications are not always clear. The categorical approach characteristic of women's studies, because it focused attention on experiences – be they disadvantages or achievements – primarily of women *per se*, found political expression in the struggle for equal rights to men. Gender theory, by contrast, introduced a relational approach that involved the study of women in their relationships with men. It is not always self-evident, however, that this opened the way for the analysis of culturally diverse forms of male power and domination over women and of what caused them historically. Only from this perspective does gender theory imply a new, subversive gender politics that challenged not only male power but also the socio-political roots of gender inequality. Moreover, from this vantage point, the goal is no longer to become as alike as possible to men, but to radically transform gender relationships, a political project which, in turn, requires overcoming all forms of social inequality (at this point admittedly a utopian dream).

Theorizing gender relations as cultural constructs entails at least two sets of analytical questions. Because gender theory challenges earlier biological essentialisms, it problematizes and opens for new scrutiny the manner in which the natural facts of sex differences are related to gender constructs. Simultaneously, the concept of gender as a socio-historical form of inequality between women and men draws attention to other categories of difference which are translated into inequality, such as race and class, and poses the question as to how they intersect (Stolcke 1981; *Signs* 1987; Showalter 1989: 3).

One crucial contentious issue in gender analysis refers to whether, and if so how, the biological facts of sex differences are interconnected with gender categories cross-culturally. In other words, what are the factual differences out of which genders are construed? Or, even more radically, does gender as a cultural construct always necessarily have something to do with the natural facts of sex differences?

Already in the early 1980s, Judith Shapiro perceived the conceptual difficulties involved in separating gender from sex.

Sex and gender serve a useful analytic purpose in contrasting a set of biological facts with a set of cultural facts. Were I to be scrupulous in my use of terms, I would use the term 'sex' only when I was speaking of biological differences between males and females, and use 'gender' whenever I was referring to the social, cultural, psychological constructs that are imposed upon these biological differences . . . Gender . . . designates a set of categories to which we can give the same label cross-linguistically, or cross-culturally, because they have some connection to sex differences. These categories are, however, conventional or arbitrary insofar as they are not reducible to, or directly derivative of, natural, biological facts; they vary from one language to another, one culture to another, in the way in which they order experience and action.

(Shapiro 1981, quoted by Collier and Yanagisako, 1987a: 33)

Collier and Yanagisako, (1987a), by contrast, have more recently defied the necessary link between sex and gender by challenging the persistent tendency in comparative studies to attribute the cultural organization of gender to the 'biological difference in the roles of women and men in sexual reproduction'. They see this as being analogous to the genealogical reifications so characteristic of conventional anthropological studies of kinship systems which Schneider (1985), for example, challenged in the United States some time ago, and of which another example is the extraordinary anthropological controversy over the alleged *ignorantia paternitatis* of certain 'primitive' peoples (Leach 1966; Delaney 1986). But while anthropologists nowadays generally acknowledge that theories of conception and kinship systems are cultural rather than biological phenomena, to question the connection between sex and gender is very novel. Collier and Yanagisako, in effect, suggest that instead of taking for granted the biological roots of gender categories, whatever their culturally specific realizations may be, we ought to start out by questioning such a universal connection: 'we argue against the notion that cross-cultural variations in gender categories and inequalities are merely diverse elaborations and extensions of the same natural fact' (1987a: 15).

Still, whereas Collier and Yanagisako question the biological rooting of gender, they take for granted sex differences as natural facts. McDonald (1989: 310) has rightly pointed out, however, that even views of biology and of physiology, and for that matter of nature as such, are socio-political conceptualizations. A cursory review of the history of biology, of embryology and of images of the body, provides abundant evidence of this (for example, see Mayr 1982; Bridenthal *et al.* 1984; Martin 1987a; Hubbard 1990; Laqueur 1991). At this point, the reader may be invaded by an eerie feeling of rootlessness. In order not to be trapped in an endless constructivist spiral, which can never provide an explanation for *why* certain 'natural' facts are conceptualized in culturally specific ways, what needs to be done is to examine the historical background which accounts for particular views of biology and nature and vice versa, i.e. to ask *why* particular social relationships are conceptualized in natural terms.

Challenges to established wisdom, such as that by Collier and Yanagisako, have a liberating effect for future cross-cultural research, even if, as they are well aware, we cannot easily jump over our own culture's conceptual shadows. But precisely for this reason, we ought to analyse also our own preconceptions. That is what I want to do here, namely to unpack and examine the cultural assumptions which inform conceptualizations of biogenetic substance and inheritance and gender constructs in bourgeois class society. This is a necessary step toward elucidating how and why class, race and sex intersect in structuring gender relations. The interpenetration of 'natural', supposedly biological facts, 'cultural' meanings and socio-economic relationships is the crucial point.

FROM RACE TO ETHNICITY AND BACK

Harding (1986) has recently drawn attention to the intersection between gender and race to show how these different forms of domination affect women and men or whites by contrast with blacks in particular ways: 'in cultures stratified by both gender and race, gender is always also a racial category and race a gender category' (Harding (1986: 18); for further references to the links between gender, class and race see Gordon (1977); Carby (1985); Haraway (1989)). For the most part, however, the interplay between gender, class and race has hitherto eluded a clear conceptualization and explanation. Analyses tend to focus on the differing socio-economic effects for women of these categorizations rather than on the roots of, and links between, these combined systems of inequality. One exception is Gordon's (1974) beautiful and early study of birth control in America. As Gordon showed, doctrines of social-cum-racial purity were the result of a particular socio-economic structure and decisively informed notions of gender and hence women's experience. Moore (1988: 86), on the other hand, has rightly insisted that the issue is not one of a mere convergence or 'coalescence', a kind of adding-up process, of several forms of oppression in the configuration of women's social condition and of gender relationships. The actual interconnections between gender, race and class remain, none the less, unclear.

By contrast with feminist scholars' awareness of 'race', a concern with gender is conspicuously absent from the recent literature on race and ethnicity. Highly politicized polemics over the conceptual meanings and social implications of race, ethnicity and racism occupy a prominent place instead. I will deal with this debate on three grounds: first, to establish the development of the contemporary usage of 'ethnicity' in addition to or replacement of 'race' in research on so-called race relations; second, to disentangle the ambivalent meaning of 'ethnicity' and 'ethnic group'; and third, to suggest that despite this conceptual shift, a continuity can be detected between what some authors in the past three decades – when analysing racial tensions in the United Kingdom and more recently in Europe – have designated the 'new racism', and older racist doctrines and discriminations.

With rare exceptions (for example, M. G. Smith 1986; van den Berghe 1986), it is now acknowledged among scholars that in biosocial terms 'races' do not exist among human beings. The alleged 'natural' basis of cultural diversity in 'race', no less than the systems of inequality and exclusion predicated on racial differences, are socio-historical constructs. On the one hand, phenotypical characteristics which tend to be interpreted as indicators of racial difference and are used to legitimate racial prejudice and discrimination reflect only a fraction of a group's genotype. On the other, there are well known instances of racism where there are not even visible and coherent phenotypical differences. To emphasize this ideological character of 'racial' discrimination, the concepts of 'ethnicity' or 'ethnic group', in the sense of cultural identity, have recently been substituted for the term 'race'.

The usage of the terms 'ethnicity' and 'ethnic group' to designate a category of people bounded by a number of common traits is recent by contrast with 'race', which is of much older origin (Corominas 1982; Conze *et al.* 1984), and 'racism', said to have become prevalent only between the world wars (Rich 1986: 12). A report published in 1935 by the Royal Anthropological Institute on *Race and Culture* distinguished racial types but also contested the strictly scientific applicability of the concept. The same year, Huxley and Haddon in *We Europeans* attacked the Nazi usage of 'race' as an adequate anthropological category and proposed the term 'ethnic' instead. This was the first symptom of a significant shift in social science vocabulary dealing with 'race' (Rich 1984: 12–13).

The term 'ethnic' came into more widespread usage in the postwar period. A humane ethical revulsion against the Nazi racial doctrines led many academics to avoid the term 'race'. The intention was to stress that human groups were historical, cultural phenomena rather than biologically determined categories of people exhibiting common hereditary moral and intellectual traits. The *Oxford English Dictionary* records the first usage of the noun 'ethnicity' in 1953 (Tonkin *et al.* 1989: 14–15).

Still, a change in terminology does not necessarily transform social reality, nor the ways of looking at it. This was evident almost from the start. The social scientists consulted under UNESCO's post-war project to demystify racist doctrines exhibited considerable conceptual and political disagreements. One group interpreted so-called racial problems as ethnic (read cultural) problems. Others accepted that racial differences were used as markers of social inequality but denied any justificatory intent. Yet others wanted to see the term race relations reserved for situations marked by racism (Rex 1986: 18*ff*).

The shift in usage from 'race' to 'ethnicity' had at least two consequences. On the one hand, it tended to downplay or side-step prevailing racism, that is, discriminations and exclusions ideologically justified as resulting from supposedly really existing racial, and hence hereditary, moral or intellectual deficiencies. On the other, 'race', by being relegated to the realm of nature, by contrast with ethnicity understood as cultural identity, was paradoxically reified as a distinct phenomenon.

Thus the American sociologists Glazer and Moynihan (1975), for example, endorsed a rather vacuous and circular 1973 definition of 'ethnicity', according to which it referred to 'the condition of belonging to a particular ethnic group'. They interpreted instances of group tension such as those between blacks and whites in the contemporary United States as 'ethnic conflicts' over access to civil rights and economic opportunity. In typical liberal fashion, they regarded the 'objective condition' (1975: 1) of ethnicity as one more criterion of social stratification which, on account of the 'ethnic revival' in the 1960s, might even have displaced social class as the main divide in modern society (Cashmore 1984, citing Glazer and Moynihan 1975). The British sociologist Rex, however, criticized this usage of the purportedly cultural notion of 'ethnic group' in the place of that of 'race' as a liberal approach to the problem of racism precisely because it neutralized the conflictual consequences of racial situations (Rex 1973: 183). Race and ethnicity were not independent elements of social stratification but ought to be understood in the context of systems of domination which they endow with meaning (Rex and Mason 1986: xii–xiii).

Yet another conceptual innovation is the growing usage of the term xenophobia. Thus, some European politicians and scholars see in the upsurge of anti-immigrant sentiment on the Continent an expression of xenophobia rather than racism, that is, an 'understandable' hostility towards strangers which is attributed to an allegedly universal antagonism towards others. As Touraine recently argued,

> The rise of xenophobia – which is not the same as racism from which it is far removed *since what is questioned here is a culture rather than a race* – forms part of a set of different and at times even opposed movements of opinion which are, nonetheless, of the same nature.
>
> (Touraine, *El Pais*, 12 June 1990: 15, *my emphasis*)

This distinction is debatable. In a somewhat later article, the same author provides a striking example of the way in which politically charged euphemisms such as ethnicity or xenophobia may serve as a cover-up for racism. Here, Touraine argues that xenophobia is a reaction against social groups which endeavour to be incorporated into the French middle class: 'Racism, by contrast, is directed against those who have marginalized themselves [*sic*] and who, being asocial [*sic*], are judged and condemned on account of their social conduct, not in social terms . . . but due to their race' (*El Pais*, 29 October 1990: 8). In fact, what Touraine means by 'self-marginalization' is the refusal to become assimilated. As examples he mentions the Negroes in the United States, and Caribbeans, Hindus and Pakistanis in the United Kingdom, all of which he designates 'ethnic groups'.

The dispute as to whether 'ethnicity' and 'race' are interconnected phenomena or whether they refer to distinct systems of social classification appears to be analogous to the puzzles over the extent to which sex differences constitute the natural basis out of which gender relationships are construed. As McDonald has recently pointed out,

> Just as there has been a move away from talking of 'race' to talk of 'ethnicity', so too there has been, over the same period, a move away from biologistic and essentialist understandings of sex differences toward an understanding of *gender*.
>
> (1989: 310, *original emphasis*)

And then she suggests that it is as impossible to get at an essential ethnic identity as it is to know what 'men' and 'women' are *really* like (McDonald 1989). Yet, I would argue that there is a factor which complicates this apparent analogy. Demonstrably, 'races' in bio-social terms do not exist among humans. Humankind can be classified in terms of a few phenotypical characteristics which express only a fraction of their genotype, but there is no evidence that moral or intellectual differences are associated with these physical characteristics. All the same, common cultural traits often tend to be attributed to 'race'. By contrast, sexual dimorphism exists among humans. Thus, the issue at stake seems to be the inverse, namely whether gender relationships in all circumstances can be attributed to this physiological 'fact'. In other words, racist discriminations are based on a natural 'fact' which is itself an ideological construct, namely 'races', while gender hierarchies seem to be rooted in the really existing natural fact of sexual dimorphism.

In a recent survey of what is commonly understood by the term, Just (1989) in effect argues that the notion of 'ethnicity' is devoid of any distinct status. Such group attributes as territory, historical continuity, language and culture merely serve as evidence for membership of a particular ethnic group but not as a definition of ethnicity: 'Ethnicity itself, ethnic identity, is left to have some independent existence, some essential definition, even if that definition remains wisely inarticulated'; yet, he adds:

> There is, however, a Joker in the pack (and it seems to be a Joker studiously avoided by the academic proponents of ethnicity): namely, race! . . . in fact the notion of race has acted (and, regrettably, continues to act) as a biological substitute for – indeed, as an earlier formulation of – ethnicity.
>
> (Just 1989: 76–7)

Morin (1980) gives an excellent review of the multiple meanings of ethnicity (and see also Nash (1989)). If we follow Just, 'ethnicity', then, on the one hand refers to shared cultural traits, which on the other, tend to be endowed with an essential reality. The long-cherished dichotomy between nature and culture becomes blurred. 'Ethnicity', which had been adopted to underline the cultural character of group attributes, tends to be itself 'naturalized'.

Another example of this blurring of the distinction between culture and nature is Tambiah's recent definition of ethnic identity as

> a self-conscious and vocalized identity that *substantializes and naturalizes* one or more attributes – the usual ones being skin color, language, religion, territorial occupation – and attaches them to collectivities as their innate possession and their mytho-historical legacy. The central components in this description of identity are ideas of inheritance, ancestry and descent, place or territory of origin, and the sharing of kinship.
>
> (Tambiah 1989: 335)

Banton (1988), on the other hand, points out the legal uncertainties surrounding the meaning 'ethnic'. Similarly, the International Convention on the Elimination of all Forms of Racial Discrimination defines as discrimination 'any distinction, exclusion, restriction or preference based on race, colour, descent or national or ethnic origin' (quoted by Banton 1988: 4).

In the above instances, cultural traits are either naturalized or they are conflated with supposed biological criteria under the heading of racial discrimination. This is what Lawrence (1982: 83) has appropriately termed 'biological culturalism'. Our puzzlement at this apparent confusion of cultural and natural criteria of social differentiation is due to two preconceptions: that there do exist two distinct realms, one cultural, the other natural, as exhibited, for example, in the conventional dichotomy between nature and culture; and that there is, after all, something like 'race' as a specific marker of human differences. By the 1970s, this conceptual confusion was transmitted to the lay public. Academic research focused on 'race' rather than ethnicity as the unit of debate (Husband 1982: 16), while political discourse tended to present the problem in terms of ethnicity (for example, see Touraine, *El Pais*, 29 October 1990). Whenever 'race' is employed as a marker of social difference and inequality, we are dealing, no less than in the case of ethnicity, with a socio-historical construct.

But is there any significant sociological difference between what are called 'ethnic relations' and those that are attributed to 'race' and, for that matter, to class? Again, scholarly opinions diverge. Rex has maintained that 'there are close similarities and a strong relationship between class conflict and race and ethnic conflict', because there is no such thing as boundary processes informed by ethnic attributes which are devoid of conflict, since they are always related to macro-political processes (Rex 1986: 1 and 96–7). At the opposite end of the analytical spectrum, Smith rejects the conflation of 'race' with 'ethnicity' because phenotypical differences[1] are hereditary and immutable and hence particularly powerful as markers of status inequalities. Ethnicity as a cultural principle of stratification is negotiable (Smith 1986: 187–225). Yet, as Rex (1986: 16) has rightly argued, if it is recognized that it is not physical characteristics *per se* but associated ideas and behaviour which are used to define a category of people, 'racial' groups may be no less flexible than those based on ethnicity.

If 'race' is not a primary biological fact but itself a social construct, 'racism' cannot, then, be derived from it; an explanation must be sought elsewhere. Conversely, without 'racism' as an ideological doctrine, 'race' would be devoid of any social significance (Rich 1986: 2). This then raises the analytically and politically crucial question why and how macro socio-political processes give rise to racial classifications and 'racism'.

Non-Marxist scholars have attributed an irreducible social role to 'race', even though the inequalities resulting from 'racial' differences have economic and political consequences. Marxist scholars have attempted to overcome the difficulty of linking 'race' and class as sources of inequality by conceptualizing the priority of class in different ways (see Wolpe (1986) for an overview). They have sought an answer not in group attributes themselves but instead have interpreted 'race' as one ideological manifestation of class struggle. As Wolpe, who rejects a purely economic conception of class and a simple reduction of 'race' to class and emphasizes the ideological dimensions of capital accumulation, has put it, 'Race may, under determinant conditions, become interiorised in the class struggle' (1986: 123). Central to this debate is the notion of class and the extent to which class conflict can account for inequalities elaborated in terms of 'race'.

One approach is class reductionism. Classes have an economic origin in the relations of production and race conflicts are ideological expressions of class struggle. Wolpe, by contrast, challenges this view of classes as unitary economic entities with shared interests, stressing that there may exist cleavages in their midst since classes are formed not only through economics but also through politics and ideology. A concrete example of such cleavages is the struggle for wages which may incorporate, beyond economic calculations, such considerations as race and gender (Wolpe 1986: 123). In other words, ideological and cultural ideas may be exploited in the interest of capital accumulation and have a divisive effect for class cohesion. But even in these analytical formulations, it is still the system of production which provides the ultimate locus of class struggle.

By contrast, I will attempt an explanation which conceives of racism and sexism as related, constituting elements of bourgeois class society.

IS SEX TO GENDER AS RACE IS TO ETHNICITY?

I believe it is warranted to retain at least the following facts at this point. 'Race' no less than 'ethnicity' are symbolic constructs used under certain socio-political circumstances to define and mark off human groups. 'Races' do not exist as natural facts among humans whereas 'ethnicity', on the other hand, tends to be 'naturalized' despite the best of intentions to preserve its cultural connotation. Sex differences, by contrast, appear to be real among humans who are a bi-sexual species. If we now turn to my initial query 'is sex to gender as race is to ethnicity?', it would appear at first sight, therefore, that this homology does not hold. Despite Collier and Yanagisako's (1987) challenge of this link, biological sex differences seem to provide, possibly not universally but frequently, the empirical material out of which historically concrete gender relationships are elaborated. None the less, as Laqueur (1991) has recently shown in a fascinating study of changing representations of the body and of sex from classical Greece to the early twentieth century, it makes no anthropological sense to suppose that a scientifically correct sex model exists nor to conceive of the modern Western two-sex model as the 'real' foundation on which gender relationships are construed.[2] Instead, the modern bi-sexual notion equally constitutes a symbolic representation linked with other traits of our culture, even if this model appears to be closer to empirical reality. It may be apposite here to quote the paleo-anthropologist Gould's opinion on Laqueur's study:

> As a practicing scientist, I cannot quite accept the argument that empirical discovery counts for nothing (or precious little) in major theoretical transitions. Yet such a claim does hold for most historical change in attitudes about race and sex – and surely for the one-sex to two-sex transition, as Laqueur so elegantly shows. I have long held . . . that such a situation applies to race because the ratio of scientific data about race to its social importance has been so strikingly low until recently. The subject is vital and we knew virtually nothing of any worth about it. In such situations, we do little more than change fuel for our unaltered prejudices when the general intellectual climate shifts. Lacquer has convinced me that we may advance the same claim of a low ratio of scientific data to social importance for sex.
>
> (Gould 1991: 13)

Hence, I want to propose that, at least in class society, the homology does hold and that there is, moreover, an ideological-political link between the two pairs of relationships. In a related manner, which I will proceed to explain, sex no less than 'race' differences have been and continue to be ideologically marked as socially significant biological 'facts' in class society as a way of naturalizing and thereby perpetuating class and, in a related way, gender inequality. In other words, social and gender inequalities are construed and legitimized by rooting them in the assumed biological 'facts' of race and sex differences. The decisive characteristic of class society, as it were, its ideological 'underpinning', in this respect is a widespread tendency to naturalize social inequality. The naturalization of social inequality constitutes, in effect, a fundamental ideological procedure in class society to overcome the contradictions inherent in it.

GENDER, RACE AND CLASS

Rich (1984: 3) has rightly called attention to the risks of 'presentism' in historical analysis, that is, to project present meanings on past phenomena. 'Race', then, needs to be studied historically to understand its meaning in each particular context (Husband 1982: 11). There is isolated evidence of the usage of the term 'race' in the romance languages from the thirteenth century. But the word seems to have been more widely adopted, also in English, only in the sixteenth century. Initially, in French and English, 'race' referred to the membership of and descent from a family, a house in the sense of a 'noble lineage', and hence had a positive connotation (Conze *et al.* 1984: 137–8). In Castillian, however, the term was contaminated from the sixteenth century onward by the doctrine of purity of blood adopted in the process of the expulsion of the Jews and Moriscos from the Iberian peninsula (Corominas 1982: 800–1). These usages apparently differ from the modern 'scientific' notion of a group of people sharing common biologically-rooted traits. At a more abstract level, however, both concepts have in common the idea that 'race' is an innate and thus hereditary condition.

One early instance of the operation of 'race' for purposes of social segregation and exclusion which already entailed a nature/culture conflation, is the Catholic doctrine of *purity of blood* which dates back at least to the thirteenth century. Until about the thirteenth century, Muslims, Jews and Christians were presented as living side by side with tolerance and in harmony. Intermarriage among families of distinction and also among the lower orders had not been uncommon. When the doctrine of *purity of blood* was introduced, it was initially intended to segregate Christians from non-Christians, specifically Muslims and Jews. The origin of the notion of blood as a vehicle initially of religious faith and later as a marker of social condition is probably related with medieval physiological theory according to which the mother's blood fed the child in the womb and then, transformed into milk, fed the baby outside the womb as well (Bynum 1989: 182*ff*). A child's substance was provided by the mother's blood. Hence, purity of blood meant descent from Christian women.

As Jews, and a century later Moriscos (converted Muslims), were expelled from the Spanish Empire, what began as a religious-cultural discrimination, which could be overcome through conversion to the true faith, by the mid-fifteenth century had been transformed into 'a racist doctrine of the original sin of the most repulsive kind'

(Kamen 1985: 158). Thereafter, descent from Jews or Muslims was regarded as a permanent and indelible stain. When this doctrine was transported to the Spanish colonies, it was gradually extended to cover Africans and their descendants in general and found expression in a heightened concern among Europeans and their descendants over endogamous marriage and legitimate birth as a means to ensure and attest racial-cum-social purity as prerequisites for social pre-eminence.

In Europe, phenotypical and cultural diversity among human beings and their place within the great chain of being, attracted more systematic attention among natural scientists by the late seventeenth century. This resulted in a series of typologies of human beings based on diverse phenotypical criteria (Jordan 1968: 216*ff*). By the late eighteenth century, the concern over 'racial' differences among human beings congealed into the first formulations of what is now conventionally known as scientific racism, namely the pseudo-scientific demonstration of the physical causation of cultural differences. These were, in addition, ordered from superior to inferior, with the so-called 'Caucasians' occupying first place. Thereupon followed more elaborate theorizations of racial-cum-socio-political inequality in the nineteenth century. In the New World, racist legitimations of slavery were by then already well developed.

As some authors have argued (e.g. Rex 1973: 75), these racial doctrines were neither a direct outcome of colonialism nor were they a special ideological outgrowth of slavery. On the contrary, such 'racist' interpretations of social-cultural differences were at least equally relevant within Europe's socio-political development as explanations for domestic political conflicts and as a tool for dealing with emerging inequalities of class (Biddiss 1972: 572; Husband 1982: 12).

All these forms of racial prejudice and discrimination have two ideological procedures in common, namely to 'naturalize' socially significant differences and interpret these differences as inequalities.

In effect, the most striking aspect of the modern debate over the place of human beings in nature is the deepening tension between man's quest to master nature on the one hand and the simultaneous tendency to 'naturalize' social women and men on the other. Consolidating class society, in the nineteenth century, generated growing social inequality. This process, none the less, was accompanied by an ethos of equal opportunities for all human beings born equal, free and hence responsible for their acts. Now, why, in a meritocratic society of self-determining individuals, does naturalization of social condition and inequality play such a central and contradictory role in sustaining class inequality?

In the nineteenth century, the bourgeoisie could no longer justify its own privileges purely in terms of an ethic of abstinence and effort, since these virtues did not account for the success of the bourgeoisie itself. The result was a kind of socio-political elitism grounded in theories of race superiority (Hobsbawm 1975). By implying that inferiority was equally innate, such doctrines of race superiority might keep the impoverished masses in their place at a time of growing political tensions. By naturalizing social position, they served to reconcile alleged equality and freedom of all men with deepening social inequalities. A developing scientific naturalism in the nineteenth century provided these contradictory phenomena with a pseudo-scientific basis in such doctrines as social Darwinism, Spencerism, Lamarckism and eugenics which could be drawn upon to disguise the socio-economic roots of inequality by attributing them to the laws of nature (Hofstadter 1955; Leeds 1972; Young 1973; Stolcke 1988a; Martinez-Alier 1989).

The illusion of equality of opportunity for all could obscure social inequalities to a degree but, by at the same time challenging class inequality, it reinforced the tendency to naturalize social relationships. If the self-determining individual, through persistent social inferiority, seemed to be incapable of making the most of the opportunities society offered to him, this then had to be due to some essential, innate and therefore hereditary deficiency. The person, or better even, his or her biological endowment, rather than the socio-economic order was to be blamed for this.

Conceptions of the self, the person, the individual, or of human nature are neither self-evident nor immutable building blocks of which societies are built (Carrithers *et al.* 1985). Social position, perceived as ascribed by descent and hence innate, was no novelty in European history. The universalist notion of the free, self-determining and responsible individual was, however, a new concept dating from the Renaissance which became consolidated with the Enlightenment. Yet contrary to what many liberal sociologists as well as Marxists have maintained, achieved status, that is, 'self-made', did not replace ascribed status. Ascription by descent, as a principle of status definition, persisted and intersected with achievement in class society.

If modern racism can be explained in the terms outlined above, I cannot see any qualitative difference between the nineteenth century variety and what some authors have termed the 'new

racism' that has raised its ugly head in the past few decades (Centre
for Contemporary Cultural Studies, University of Birmingham
1982). Both instances are ideological constructs generated by the
contradictions inherent in capitalist society between an ethos of
equality of opportunity of all and existing national as well as international socio-economic inequality and domination.

In the United States, as well as in Europe, racial violence and
conflicts have occurred with increasing frequency since the 1960s.
The present wave of aggressions against 'non-communitarian' immigrants by extreme right groups, and the electoral success of
explicitly racist parties, are the most recent and tangible expressions
of the more subtle forms of racial prejudice and discrimination in
countries such as Germany, France and also in Spain and Italy
(Rose 1969; Husband 1982; Centre for Contemporary Cultural
Studies, University of Birmingham 1982; Rich 1984; Rex and Mason
1986; Jenkins and Solomos 1987; Solomos 1988; Caritas Española
1988; Banton 1989; Europäisches Parlament 1990). And scientific
race theories resurfaced again, for example, in Jensen's (1969) pol-
emical article purporting to demonstrate blacks' innate mental
inferiority which came precisely at a time when blacks in the United
States were mobilizing to demand equal rights.

As I have shown, one characteristic of racism is the naturalization
of social and/or cultural differences to justify exclusion and discrimination. In other words, racism is an ideological doctrine which
presents systems of social inequality as in the natural order of
things. To interpret European anti-immigrant sentiment as xenophobia means minimizing the problem by disguising its perverse
racist content, more so when this hostility is defined as a universal
human trait. This is, in effect, no different from British racialists'
propaganda which attributed the social tensions generated by the
growing presence of people from the ex-colonies with 'alien' cultures to immigration rather than 'race' (Barker 1981). In the 1970s,
the British Conservative Member of Parliament, Ivor Stanbrook,
provided a revealing example of this misrepresentation: 'Let there
be no beating about the bush. The average coloured immigrant has
a different culture, a different religion and a different language.
This is what creates the problem. It is not *just* because of race'.
And then he added, 'I believe that a preference for one's own race
is as *natural* as a preference for one's own family' (Stanbrook,
Hansard, p. 1409, quoted in Lawrence 1982: 82; my emphasis).

The concrete historical circumstances under which politics
become overtly racialized, the social groups which are racially dis-

criminated against and the severity of its consequences, may be distinct. But there is an underlying common element. Racism is always latent in class society and becomes overt at times of socio-economic and political polarization to legitimate socio-economic inequality. Yet because of the ethos of equality of opportunity, on the other hand, racial discrimination can also be challenged.

Now, what does this naturalization of social inequality have to do with the gender hierarchies prevailing in class society? As I have shown elsewhere (Stolcke 1988a), doctrines of biologically grounded inequality have served to consolidate the notion of the genetic family construed as the basic, natural and hence universal cell of society providing for the reproduction of socio-cum-racial pre-eminence. It has reinforced a notion of parenthood as resting on an individualized biological bond, and of the parent–child relationship as a 'blood tie'. The well-known English proverb that 'blood is thicker than water', reveals nicely the essential distinction between kin and relationships based on personal affinity. One result of this is the strong desire, especially of men, for immortality by perpetuating their genes through the generations and relatedly the image of women primarily destined by their biology to motherhood and domesticity in the service of the male. If social position expresses biological endowment, then for the privileged class, endogamy is crucial to protect their social pre-eminence. The lower orders cannot do otherwise by default. One well-known way to achieve endogamous reproduction is through the control of women's sexuality by men. This control was translated into women's need for male protection and hence their dependence on men. Precisely because women are thought to play the principal role in social reproduction, they need to be controlled.

All this may sound very Victorian. It may be argued that, although class society has not changed in a fundamental way, the sexual revolution and contraception have done away with this tangle of sexual restraints and, moreover, that the traditional monogamous nuclear family is falling to pieces anyway. This is true to an extent. In effect, a shift in meaning has occurred that affects the way the image of women is construed. In an increasingly competitive society, fragmented by the social division of labour into a milliard of hierarchically ordered functions, individual achievement and function are thought to determine a person's social position almost to the exclusion of such other criteria as family origin. A person's place within the social division of labour, however, in contradiction with the value attached to individual achievement, is also attributed to natural ability. As Durkheim revealingly argued almost a century ago,

> the only cause determining the manner in which work is divided, then, is the diversity of capacity . . . labour is divided spontaneously (and generates solidarity rather than conflict), only if society is constituted in such a way that *social inequalities exactly express natural inequalities.*
>
> (Durkheim 1964: 378, *my emphasis*)

Sex differences have acquired a singular meaning as one of the natural sources of social differentiation. In the nineteenth century, during the formative process of class society, women were assigned the instrumental role of mediating between biologically conceived purity and social pre-eminence. With a new turn of the naturalist screw, in advanced industrial society, women tend in addition to be defined in an unmediated way by their sexual characteristics as first and foremost mothers and as the essential, incommensurable, biological others to men. Due to the growing importance attached to achievement, women are now regarded as inferior and dependent on men in themselves: on account of their 'natural' function as mothers, they cannot compete on equal terms with them. Discrimination in the labour market, differential wages and the exclusion from politics, are only the results of this.

The recent alarm over declining birth rates in some European countries and the natalism which this concern has fomented is only one more instance of the racism which reinforces women's maternal role. If falling birth rates were, as some conservative politicians in these countries argue, threatening the so-called welfare states, one solution would surely be to provide employment for the unemployed and/or to open their frontiers to the poor millions of the Third World, but then they are generally not 'white'.

Let me sum up my argument. I have attempted to suggest how and why gender, class and 'race' intersect in the formation and perpetuation of class society, a society which is profoundly unequal and contradictory. Class conflict, even in these times of disillusion and political demobilization, not only lurks always under the surface but has also become internationalized. Growing inequalities and tensions between North and South are proof of this. The liberal illusion that socio-economic success only depends on the goodwill and effort of the individual is an ideological trap which diverts attention from the true causes of inequality in the unequal access to power and property. It thus undermines possibilities for collective resistance. But the notion of equality of opportunity for all also provides the stuff for challenging really existing inequalities. The naturalization of social inequalities – that is, racism – is a fundamental ideological-political doctrine designed to reconcile, though obviously unsuccessfully, equality of opportunities with inequality in reality. Whenever social condition is attributed to natural deficiencies, women move onto centre stage as mothers, be it as bearers and reproducers for a class or for a 'nation'. If class or nation are conceptualized in essential terms, women's procreative capacity needs controlling to perpetuate class and national-cum-racial privileges. And control implies domination by men. I am not suggesting, however, that gender inequalities are an epiphenomenon of macro-social processes. On the contrary, they are central to them. The contemporary paradox between pro-natalist conceptive policies in the so-called First World and aggressive population control policies in the Third World are exemplary of this racist-cum-sexist ideology. It is this complex constellation of economic and politico-ideological elements which in class society roots gender relations in sex differences and ethnicity in 'race'. Women's diverse experiences of oppression depending on their class and/or 'race' are one important manifestation of this. However, this 'naturalization' does not go uncontested precisely because the notion of the self-determining individual is one of its constitutive elements.

NOTES

1 Note the confusion between phenotype and race.
2 I want to thank Professor Raymond Smith very specially for his comments on this chapter and for drawing my attention to this book.

2 The study of kinship; the study of person; a study of gender?

Signe Howell and Marit Melhuus

The last two decades in anthropological research have seen an overwhelming interest in gender and the meaning of gender for the understanding of cultural systems. The seminal edited volumes by Rosaldo and Lamphere (1974), Reiter (1975), Ardener (1975a), MacCormack and Strathern (1980), Ortner and Whitehead (1981), Hirschon (1984), as well as the more recent studies by Collier and Yanagisako (1987a), Strathern (1987, 1988), and Moore (1988) to name but a few, seem to us to have discussed the complexity involved in gender studies from many different angles. Numerous excellent enthnographic studies have been published of male and female roles, of the significance of the sexual division of labour, on the ideology of gender relations and the importance of gender identity for cultural understanding. We have, in many cases, been given alternative interpretations of social institutions, the most well-known perhaps being the study by Weiner (1976) from the Trobri-and Islands, which has given new insight into that famous society. In a different vein, Bell (1983) has shown how aboriginal Australian women have their own versions of the cosmology and ritual which force one to rethink the 'meaning' of aboriginal societies.

Given this richness in research on gender issues, our initial intention was to rethink the scope and meaning of kinship in light of recent theoretical advances in the study of gender. It was our general impression that the area of kinship had been left out of these studies, and we thought that this was odd – given the inherent 'genderness' of kinship. However, reading and re-reading the 'anthropology of women' literature, we realized that much of what we wanted to say has, in fact, already been said, or intimated, although few have made kinship the main focus of their debates (the exception is Collier and Yanagisako 1987a). It was, therefore, rather confounding to discover that, despite the advances that have been made with respect to gender, as well as more specifically gender and kinship, very little of it seems to filter through to 'mainstream' anthropological kinship waters. A rapid review of articles on kinship and marriage in two of the major anthropological journals over the past ten years indicates – with a few notable exceptions – no general shift in focus. This is not merely distressing, but an illustration of a serious flaw in our construction of knowledge. It not only raises the question of which voices are heard by whom and when, but also confirms an inkling echoed by many feminist scholars,[1] that feminism, as a contribution to scientific theory, is not acknowledged.

It is, therefore, important to confront the lack of impact of gender studies on the discipline as a whole. The anthropological study of gender started as a study of women. By and large, 'women' were perceived by male anthropologists as being of concern to women anthropologists; of special interest on a par with the anthropology of art. One might add, most women anthropologists thought much the same (see E. Ardener 1975). Only more recently have 'gender', or 'gendered', become more commonly used expressions. Yet gender is as often as not still read as 'women' or, more specifically, as 'the position of women'. There appears to be a lack of willingness to accept the fact that males and females are constituted in relation to each other, and that, in and of itself, gender is relational.

As a result of our perusal of the literature, we changed our original aim somewhat, as well as broadening our scope to include some new trends in social anthropology. The first part of our paper is an attempt to recover some of the ground gained with respect to gender and kinship. We will most likely reiterate points and positions that have been made before, but do it with the confidence that a good thing cannot be repeated too often. If we seem to be flogging dead horses, we will counter that; outside the confines of the converted, there appears to be a lot of life left in them still. In the second part, we wish to extend the discussion into another central area of anthropological research in recent years, namely the study of self, personhood, human nature and the related topic of emotions.

We wish to suggest that as kinship studies lost their centrality in anthropology during the 1970s and 1980s, their place was taken, towards the end of that period, by studies on personhood. However, just as gender was absent in kinship studies, so it is in person studies. We are convinced that this is not a mere coincidence.

Although actual reasons – historical and sociological – for gender blindness in these areas of anthropological investigations are very different, we nevertheless will argue that underlying both constructions are particular notions of the gender relation which seem to be peculiar to certain dominant parts of modern discourse. Central to our discussion is the challenge of androcentrism (and of ethnocentrism) and its implications for anthropological analysis. In fact, following a tradition of what has aptly been termed a 'hermeneutics of suspicion' (Fiorenza 1988: xxiii), we question the hold of androcentrism on our concepts, models and hence on our interpretation of 'the other'.

IN THE BEGINNING WAS KINSHIP

The following quotations are chosen so as to set the scene for our further deliberations. They concern kinship and its place in the anthropological discipline.

In the Preface to his widely used textbook *Kin Groups and Social Structure*, Keesing says,

> Acquiring a measure of technical competence in kinship theory is crucial in cultural anthropology, even for the student who does not aspire to professional specialization in kinship studies. Without such competence, one cannot read with comprehension the major anthropological journals . . . and one cannot adequately understand anthropological monographs on tribal peoples.
>
> (Keesing 1975: vi)

He even goes so far as to say,

> Without it, one cannot understand the development of theory in social anthropology – for many fundamental issues about human social life have been debated in the arena of kinship.
>
> (1975: vi)

In a similar vein, Needham is, perhaps, even more insistent. He says,

> . . . Lafitau began the comparative study of unilineal descent and classificatory terminologies as long ago as 1724, and Morgan inaugurated in 1871 what has since become a recognized topic of academic investigation and theory. The syllabuses of university instruction in anthropology now invariably include kinship; no

textbook is thought adequate without some treatment of it; and in all the variety of examinations in anthropology it occupies a central and unavoidable position. You cannot gain a certificate of competence as a social anthropologist without demonstrating a command of kinship theory, and it is expected of most anthropologists that they will make some contribution to it. Indeed, most of those who have great names in anthropology – e.g. Rivers, Kroeber, Radcliffe-Brown, Lévi-Strauss – have gained their prominence largely by their publications on kinship. If there is one topic which is indispensable to social anthropology, and which defines what social anthropologists essentially do, it would appear to be kinship . . .

(Needham 1971: 1)

This long quotation from Needham's iconoclastic 'Introduction' to the 1971 ASA volume *Rethinking Kinship and Marriage* sums up the discipline's attitude to the topic. That Needham then proceeds to deny that there is anything which may be usefully called kinship does not detract from the sentiments already expressed. Needham does not deny that anthropologists will continue to study a particular kinship system in a particular society – and gain much understanding from such a study; he asserts that, at the analytical level, with a view to rigorous comparative analysis, there is no such thing as kinship. He makes the significant point that the dearth of theoretical advances within kinship studies is not due to lack of data, but to the conceptual framework of analysis. He says,

> The current theoretical position is obscure and confused, and there is little clear indication of what future developments we can expect or should encourage . . . Obviously, after so long a time, and so much field research, it is not just facts that we need. Something more fundamental seems to have gone wrong. What we have to look for, perhaps, is some radical flaw in analysis, some initial defect in the way we approach the phenomena. . . . A possible diagnosis may be that the trouble lies not so much in the substantive study of institutions of kinship and marriage as in *our conceptual premises*, and most decisively in the way we conceive the classification of phenomena.
>
> (1971: 2, *our emphasis*)

Yes indeed! Needham then mentions, but rejects as uninteresting, the possibility that sexual categories might provide such a framework:

It is true that the possession and exercise of these rights is
defined by reference to the sex of the persons thus related; but
then so is the division of labour in the simpler societies, yet we
do not for that reason think this method of distinguishing statuses
so remarkable as to deserve a special designation and to call for
a distinct type of theory.

(1971: 4)

Here we disagree with him. Not only is the division of labour by
gender so remarkable as to warrant a distinct theory (and feminist
studies over the past two decades have provided theories), but more
importantly for our present purposes, the sex of the person in a
kinship system – or rather the fact that kinship systems are
inherently gendered – is of such importance as to call for a distinct
type of theory. It is not our intention to present such a theory in
this paper. Some attempts have been made by others and we will
refer to these, but much challenging work remains to be done.
Rather, in this paper we will try to identify our own perplexity with
respect to the relations between kinship and gender – and following
on from that, between personhood and gender.

GENDERED KINSHIP?

Our considerations have been prompted by an observation we perceive as puzzling and in need of some comment. The observation
is the existence of a gap – and this gap is in itself the problem, or
rather a paradox. The gap is between two central areas of study in
social anthropology: kinship and gender. The paradox is that in
kinship studies, from the earliest days, the central characters are
quite literally men and women and the various relations between
them. These are represented through kinship diagrams made up by
circles and triangles to denote the two sexes. Although the central
concern of anthropology has, therefore, on the face of it, been
about relations between men and women, the way that this has
been pursued tells us, in our opinion, virtually nothing about gender
in the societies described and discussed. Ortner and Whitehead
observe something similar:

The sphere of kinship and marriage relations then is clearly
consequential in various ways for cultural notions of gender and
sexuality. . . . Yet although we might suppose, in a common-
sense way, that cultural notions of gender, sexuality and reproduction would reflect directly the shape of kinship, marriage and

other structurally and affectively important cross-sex bonds, the ethnographic record has proven frustrating in this regard. The obvious (to us) connections are often missing.

(Ortner and Whitehead 1981: 11)

As Rubin pointed out eighteen years ago, 'kinship systems are observable and empirical forms of sex/gender systems' (1975: 169). Her essay was in many ways ahead of its time, so much so as not to receive its just impact. Not only did she go to the core of what studies of kinship systems seem to be all about, namely the cultural construction of gender activated in social relations, she also refuted all claims that women's oppression is derived from a biological necessity. She critically examines aspects of the works of Lévi-Strauss, Marx, Freud and Lacan, and she points out that while both Freud and Lévi-Strauss centred their theories upon sexuality, this was sexuality predicated upon a presumed and unquestioned universal male experience. In the case of Freud, attempts were made to account for female sexuality within a framework of males *manqués*, whereas Lévi Strauss hardly thought it worth considering. Interestingly, both Freud and Lévi-Strauss – in their different ways and with different aims – theorize around sexuality (not gender) within a parameter of kinship and marriage. To Lévi-Strauss, marriage was, of course, to be understood as the mechanism that created social relations and, ultimately, culture. Through exchanging women (sisters or daughters), groups of men are able to reproduce while avoiding incestuous marriage. Exogamy becomes a male prerogative as a way to curb and channel male sexuality into instituted (male) social groups.

Many anthropologists, when giving an account of 'women's studies' within the discipline, will immediately draw attention to the centrality of kinship and kinship studies in the development of the discipline, thereby implying a continued presence of women in anthropological studies. There is, however, an important difference between the *study* of kinship systems as 'latently "genderized" ' (Ortner and Whitehead 1981: 10) and the *empirical phenomenon* of kinship as composed of members of both sexes. Not distinguishing between the two is, of course, a grave category mistake. Kinship (as we are not the first to point out) has remained a study of relations between men, with women filling subordinated roles as mothers, sisters, daughters or wives. Moore substantiates this view:

Kinship relations, particularly when they are examined in terms of their role in political and jural structures, can turn out to be the study of kin-based links between men, and women are considered merely one of the mechanisms for establishing those links.

(Moore 1988: 132)

So while sexual categories abound in the central anthropological concerns for more than a century, gender and gender relations as part and parcel of social and symbolic relations are not given due attention. Paradoxically, the inherent values of maleness and femaleness in kinship and marriage ideologies and practices have not been investigated.

SACRED TEXTS

We wish to pursue a little further the centrality of kinship. In his textbook *Kinship and Marriage*, Fox (1967: 10) says, 'Kinship is to anthropology what logic is to philosophy or the nude is to art'. May we add to the list of analogies 'as the Bible is to Christian theology'? Fox continues, 'it is the basic discipline of the subject'. From this and other quotations given above, it appears incontrovertible to suggest that kinship has an aura of sacredness attached to it. Not only does it seem to generate awe, but also, in some cases, it creates a certain fear (cf. Needham 1971: 12). In fact, insofar as kinship is concerned, many (anthropologists) have in recent years become agnostics without taking on the intellectual tasks of presenting their argument. Uneasily, but without any real debate, kinship has lost its central position. Rather than take up the challenges offered by the theoretical insights gained in gender studies, anthropologists have turned their backs on kinship.[2]

In juxtaposing the Bible and theology with kinship and anthropology, we are not just trying to introduce another metaphor with which to think about kinship. Rather, as different forms of cultural texts, the Bible and kinship seem to produce the same type of dilemma for feminists who wish to read them with a critical eye. The problem has to do with accepted truths, the relation between such truths, and what they represent. Depending on how 'close' you are to the text, and how much it means to you, this problem of representation will take on different forms with very different consequences. For example: although feminist theologians may agree to the fact that the Bible is androcentric, the implication this has for their relationship to the Bible, as a text, will differ. Some will continue to accept the Bible as sacred, the word as authoritative, but through careful exegesis construct new meanings, which include and even enhance women (e.g. Fiorenza 1988, 1989). Others may insist on historical contextualization of the events recorded and thus challenge the very status of the Bible (e.g. Fatum 1989). Others yet again may choose to put away the Bible altogether (e.g. Daly 1973). While feminist anthropologists cannot be divided into similar groupings with regard to their attitudes to kinship, there is, nevertheless, little doubt that kinship in itself presents problems that are analogous to those of the theologians. If we put away kinship, we are putting away our very creed. Insofar as kinship relations structure society (at the cosmological level as well as the social, economic, political and institutional), there can be no understanding of society without an understanding of kinship – or can there? One of the main problems we have had in composing this article is to define for ourselves what the problem actually is. Kinship seems to escape critical scrutiny – maybe because it is one of those areas where it is impossible to think that our thinking is wrong – and hence prevents a dispassionate positioning outside the discourse as this has been handed down.

It could be argued that in the case of kinship, and its place in anthropological discourse, the old masters were right: that despite their analytic blindness to human females and issues of gender, their presentation of social organization and ideology may, in fact, be representative of a large number, perhaps the majority, of human societies. In other words, we may rage over Lévi-Strauss' clear neglect of women in his model of social relations, but it may be that his theories do reflect the ideological state of affairs. Much recent empirical research appears to substantiate the model of a male encompassing (*viz.* Dumont e.g. 1986) the female in any number of, but by no means all, societies (e.g. Howell 1984). However, this does not preclude a reformulation of questions asked and models created with a view to making gender more problematic. Gender relations are as much about same-sex relations as they are about cross-sex relations, yet the quality of same-gender relations is predicated upon opposite-gender relations in each sociocultural instance. Same-sex relations take on specificity of meaning only if we view these within an overarching reference to cross-sex relations. Moreover, within any one society, we must be open to the possibility that persons of the same sex are not necessarily of a kind; both category and age may further complicate the gender picture.

Another, but related, issue in the study of gender and kinship is the question of difference and sameness. This is also addressed by Collier and Yanagisako (1987b), and their analytic stategy is to question whether the biological difference between 'male' and 'female' is what will always structure the relation between them, i.e. 'whether these differences are the universal basis for the cultural categories "male" and "female" ' (1987b: 15). They argue – along lines taken up elsewhere by Strathern (e.g. 1988) – that a number of the analytical dichotomies that have guided gender studies (domestic/public; nature/culture; reproduction/production) assume that gender is everywhere rooted in the same difference, and hence 'take for granted what they should explain' (Collier and Yanagisako 1987b: 17). With respect to gender and kinship, they hold that both fields of study have been defined 'by our folk conception of the same thing, namely, the biological facts of sexual reproduction' (1987b: 17). While we agree with the gist of their argument, we do not go along with the complete open-endedness with regard to biological sex. Although theories of procreation certainly vary dramatically, this does not mean that physiological differences between men and women are not universally acknowledged. What matters, anthropologically, is the way that this fact is used for the creation of meanings and values. Androgynous conceptions, homosexual conceptions and other possible sexual conceptions can be understood only in relation to ideas about maleness and femaleness. What we *must* avoid is unthinkingly to maintain the boundaries of our own dichotomies when confronting alien constructions.

FROM KINSHIP STUDIES TO PERSON STUDIES

The past years have seen a significant shift in theoretical concerns in social anthropology; kinship, a former central theme, is noticeable only by its absence in ethnographic studies. What is emerging as a major concern is explication around indigenous concepts of personhood. The empirical research into notions about what different societies hold to be human nature and the various perceived attributes and values associated with this are rapidly becoming important ethnographic and anthropological themes. However, in the excitement of finding and exploring a novel ethnographic perspective, anthropologists yet again fail to take proper account of gender. Specific indigenous notions of human nature are all too often explored and explained as if this is a uniform concept, applying equally to every member of a society, regardless not only of gender but also of social category.[3]

Examples are numerous. Let us mention just a few. In his contribution to the French symposium on 'Concept of Personhood in Black Africa' held in 1971 (one of the earliest forums for deliberations along such lines), Fortes discusses what he calls the concept of person among the Tallensi. The paper is a subtle and detailed investigation into aspects of what Tallensi perceive significant and valuable in human beings. Fortes is particularly concerned with elaborating the moral and jural capacities and qualities that constitute the *personne morale*. It is 'by observing and conversing with the *common man*, so to speak, that one could see how the ideas and beliefs relating to such abstract notions as that of the person were channelled through *his* daily activities' (1987: 248, *our emphasis*). What we end up with is a picture of what the Tallensi head of a patrilineage ought to be like. It emerges that Tallensi women have no possibility of becoming persons, but this fact is not made an issue of, either ethnographically or theoretically.

Fortes takes as his starting point Mauss' famous essay on 'A category of the human mind: the notion of person, the notions of "self",' (in Mauss 1979), an essay which also was made the basis for a conference and subsequently an edited volume published in 1985. The editors of the volume (Carrithers *et al.*) do not even mention gender as an aspect of the empirical comparative study of personhood. A whole series of other edited volumes devoted to the anthropological study of personhood and self, for example Heelas and Lock (1981), Jacobsen-Widding (1983), Shweder and Levine (1984), include no index entry under 'gender' and hardly any under 'women' or 'men'. With a few notable exceptions, those anthropologists who write on these issues treat the concept of the person as a unified concept, and one presented in the male idiom. That Mauss (and possibly also Fortes) was blind to questions of gendered selves – as social facts – is perhaps not surprising; that the same is true for young anthropologists writing today and having gained their training in the midst of feminism and countless ethnographic studies of women in society, *is* surprising.

Why is it that the excellent critiques of male bias in the anthropological praxis have failed to affect such a central concern as indigenous concepts of human nature? A focus such as personhood and human nature should, on the face of it, lead directly to questions of gender. Yet the two discourses have been developed in parallel. Not only have they not been integrated, more importantly they are barely partners in dialogue. If nothing else, this tells us much about the insidiousness of androcentrism.

At a certain level, one may grant that, insofar as models of kinship and marriage reflect empirical situations, then a model of male encompassment standing for the whole is justifiable. However, when we turn to the study of personhood, the empirical base for such a model is questionable. In studying indigenous concepts of human nature, person, and emotions, we seem to continue a philosophical debate which has been part of Western traditions since the Greeks. Unreflectingly, Western philosophers have pursued truth about human nature from the point of view of the aristocratic (reasoning) male. Unreflectingly, this exclusive bias has, by and large, continued when Western anthropologists have sought comparative conceptions. We are here confronted with a blindness to empirical realities, surprising in a discipline which prides itself on working from within native categories. Non-Western ideologies may operate with several categories of human nature, not just one. Not only are there gender differences in concepts and attributes of personhood, there are also age and class differences. Slaves, as is well known from the days of the Greek city states, lack some quality, which debars them from the status of full human beings. The Tallensi example illustrates that women (and junior lineage male members) also lack vital qualities which – in the case of Tallensi women – they are *inherently* incapable of acquiring. It goes with being born female. Hence, can we with any legitimacy talk of the Tallensi concept of personhood? Geertz, who has advocated the anthropological pursuit of the cultural construction of personhood, similarly fails to take account of structural variability of person categories and qualities within any one society. His much-quoted essay 'From the native's point of view' (Geertz 1984), strongly advocates the interpretative usefulness of 'experience-near concepts'. By this he means, in effect, employing concepts of self as the starting point for interpretation. However, in his three ethnographic examples, he does not differentiate according to sex, gender or social category. Rather, we are presented with thumbnail sketches of the Balinese, Javanese and Moroccan concepts of self – all of which turn out on closer inspection to be male as well as aristocratic.

A kinship diagram is blatantly 'sexed'. In the words of Rubin, 'It is a description of society which does not assume a genderless human subject. On the contrary, the human subject . . . is always either male or female' (Rubin 1975: 171). This is a truism, but as we have been arguing, it has not affected analysis; persons are, in the anthropological literature, generally presented as sexless.

Authors seem at the outset to assume an abstract genderless human subject. Yet to our knowledge not only are persons invariably gendered, but so also are many human qualities, and we would question whether there exists an idea of personhood which is not gendered. Just as men and women in kinship systems are constituted in relation to each other, so also are they in conceptions of personhood. However, there is a difference. In kinship studies, men and women are, by way of the diagram, 'visible', hence the analysis purportedly includes men and women. In person studies, neither characters nor characteristics are similarly 'visible', being glossed over by the very concept of the person.

Insofar as ethnographic investigations on the theme of human nature have been couched in male categories, this may be the result of Western androcentricity and a failure to let the native categories speak for themselves. This may, perhaps, partly be accounted for by the fact that the majority of ethnographic studies on gender relations have been conducted in terms of relative status and power. Few have extended their studies into other traditional anthropological issues such as religion, cosmology, ritual or kinship – although this is now changing. Fewer still have explored the hypothesis that societies are, in their very essence, gendered. In order to truly take account of such an iconoclastic assertion, it is not enough to take up old anthropological themes in the same way, but with an inserted gender aspect. Gender is not a matter that, having once been ignored can now be added. On the contrary, as is being shown again and again, taking gender seriously requires some basic rethinking of our concepts, as few can be taken as *a priori* relevant or useful. Although this fact has long been recognized, the painstaking work of the deconstruction of theoretical concepts has just started, of which Strathern's (1988) recent book is a good example. She not only questions the theoretical constellations of individual and society, but also puts a question mark on the concepts of men and women and, by implication, on the very notion of gender.

SAMENESS AND DIFFERENCE

While gender studies may have been influenced by a Western tendency to look for dichotomies (Collier and Yanagisako 1987a), person studies appear to be influenced by another, but equally pervasive, Western tendency to look for unity. Monotheism may guide Western thinking towards 'monohomoism'. In this particular enterprise, we may further have been guided by our commitment to the idea of universal human rights, whereby all human beings are held to be existentially and morally alike.

Feminist anthropologists have been slow to embrace the focus of human nature. This is surprising, as such a focus could provide both the essentialists as well as the relativists with further ammunition. Either way, the potential for broadening the discussion away from relations of production, from prestige systems, from social institutions such as bridewealth/brideservice, are, as yet, largely unexplored. Ultimately, the focus on indigenous conceptions of human nature brings up, perhaps even more than the focus on kinship, fundamental problems concerning sameness and difference. Are societies fundamentally (formally) identical? Are cultures fundamentally (formally) identical? Are human natures fundamentally (formally) identical? Are men fundamentally (formally) identical? And are women fundamentally (formally) identical? We are not going to attempt to answer any of these questions; we wish merely to pose them within the present framework.

Nevertheless, it seems to us that both anthropological and feminist thinking converge in a renewed – and vitalized – interest in notions surrounding sameness and difference. These notions have always permeated the anthropological enterprise, premised as this is on comparison. They also permeate the study of gender and, in recent feminist debates, have been made the centre for major controversies (e.g. Spelman 1988). Central to these debates is how to tackle not only differences between men and women, but differences between women (and presumably between men), and, perhaps more importantly, how to establish and account for the differences which make a difference!

Rubin, in the essay referred to, raises the question of sexual difference. She says, 'The idea that men and women are more different from one another than either is from anything else must come from somewhere other than nature' (1975: 179). She argues that the sexual division of labour, and its ideological underpinnings, is based precisely on difference, and this is to be understood as a 'taboo against the sameness of men and women' in order to sustain – or perhaps it presupposes – the heterosexual marriage. Collier and Yanagisako (1987a) base their whole argument on *our* notions of sameness and difference. When discussing the mutual constitution of kinship and gender, they state,

Both 'gender' and 'kinship' studies have been concerned with understanding the rights and duties that order relations between people defined by difference. Both begin by taking 'difference' for granted and treating it as a presocial fact. Although social constructions are built on it, the difference itself is not viewed as a social construction.

(Collier and Yanagisako 1987a: 29)

In line with Rubin (to whom they do not refer),[4] they posit sexual procreation as the basis for Western thinking about gender which, as a result, places all value on the heterosexual couple and informs our approach to and understanding of other societies. They suggest that, 'the conviction that the biological *difference* in the roles of women and men in sexual reproduction lies at the core of the cultural organization of gender persists in comparative analysis' (1987b: 32, *original emphasis*). Their answer is, of course, to transcend this legacy, firstly by not assuming any presocial facts and, secondly, by not reinventing dichotomies. Instead, they propose a strategy based on the premise 'that social systems are, by definition, systems of inequality', a society being a 'system of social relationships and values' and, moreover, that 'values entail evaluation' (1987b: 32). These statements beg as many questions as they answer. On the one hand, they do away with any basis for a psychic and cognitive unity of humanity (no presocial facts); on the other hand, they posit what must surely be understood as a presocial fact, namely that all social systems are systems of inequality.

CONCLUDING REMARKS

The development of a feminist anthropology has been a process of many phases. The main transitions can perhaps briefly be stated as follows: the 'discovery' of male bias; making women visible; and the emergence of gender relations as a basic conceptual premise. Though all three phases interlock, the shift of focus from women to gender has implied a major rethinking, not only with respect to anthropological theory, but more generally with respect to scientific theory. Indeed, there are those who will claim that feminist theory poses today the most challenging questions to established theoretical premises.

However, it seems that although the issue of male bias in anthropology has been recognized, we have yet to draw its full implications. In fact, some may be content to leave it at that. Redressing androcentrism is in itself an arduous task, as it takes us to the very core of our own cultural heritage and, hence, to our concepts of knowledge. But we are not convinced that there is a general consensus about the meaning of male bias, nor are we certain that it is possible, in the last instance, to escape it. On the contrary, if gender categories are, as some modern feminist thinkers would hold, not just *one* of many variables determining cultural forms, but *the* governing principle by which meaning is constructed in *modern* Western society; and moreover, if gender is the basis whereby we construct difference, and hence underpins our perception of 'the other', our analyses will invariably be infused with a Western perception of gender (see Borchgrevink and Solheim 1989; Nader 1989). However, the very fact that we are in a position to even recognize this possiblilty, that we are able to think not only within our own culture but also about it, creates, perhaps, a space – or a vantage point – from which we can critically apprehend our own androcentrism and ethnocentrism.

Moreover, the task can be facilitated through knowledge and comparative studies of other cultures where not only gender, but also the notion of difference, may be encoded in ways distinct from ours. However, a precondition for even seeing differences – or sameness – is an acute awareness of how gender permeates our thinking, and perhaps in particular our academic thinking. In other words, we are saying that the more we understand about what informs *our* way of thinking, the more we are able to grasp other ways of thinking. In the process, we may be able to contribute not only to new knowledge, but also to other forms of generating knowledge. Ultimately, that is what the academic endeavour is all about. Our approach to knowledge follows, to some extent, what Harding posits as the 'valueladenness of knowledge seeking' (1986: 22) and we may do well to recall her position: 'What counts as knowledge must be grounded on experience. Human experience differs according to the kinds of activities and social relations in which humans engage' (1986: 22).[5] This applies equally to us as it does to people of other cultures.

Hence, to accept the fact of androcentrism is not just to launch a critique of established theory; it is also a step – or, to put it even more strongly, a commitment – towards creating new theoretical paradigms. In feminist scholarship these steps are now being taken within most disciplines, and there is much to be gained from this work. In fact, feminism seems to converge in an interdisciplinary effort in which anthropologists are also partaking. Our wish is that both male and female anthropologists will engage in the debates and take up the challenges so that the anthropology of the future will be a truly representative discipline.

NOTES

1 Our use of the words 'feminist' and 'feminist studies' is to be taken loosely to mean those scholars who seriously incorporate questions of gender in their studies.

2 Surprisingly, in between the presentation of this paper and the rewriting of it for publication, an issue of *Man* appeared which is devoted exclusively to ethnographic studies of kinship and marriage (25, 3 September 1990). Although we have not had the time to read them fully, our impression is that some of the articles follow the paths of traditional studies on kinship and alliance, while others, in varying degrees, take account of sex and gender.

3 The role of the anthropologist in a field situation, and the role and status of the text subsequent to fieldwork, have become the topic of much recent debate. Reflexivity, intersubjectivity, fluidity in epistemologies and even ontologies are topics of theoretical concern. One striking feature of the debate, as it is being carried out, is the virtual absence of females. Women as anthropologists, women as the 'other' in field situations, women as acknowledged sources of many of the general ideas propounded, are mute and invisible. In a recent article, Mascia-Lees *et al.* (1989) claim – with good reason – that the thrust of postmodernism in anthropology parallels ideas explored by feminist anthropologists (and others) for more than two decades. This, however, is passed over in silence by male anthropolgists.

4 Despite this omission, we nevertheless wish to note that their references are virtually exclusively to North American writers – anthropologists and others. While their Introduction takes up many important issues, this gives the uninitiated student an incomplete picture of the history of anthropological studies on women and on gender. British and other European scholars have been debating the themes for many years, and have contributed original ethnographic as well as theoretical material.

5 In exploring the relation between gender and religion with respect to religious experience, Bynum states, '. . . all human beings are "gendered" – that is, there is no such thing as generic *homo religiosus*. Religious experience is the experience of men and women, and in no known society is this experience the same' (1986: 2).

3 The illusion of dualism in Samoa

'Brothers-and-sisters' are not 'men-and-women'

Serge Tcherkezoff
Translated by Sarah Manbury Tenison

THE FRONTIER OF THE SEXES

The anthropological study of 'gender' involves enquiring into all the ways employed by a given society to define and distinguish between individuals, as well as any other elements in the universe, by analogy with the sex difference in humans, which we usually call anatomical. The problem is that this question, while apparently universal, is in fact predetermined by a particular culture. It introduces a Western concept, that of complementarity or symmetry, as applied to an object, humanity. In this case, the opposition is distinctive and the difference *symmetrical* (meaning that the relationship of each of these terms is identical with reference to the opposition). We are dealing here with 'male' and 'female', in the same way as one would distinguish between 'right' and 'left' on a horizontal axis and between even and odd numbers among the sum of integers, and so on. However, when we want to analyse this sort of difference, whether it be sexual identity, or right and left etc., within a particular society, we have to ask this society how our question, and thus *our* view of this difference (what we call 'gender' or 'lateralization' etc.), may be set within a specific whole. In order to obtain an answer that is expressed in terms of the society under investigation, we have to endow the society as a whole with formal epistemological status, thus allowing our question to be deduced from this whole.

This is where the formal logic of encompassment can be useful. It enables us to establish that a second level, at which the part is contrary to the whole, is, by means of another transformation, a form of reversal of a first level, at which this part is identical to the whole (Dumont 1979, 1983; Tcherkezoff 1983, 1985).[1] In fact, if we want to deduce our question (which refers to a distinctive opposition) from the society as a whole, we have to establish the point at which a male/female contrarity happens to reverse another relationship in which one of the two terms mentioned above is equal to the whole (although, generally speaking, under a different and possibly unrecognizable form; hence the need to rely on a transformation between relationships, without dwelling on the substance of the terms). We must thus 'translate' the second level through its opposition to the first one. The implication is that ethnographical research should concentrate on the points at which what we should recognize as male or female is linked to the whole in an ambivalent manner.

This method is very different from the 'external' point of view, whereby the observer translates the 'whole' and the 'part' separately, simply as two symmetrical sides of a world-view or social structure. The sort of answer elicited by this external method is, in fact, a monologue which restricts itself to paraphrasing the initial question. An analysis that starts from a male/female pairing will simply produce further dichotomies: control versus freedom, social norms versus self-interest, giving out versus keeping in, the reproduction of the group as such versus exchanges between individuals, or classical dichotomies such as sacred versus profane or culture versus nature (in the sense of two opposed representations of the person in a given culture) and any other such pairings.

In our case, 'reversal' does not merely represent a change of context; it is not simply a binary distinction. We have a particularly clear example of this which leads us instantly into the configuration of gender: 'female' sexuality in Samoa. It is a fact well known in Samoa that a girl is supposed to remain a virgin until marriage. Furthermore, a wife is expected to keep her 'sexual' relations outside 'her home' (meaning her village). She must marry outside, *i fafo*, even though the Samoan village does not consist solely of relatives. She must also not show herself there as a *fafine*, a female defined as a woman *because she has a male sexual partner* (whether real or merely rumoured). Hence a variety of gestures and words, however tender and innocent they may seem to us, are proscribed, even when the woman is legally married. In short, what we would term 'free sex' (or 'free love') belongs to a context which is clearly opposed to something. This freedom involves pre-marital relations, adultery sought by a woman or a tacit consent by a woman to her husband's adultery, as well as explicit references to the sex act in relation to herself – although jokes at other people's expense, which can be very crude, are common currency. We shall leave aside male-initiated 'free-sex' contexts. We need simply mention that 'free sex' is advocated by the young men and recognized to a certain extent by the general ceremonial set-up, and that it is one of those faults which are, by definition, permitted in the case of high-ranking men. Such male contexts are not defined by taboos; thus they do not appear in a primary place within the general discourse about norms.[2]

Two methodological approaches are now possible. With the first, we would be content with what this society had told us up till now; we would have found a particularly relevant opposition in their culture: in the case of women, free sex versus non-free sex. More precisely, we would feel we had found that behaviour such as all that covered by our expression 'free sex' is so unacceptable in Samoa and is so bound by various taboos that we could actually call it 'non-free sex' if we were to name that part of Samoan culture using an appropriate term from our culture (even if this is a negative assimilation: what they seem to forbid is what we call in our culture 'free sex').[3] As a result, we would retreat to our study to work out suitable hypotheses.

Non-free sex could be explained in terms of the requirements of a social order whereby the males 'hold on' to their female kin so as not to disperse rank through unplanned progeny. This society is, after all, dominated by the idea of rank (Ortner 1981). Or more generally, we (our European interpretation of the Samoan culture) would tend to think that we are facing the constraints of a cultural system that Samoans represent to themselves (without giving any further reasons or explanations to themselves) – and then explain to the foreigner – as a world of generalized control exerted on anything that looks near to self assertion, a world where this kind of assertion is understood as a threat to the social system of control, and where this control is cared for because it is seen as the source of all social contractual relationships, originating through God and flowing through the family system of titles which gives rank to everybody in society (Shore 1976, 1981, 1982). Or again, whether as well or instead of the second view, one might also think that the women here have a sacred role, precisely that of transmitting *mana*, sacredness, and that this role involves constraints (which is true) (Schoeffel 1978, 1979). However, the question is one of knowing whether this is a role and a position which complements that of the secular authority (pertaining to men) (Schoeffel 1978, 1979) – the mystical/pragmatic 'complementary' opposition – or whether it involves a certain context of relations that summons up others to create a coherent social whole, which also signifies that we have to integrate within this picture (at what level?) other less valued or devalued female roles (such as wife, sexual partner).

In this case, the methodological error is to think that a single ethnographical fact, or cluster of facts, can in itself have meaning in terms of anthropology. In actuality, it will only acquire a specific meaning when we can perceive its place in relation to the whole society. Are we dealing with something 'encompassing', oriented towards value, that indicates directly that it *belongs to* this specific society, such as sacredness in the Maussian sense? If so, we have to find out what it encompasses, in order to see its specific involvement with value (we also have to observe what other facts are confronted by value when our question thus intrudes in the society). Or is it a substantive context, organized by distinctive oppositions? If so, we have to discover the point at which this context is encompassed by the society, so that our recognition of an 'empirical' fact is inserted within a specific socio-cultural entity.

Thus, with the second method, the observer continues to observe Samoan practice in order to discover (within the society and not in his or her study) the other context to which 'free sex' (our initial label) is opposed. In short, he or she has to find the link to the whole that gives rise to an ambivalence which itself presents the possibility of an opposition of practices. This must then be analysed as a two-level practice. In the present case, it would appear that free sex is a reversal of the 'brother–sister relationship'. This is a general observation not limited to circumstances in which this 'freedom' could have led to incest between siblings (although it is significant that this theme is present in their mythology and in village gossip). Every practice of the type referred to in connection with 'free sex' is a reversal of the ideology that is represented in emblematic terms as the 'brother–sister relationship' (*feagaiga, alofa, faaaloalo*).

How do Samoans express this reversal? (We will see what makes it a reversal later on.) For instance, they say that a young man's intention to seduce a girl (including, of course, a married woman) is 'not *alofa*' (*e le alofa*). The same term is used to qualify the possible outcome of such a case, as well as the woman's attitude if she responds to his advances. My informant would utter this term spontaneously, without the slightest encouragement from the anthropologist through his questions. Then, when one asks for examples of *alofa* behaviour and an *alofa* relationship, the first replies given will almost always point to *feagaiga*, the brother–sister relationship. The relationship between God and humans is also referred to, as is that between the pastor and the village. Sometimes the list will even include a couple married in the best possible way: in church, with the wife having retained her reputation as 'daughter of the village' and 'sister of the family', in other words, her reputation as a virgin and hence an exemplary attitude of non-free sex.[4]

I must point out here that these examples do not constitute a heterogeneous list. The pastor was able, right from the start, to secure a central place in Samoan culture because he was immediately attributed the position of 'sister of the village'. At present he is designated the 'celestial brother–sister bond' or 'like a brother–sister bond'. What is more, the Divine, the one prior to the Mission as well as the new one, is the apex (and even the whole) of the system of titles which constitutes the whole social order. The sisters are its intermediaries, through whom sacredness is actualized, and who give 'life' to their ancestral family name (the 'title') and to those who form a 'family' around this name. It was this symbolic position which enabled the Mission to render sacred a form of marriage which appears to be analogous to the brother–sister relationship. Hence, according to our hypothesis, there is the absolute avoidance by couples married in church of any reference, whether by word or gesture, to the sex act in front of a third party, although the idea of the sex act has in itself never become shameful or indicative of sin in Samoa. In short, the unity that underlies these examples points to the brother–sister relationship as an emblem of *alofa*, as the opposite to not-*alofa*.

Other types of situation reveal the same pattern. When the anthropologist expresses notions referring specifically to the 'anatomical' (my word) difference between the sexes, and thus to a 'sexual' difference in Samoan (see above – re. the word *fafine* – and below) – for example, when he or she mentions the transmission of substances (blood lines etc.) through men versus through women in the course of a discussion centred on titles, genealogy, rank and the perpetuation of 'families' – he or she is told that it is 'disgraceful' to express such notions; to do so is not only irrelevant and inappropriate to the context, but, they will stress, it is ethically *antinomic*.

Furthermore, we can watch a recent interview with a Samoan man in a video filmed by George Milner, well-known as a specialist in the Samoan language and author of an English–Samoan dictionary. The fact that the interviewee is a pastor does not present an obstacle (unless the fact that his replies invoke *feagaiga* so directly constitutes one), as is made clear by listening to the whole of the interview. Generally speaking, Samoan pastors are first and foremost Samoans, members of a culture which they glorify as much as other Samoans. For them, as for all Samoans, the arrival of the Mission is included in their accounts of the origin of their 'culture' and 'tradition', which basically refer back to the nineteenth century. This having been stipulated, it can be said that the pastors are very keen to maintain 'the custom', *aganuu faaSamoa*, since the new Church has moulded itself to the existing system rather than creating its own set of values. The only notable change that took place affected marriage. In this case too, however, the change was a result of the indirect assimilation of marriage to a value that was already present. Although the pastor had become a 'sister', at the same time some of them had wives and were centring their instruction about the Christian sacrament of marriage on love, which they translated as *alofa*; a term which immediately evoked the brother–sister relationship for their listeners. To return to the interview: when the interviewing anthropologist (Christina Toren) asked the pastor (O Le Faafeagaiga Kamu) to explain what sort of value is attached to the virginity of unmarried girls and to comment on the place of these ceremonial virgins who represent their family and the whole village towards another village, he did not discuss 'the status of women' (or 'of the sexes') in his reply but said straight away that 'this relates to what I would call the brother–sister relationship'; but he did not comment further (Kamu 1988).

Much more data could be added to this. The overall picture is that of a broad opposition between two sets of facts and relationships. On the one hand, we can see the trans-generational continuity of the family group, the brother–sister bond (as well as the bond between the descendants of both sexes from a woman and her brother, themselves the children of an eponymous ancestor or who, lower down the whole family genealogy, form the point of reference for this particular discussion), the virginity, *teine muli*, of unmarried girls and, in a wider sense, what we here call 'non-free sex'. It is now permissible to use the term because it has already been invested with the reality which our enquiry gave it: the brother–sister relationship, *feagaiga*, and its synonyms which constitute the opposite of what we began by recognizing through assimilation to our culture – that is, the question of 'free sex'. On the other hand, we have an attitude or actions which indicate 'free sex'. We should add at once that the vocabulary used in this latter context (free *sex*) distinguishes between men (a relatively ambiguous semantic field) and women (a clear and restrictive definition meaning individuals engaged in a sexual relationship with a man), with the former as 'strong' beings and the second as 'weak' (vocabulary relating to fishing and war).[5]

At this point of our analysis of the opposition between the two sets, we have already penetrated into a specificity. There is still some way to go. If we have understood correctly and these two sets are indeed opposed within Samoan practice, we should be able to observe two things. First is an orientation to the whole, because any pertinent sociological opposition between two fields which are already defined by a relationship – in short, a relation of relations – cannot be symmetrical and must be orientated towards value (if, at least, we intend to study the society as a concrete reality and not simply as an analogous collection of mental classifications, which are thought but not lived (Tcherkezoff 1983)). We also have to see at the same point a transformation, which can be a reversal, from one relation to another. The question is knowing which relationship, in this link between relationships, is representative (or more representative) of the whole. The second relation constitutes a modification, if it is well and truly distinguished from the first one, although the modification only applies at a lower level. In a system consisting only of relations, differences between situations are revealed by transformations of the relations and/or of their order between themselves. It is not simply a case of different contexts (in which case the relations could be heterogeneous to one another, without any mutual link), since we are postulating a system: the whole of the social body, or a part which stands as a whole with regard to our present enquiry. Consequently, the successive transformations themselves trace an order; certain relations determine others and do so in a non-reciprocal manner.

SAMOA

The Samoan society considered here is basically the present State of Western Samoa, where I carried out several surveys, particularly in 1981–2, during a fourteen-month stay. I was able briefly to examine the American territory of Eastern Samoa which seems to be basically similar. There is a specific Samoan society. Everyone there speaks and thinks in Samoan. Furthermore, everyone's identity is conceived as part of an overall 'system of title-holders', or *faamatai*. This is a system of ancestral names, and consequently a system of groups of people who belong to that particular name (and to sets of names), and a system of lands, each associated with a name. Everyone who can trace a line to a title-holder, whether dead or alive, whether through blood kinship (paternal or maternal), adoption or marriage, and who puts this link into practice by means of participation (contributing ceremonial goods to exchanges between their group and other groups), forms part of the group which is defined by its title (or by a set of titles) and consists of those who put this 'familial' link, or *aiga*, into practice.

All these titles belong within one hierarchy which should not be understood in terms of social stratification (as in the case of an ordered and fixed list of names, in which the absolute position of each one can be determined). This hierarchy is quite different, since it implies that the representatives of different titles are able, when they meet up, to sit 'together' 'in a circle', this being the circumference of the ceremonial house in which every position is different at the same time as belonging to a single circle. The actual *hierarchy* pertains to the differences which are the *logical outcome of belonging to one and the same whole*, indicating that, although their practices take place at a level that relates to their 'difference' and so creates inequality, this level will always be encompassed by a further level at which 'belonging to one whole' sets the value. Thus, the first level is the one at which they share the ceremonial food, the speeches and the giving of gifts. This 'sharing' is a fact and is constantly invoked in their formal speeches, because each (of the title-holders) has access to these activities; the latter constitute the 'circle' and all those sitting in the circle participate.

The outcome of these exchanges of speeches and gift-giving, whether within the village or between villages, is to introduce differences which can be observed from the way the various participants take their places within the circle. Some differences have undoubtedly been established for centuries, as witnessed by the genealogical accounts, and others can be seen to change over a few days or weeks. These differences are everywhere; all the positions on the circle are different (there are also several ways of differentiating several subsystems operating simultaneously). However, the general idea holds good. These differences do not form an eternally established system of places granting unequal access to a shared substantive value; they are not external to the shared identity (such as unequal access to land and resources, when land is limited). They only apply within a second level in relation to the circle, which is 'complete' in itself. This 'circle' has four sides (four named parts) and, generally speaking, to be 'four-sided' is to be 'complete' in

Samoa. It is significant that the hierarchical differences between positions on the circle, where equality of membership comes first, refer us to the circle or semicircle of lands surrounding a village. Each name (title) is attached to a land which starts at the village and extends outwards, widening as it goes, towards the forest or sea. Both the statutory high positions on the circle and the less high ones have relatively similar shares, with low and high lands (the ground often rises steeply behind the villages, which are generally coastal). Were this not the case, the *hierarchy* would be a *stratification* (i.e. unequal access to things external to the whole constituted by differentiated terms).

This ranking or statutory system is firstly a system of belonging to one 'identity of a community', *aganuu* (the usual word for 'custom', constructed from *aga*, identity, essence and *nuu* village, social group), through a person's title or through the mediation of a title-holder, who, when enthroned, becomes head of family and thus the representative of the family to which one belongs. The system is both flexible and open. Each person is linked to several titles, and one in every eight adults (recently, one in four) bears a title (he is a title-holder). Thus it is not a 'chieftainship', nor a class system, nor a set of feudal orders. The title-holder is simply one to whom the 'whole family', *aiga potopoto* (the family in a circle), has decided to entrust its name and title; the family may subsequently change its mind. The title-holder administers the land, and this land cannot be alienated (sold, given as a guarantee to a private party, etc.). More than three-quarters of the country is still 'customary land', i.e. land which is attached to titles and cannot be sold (although there are problems arising in some areas between communal and individual control, cf. Tcherkezoff forthcoming b).

GENDER

Samoa constitutes a specific society, which means that the Samoan system is relevant to the study of gender in anthropology. This, however, is one of the reasons why Samoa has become a major example in this field. Unfortunately, the ethnographical specificity ascribed to Samoa by research of this kind reflects an imported ideology (*papalagi*, as the Samoans say, an 'intruder in the Samoan sky') rather than any empirical observation of the facts, compared at least with what I saw and heard for myself in Samoa.

All these various current analyses have somehow co-operated in their attempt to reveal a dualist scheme, even though Schoeffel has on several occasions sharply criticized Ortner's and Shore's views on gender (Schoeffel 1985, 1987).

For Ortner, Polynesia in general, with Samoa as a representative example, has a social organization based both on a male-orientated 'prestige' system, in which value pertains to rank and kinship and the maintenance of rank through descendants, and, to a certain extent, on kinship as something counter to affinity (by 'encompassing' affinity, in the sense of including that which is contrary, according to the author (Ortner 1981)). Men 'hold on' to female kindred, for women also transmit their rank. Female blood relatives are valued (but as intermediaries, in a system orientated towards men). Consequently, all other types of female status are more or less 'devalued' (such as lover, wife or mother); which, as should be pointed out, is not at all a necessary consequence of the first statement and which is furthermore wrong with regard to the relation of Ego to his mother. This strange reasoning is intended to explain the peculiar – albeit correct, in Western Polynesia at least – fact that a man's intention to engage in a sexual relationship, even when his aim is marriage, is generally viewed as something that must be 'stolen' (as Ortner says).

This model does not correspond with my own observations. While it is correct that the relationship between 'male' and 'female' is difficult and unequal, this is the consequence of an order that is orientated towards 'sisters' and not 'men'. My only comment for the moment is that if Ortner is correct, this would imply, as she says explicitly in the introduction to *Sexual Meanings* (Ortner and Whitehead 1981), that all female positions are defined relative to male positions. As it is, what is true for wives is not true for sisters. A wife is always designated according to her husband's status.[6] However, the vocabulary that is applied to a sister reveals a different orientation. She is called '*feagaiga*', 'the fact of having a face-to-face relationship'. On an everyday basis, she is properly called by the word that designates the brother–sister relationship (or, rather, the sister–brother relation) and the relationship between a sister's descendants (of both sexes) and her brother's descendants. A brother, for his part, is not called by this word. It should be added that the 'face-to-face relationship' (*aga* + *fe . . . i* (being 'in front of' + a 'mutual' relation) underlies the area of the ceremonial circle which defines a community. Rivalry is not involved; we are dealing with an encompassing relation in which one term 'is' the whole circle, and the other is part of the circle.

From this point of view, sister is an 'encompassing' term (within a two-level social logic (Dumont 1979; Tcherkezoff 1983)). She 'is' absolutely and the brother is 'the other' in this relationship; in short, between siblings of different sexes, only the man is sibling to the woman. While this linguistic form does serve as a useful indicator, it is in itself insufficient proof, simply telling us to observe the practices while paying attention to the possibility of encompassment – as is the case here. The brother is the 'trustee' of a name (title) which is made 'alive' (and can thus be transmitted) by his sister. Her brother procures the cooked food, his sister weaves the 'fine mat' of pandanus; both in myth and in ritual a person and a life spared through the blood-price given following a murder are, in fact, represented by the cooked (or to be cooked) food, primarily pork, covered with the mat. Furthermore, the sister represents the side of the sky and the light, that of life and of the mat – as an effective life-giving ritual object – and that of the ritual perpetuation of the family title. She has to be there, even if she just keeps quiet, to indicate or somehow to reveal who should be chosen trustee for the title when a title-holder dies or is deposed by this same assembly. Her body, too, is treated as though it were the matrix of the title.[7]

In Shore's (1981, 1982) analysis, female gender is represented by the status of sister. This seems a reasonable option, since this status epitomizes the part that is valued by Samoans, both male and female, of the broader set of data which constitutes (for us) female status in Samoa. However, this method of reducing Samoan classification to our own – in fact subordinating the former to the latter since we define the female sphere and the Samoans fill it out with their cultural preferences – leads our analysis to enter all this data forcibly onto a two-column scheme featuring only Female and Male and no third category or any other possible level at which the binary opposition of the sexes could be transformed into another relation. Consequently, to take one example, 'When we examine the relations between sister and wife, however, there is a weak replication of the Female–Male dichotomy, in which "wife" is symbolically a more "Male" status than is sister, which remains quintessentially Female' (Shore 1981: 208). To take another example, because sitting chiefs share some points in common with sisters (attitudes, sitting positions, honours received), they belong to the Female by analogy with the two distinctions, one between sitting chiefs *alii* and standing chiefs *tulafale* and the other between sister and brother (Shore 1981, 1982).

We are now rapidly being faced with an alternative, as is the case with the whole tradition of binary schemes in anthropology. On the one hand, is all this not so much an attempt at inter-cultural dialogue as simply a structural way of proving that, ideally, any observer can, by observing particular transformations, 'think up' the socio-cultural configurations of all these cultures and thus construct a picture of the human mind (Needham 1980, 1987)? In which case, while restricting things to a single, very poor logic, that of the analogy between symmetrical pairs, we are simply reiterating things that needed to be said in the 1950s (Lévi-Strauss 1958, 1962) but which no longer need to be postulated today – at least when no new form is elicited by repeating the project (which, fortunately, is not the case with many other contemporary structural research projects). Repetition and reduction are all the more a waste of time in that we are in a period when the idea of the unity of the human mind across cultures has gained the upper hand, but also when dialogue between different cultures is becoming increasingly difficult. On the other hand, this binary exercise is attempting, even implicitly, to tell us something specific about the 'order' that is present between terms encountered during classification of a society, between social relationships, and between persons. In which case, we are moving on to something else; we are talking about 'power' or 'dominance' and about 'sexual or gender asymmetry', in an attempt to show that one of the two columns in our scheme expresses a cultural concept or a social function which somehow dominates (controls, etc.) that which is expressed by the other column. However, if this is the case, establishing this double monism involves a serious problem of translation.

Consequently, no single fact that appears on the scene can be dismissed. However, as I have tried to demonstrate elsewhere, the analysis (based on an African example) underpinning this form of structural functionalism (the symbolic structure reveals by analogy – with or without an assumed 'reflection' – the relations between cultural categories and/or socio-cultural functions) had to dismiss certain facts which did not fit neatly into the picture.[8] The same problem arises in Shore's (1981) study on Samoan 'gender'; according to him, the situation is a consequence of a huge dualist configuration of the whole Samoan culture (as developed in Shore 1982). The binary scheme developed by Shore links more than eighty pairs and thus goes way beyond the records set in the collective work *Right and Left*, supervised by Needham earlier on (Needham 1973). One column represents social control (with the sister representing the Female here) and the other individual free will, which tends fairly often to be spontaneously anti-social and thus to demand its complement, which is harmoniously assumed to be 'social control' and the cultural forms of 'formal' authority as opposed to instrumental power. Note that Shore does not refer in any way to work of the kind contained in *Right and Left*, and that these writings do not explicitly purport to expose power relations, although they end up so doing (Tcherkezoff forthcoming c) and Shore's analysis is actually a good example of the possible consequences of this method.

There is no space here to take a close look at Shore's hypothesis, according to which two concepts of Samoan culture, *aga* and *amio*, are treated by all the inhabitants as explicit titles for the two great categories isolated by his binary analysis.[9] Two points should be mentioned here: Shore is mistaken in his usage and extension of these words. For instance, he reduces *aga* to social control and to human action in conformity to norms, whereas the word designates universal norms and can apply to a tree or a stone, for it signifies 'nature, essence, identity', within the whole formed by the 'social custom' *aganuu* (precise meaning 'the essence of the group'), from the 'family' group to the 'village' to the 'world' or *lalolagi* (under-the-sky), which itself is bounded by a semi-circle, the vault of the sky. What is more, the author thinks that *amio* designates an anti-social attitude, whereas the word designates any kind of comportment (by gods, men or animals), which can be 'good' or 'bad'.

In the same way as Needham's (1960) wish to present a binary Left and Right scheme led him, in the case of the Meru, to fall into sometimes flagrant misconceptions (see *supra* note 8), Shore's occasionally erroneous interpretation of these terms also betrays the obsession with the pair 'society versus individuals' and the preconception in anthropological terms of a social body which is *a priori* a control of individuals. The contrary applies in the case of Samoa, where, if one wants to talk about their world-view, one has to stress the fundamental premise that every being and thing takes its meaning and existence from 'above' ('God' and the 'essence-of-the-group'). This includes what and who will eventually behave in an anti-social way contrary to this 'essence' and what and who will thus 'dwell' in Night instead of living in Day (here indeed are two cosmological sides, but one encompasses the other), by 'stepping into the Night' and by leaving the 'Day' (this is what the violation of a prohibition is called in their mythology). On the side of Night is found violence and loneliness but these constitute a *transformation* of relations during the Day.[10] In Samoa, he who enters into

Night, so to speak, can only find unhappiness there (in combat against others or oneself; it is the domain of violence, murder and also of suicide). If it were really a world or a side of a world that was significant in itself (such as the idea of 'night' in *distinctive* opposition to that of 'day'), the individuals who turned up there would not be so weak, like the grasshopper in the fable who is caught out by winter when she has known and thought only of summer. If there were a sort of anti-social *amio* world, this anti-structure, so to speak, would be precisely ordered in a way which would constitute a distinctive opposition to the world of the (social) 'structure'. Those persons who turned up there would not perceive themselves as 'lost' (the current expression when the informant is speaking English). This, however, is indeed how Samoans perceive this side. This is also what makes adolescence difficult in Samoa, at least in connection with sexual desire and acts, for this life context pertains hugely to the Night.

Let us finish with a word about Schoeffel's (1978, 1979, 1985, 1987) analyses. The author stresses correctly that 'gender' does not constitute a predominant principle in Samoan culture in general and in male/female relationships that are in process of being established. Nevertheless, although the author does mention 'encompassment' by referring to Louis Dumont for this logical notion relative to the sacred, her analysis puts forward a view of a male world of secular power encompassed by a female world of sacred power. We have come back to 'women'. They are indeed valued in their position as sisters because it is they who transmit *mana*, the sacred power which is thought to encompass *pule*, the secular power (Schoeffel 1979, 1987). Here, the substantialism which was avoided by thinking critically about 'gender' re-emerges in the idea of reproduction: the transmission of a mystical substance which itself actually leads back to a gender or simply a sexual category (women). As it is, *mana* cannot be transmitted solely by one side of the relationship (whether the latter is man versus woman or brother versus sister). Each time I tried to induce an informant to establish an analogous relationship between a distinction *mana* (or *mamalu*, the dignity of rank)/*pule* and a distinctive opposition of gender, sex or whatever (I was pursuing that idea in 1982), the reply would be that these notions were both something 'of the title' and not properties attached to persons, to whom one could then attribute possession and the transmission of a particular property. This is to say that distinctions are to be observed as the product of *the social reproduction of titles*. As it is, in these places, the brother versus sister relationship is the agent – rather than the-power-of-the-brother or the-sacred-that-pertains-to-the-sister – since when given substance in this way (as if each one could function and/or have meaning in itself) these notions do not exist in Samoan consciousness. Furthermore, the point that the agent is, in fact, a relationship is obvious when one considers that the object, the title, is itself a relationship (of belonging), a bond between a group of persons and one or more ancestors, and not an object of power, whether secular, sacred or whatever.

TWO LEVELS

We have mentioned the fact that, where female sexuality is concerned, Samoans view as contradictory any reference to sexual distinctions within a genealogical context. Shore (1982), however, attempts to retain a distinction in terms of blood-lines, between a 'strong' side (through men) and a 'weak' side (through women). However, the Samoans are very clear on this point. I have often heard this 'strong versus weak' opposition applied to contexts in which a distinction is made between a 'man' *tamaloa* (in the sense of the Latin *vir*) and a woman *fafine* (in the sense of 'female'), by imagining humanity as included in or equivalent to their representation of the animal realm. However, were I to bring this distinction into a conversation about genealogy, I would be told that these terms (strong and weak) are 'disgraceful' and that one must discuss it in terms of *tamatane* and *tamafafine*, which designate the descendants (of both sexes) of a man and his sister respectively.

Why is it 'disgraceful' to superimpose contexts in this way and to mention the man versus woman difference when referring to the brother versus sister relation (we know that this orders the genealogical reference)? It is because, when we translate '*tamaloa* versus *fafine*' as 'man versus woman' (indeed, there are no other possible translations) we are, as far as Samoans are concerned, actually denoting the *sexual* relationship. We have already noted that this happens to be 'contrary' (not *alofa*) to contexts defined by the brother–sister relationship.

Let us observe first of all that every Samoan representation of a person is defined in a relationship (according to our sense of the concept). This is the case with women, with one peculiarity. Femaleness and the female gender are not directly comprehensible; the only word that seems to approach this meaning, *fafine*, involves a relationship, albeit a very restrictive one. A person is *fafine* because she is sexually active, engaged in a relationship with a man. But this 'sexual relationship', as we put it, is not a 'relationship' in Samoan, at least if one observes the usage of terms generally employed to designate a 'bond' or a 'space' linking two objects or persons, the reciprocal nature of prestations, etc. (*va, feagaiga*). For the Samoans say that the sexual bond is something that one 'does'. The relationship between the partners is thus one between two agents and it measures their equality or inequality of action (to do, to act, is called *fai*). It is here that Samoan practice and speech about the *inequality of the sexes* is articulated ('strength' versus 'weakness'), for in the sexual relation, the man's action is thought as 'strong' and the woman's as 'weak'. In fact, what we have now is a logic of the *stratification* type, in the sense that we have distinguished this concept from the concept *hierarchy*, thereby adopting a distinction which was elaborated by Dumont in a completely different field (i.e. with respect to economic classes, or groups segregated according to 'race' in the West, and the caste system in India; Dumont 1966: Appendix A). The connection between the persons is mediated by a measure of each one's connection to things and substances (even those which we call 'symbolic'). This access can be equal or unequal, being access to a substantive identity. This substantialism (logical, not mystical) is apparent in expressions currently used by Samoans to designate the sex act: *fai*, to have sex; *fai amio*, to do the behaviour; *fai aiga*, to make a family; *fai mea*, to do the thing.[11]

In contrast, the brother–sister relationship is not a connection between two agents and two measurable forms of access to a substantive quality. It is part of the 'relations' (in Samoan) in which one term, the one which 'does' things at a certain level, is encompassed by another which somehow constitutes the matrix of the former and which defines the space for applying the relation, thus making an action possible. The Samoans express this through the concept and practice of *tapuaiga* where a person (representing a group 'in the circle') 'puts himself in silent communion with the divine', which enables an action to take place during this time with some chance of success. This is the brother–sister relationship, whereby the sister represents the group in relation to its origin, thus enabling the brother to represent the group in relation to other groups. The main thing is to understand that title-holding (by the brother) is a representation that involves being active (preparing successful exchanges, for instance, by organizing work in the plantations and collecting money gained from paid work), and that this representation is dependent on another representation of the group, which is called 'immobile', *nofo*, in which the life of the title, itself the sum of their ancestors, is actualized (thus the person who presides over a man's funeral is a 'sister').

We have emphasized a primary methodological necessity: that of following to the end the relation encountered and recognized by us, in order to see where it stops applying and what other relation it then confronts. Our question about 'gender' leads us to the sex difference, which is in Samoa a 'sexual' difference that is in opposition to the brother–sister relation. Or, by following Shore or Schoeffel, our enquiry into 'gender' reveals the central position of the brother–sister relationship, on condition, however, that we claim, like Schoeffel and if need be more clearly than her, that this is not a 'gender' relation in Samoan practice – and that this relationship reveals an opposite element, that of the sex relation (our word) in 'sexual' terms (thus translating the Samoan 'to have sex' in a 'strong' or 'weak' manner). Now, we have to observe the orientation of this opposition between two relations.

Part of our work has already been done. These two relations are not analogous. One of them involves 'holistic' inclusion or *encompassment*: one of the two terms 'is' (designates in linguistic terms and represents in practice) the entire relationship between the two terms; and the superiority of this term over the other is then 'absolute', obvious and without appeal to a form of measurement involving access to a substance. The other is *unequal* in the stratification sense. Thus, we already know which of the two relations we must begin with in order to observe the whole of the picture. In any case, for comparative reasons which constitute a preliminary generalization, we did in fact agree to submit our question to a 'whole' even before entering into the nature of a particular society. Thus we must establish at a first level the relation or relationships with a 'holistic nature' that we may encounter. However, we can only do so definitively in our final model if we verify the existence of a transformation between the first and the second set of relations and whether this is irreversible or, at least, not reciprocal. If we are indeed dealing with one single relation of relations, the second relationship is not a context but a level in relation to the first.[12]

We must thus observe whether the brother–sister connection can lead to a form in which we would rediscover the sexed–sexual man versus woman pair. The first question is undoubtedly as follows: is 'gender' already present somehow in this relationship? If the distinction between 'genders' were fundamental in Samoa, it would appear in this society's holistic relations and in the encompassing term of each of these relations. However, this is not the case. No speech or practice concerning sisterhood suggests that we should define it as the female half of the world or of society; nor is this the case in English-speaking Samoan discourse, although English-speaking Samoans would be able to express such a concept, and nor in Samoan where the very word is absent, although everyone is familiar with the English words 'woman' and 'female'. There is no reason why this should surprise us. They have no substantive and definitive definition because sisterhood is defined as encompassing; in short, it is a category that can only be defined or 'translated' for the observer by his recognition of what it encompasses (the sister is not sister 'of' whomsoever, she 'is', and the brother is 'brother of' the *feagaiga*).

Turning to the brother, we do find a certain presence of gender here, but at a second level. At the first level, where the brother is, so to speak, defined by his sister, we see the brother holding the family title (depending on circumstances – one man in eight was a title-holder prior to the recent multiplication of titles) and thus actualizing a continuity that is represented by his sister. He is the one who uses his eyes to 'see' the empirical world (the 'title-holder' is *matai*; *mata* = eyes, face); but the 'apple' of his eyes 'is his sister', *ioimata*; the 'stem', the 'root' *io* of his capacity for 'seeing' *matamata*). This aspect defining the brother is relevant at the level where the brother bears the name and thus 'serves' the name, *tautua*, the family and his sisters in particular; being 'head of the family', as we put it, in Samoa means 'putting oneself at the service' of the group, at least at the service of the group's name, and thus at the service of a certain form of ancestor worship, which here takes the form of maintaining a genealogy. At another level, when commenting specifically on the content of this 'service' as the work of the chief (*galuega*), being 'strong as a man' (*tamaloa*) is one of the qualities required. In fact, most title-holders are men (though this job is not expressly limited to the male sex). There are some (less than 10 per cent) title-holders who are indeed women; in which case it is said that the woman has agreed to abandon her role as *feagaiga* and to comply with her family's wishes in considering her alone capable of the job (implying that she can deliver persuasive speeches and make every member desire to contribute to the collective good during the preparation of exchanges). But, it is precisely in such cases that the Samoans say also that this person is chosen because 'we know that she is capable of being strong like a man'.

Is this appearance of the male gender within the encompassed term of the first relationship ('brother') coherent with the whole set of data? Does its presence imply that this term should also be considered as pertaining to a second level? We are invited to think so because 'gender' is not implied in the Samoan definition of the encompassing term ('sister'); indeed, the role of sister can be held by a male title-holder, whose genealogy places him in a 'sister' relationship with another title; and this relationship alone will count and not the person's sexual identity. Also, we know that calling a sister *fafine* (within her social roles as a 'sister') would bring serious trouble. As for the 'gender' identity of a title-holder, we have just said that it is, at a certain level, male. This does not hinder the fact that a man can, for instance, hold a sister role at funerals: it does not bring up any affirmation of maleness in the role of sister in general. Sisterhood is neither 'female' (it cannot be called *fafine*) nor 'male' (it is not said that one should be 'strong' in order to be a sister). On the other hand, while there are indeed female title-holders alongside a male majority, they are assimilated to men when a particular content of their work comes into consideration. In which case, and in order to be sure that this second stage is a level and not merely a different context, we should look at a stage at which the 'strong-male' aspect of the brother emerges not only as secondary in relation to his sister, but also as a determinant element when considered on this second level. We should insist on this logical constraint, which will undoubtedly appear superfluous to the reader. If there is indeed a value relationship between our two initial relationships, the change of level must affect the entire first relation and not simply emerge as a lower version of one of the two terms.

This observation is very clear. When a sister, considered as such (i.e. 'non-free sex'), behaves in a way which makes the group think that she is behaving in a context of free sex (to retain our own vocabulary which encapsulates the data referred to above), and that she is thus a *fafine*, it is precisely her brother who is supposed to act against her and 'with strength' – 'because it is he who is the man' (*tamaloa*) – in order to stop or even punish her (with words but, where necessary, also with blows). The case is clear-cut when dealing with an unmarried sister. It is less so when the sister is married. Firstly, the infringement of the prohibitions is always less serious (they would refer rather to proper conduct, reputation and such). Next, there is the idea, albeit not elaborated, that in this event she is 'elder' and 'so, I can tell her what I think but it is hard for me to raise my voice or threaten her'.

We should add that the brother can act with 'strength' against his sister only if he is older than her. This is at first surprising, because the observer is used to the notion that being first-born is not relevant to the brother–sister relationship (generation or *tupulaga* being the only notion that counts). On the other hand, the consideration of being first-born is constantly present between siblings of the same sex. Next, we tell ourselves that we should actually have expected this fact. We have arrived at and, within the chronology of our observations, returned to a relation in which the two persons are distinguished by their inequality of access (access to sex as a gender category – 'strong' sex versus 'weak' sex – and access to sexual activity – to do *fai*. Being unequal and thereby identical in substance (and different in terms of external measurement), they can be compared, and the presence of this other substantive measurement, that of being first-born, is certainly not incongruous, even if it is not a logical necessity here.

It should be added that Samoans are very conscious of this change of level between one side where there is no substantive comparison to another level where there is. Man (*tamaloa*) and woman (as *fafine*) are more/less strong/weak, as same-sex siblings are 'bigger-older/smaller-younger' (*matua/laitiiti*). And anyone who would forget his or her place within those scales is *tautalaitiiti*, he or she who speaks above the smallness of his or her position: e.g. a child using unrespectful words, or a girl (or a young woman, or even mature) who seems to be sending signs of seduction to men (or to a man) (the man's seduction is not *tautalaitiiti*, because he is on the strong side; it is just 'bad' *leaga* and 'not *alofa*', because inducing *teine* or women into sex is a move contrary to *alofa*, as we have noted). But if we consider the first level, where relations, like that of sister–brother and others, are of the *tapuai/fai* type (the divine-human identity encompasses the human agency), we meet with sayings such as: 'he who is on the side of doing cannot be superior to the side of *tapuai*'. The saying, used in a variety of contexts (from ritual to modern sport games, where the *tapuai* side is constituted by the people supporting their village), does not set a given substantive comparison (saying that A 'is superior' to B), but denies the comparison (. . . *e le sili* . . .) (cf. Tcherkezoff forthcoming a). With encompassment, the superiority is absolute: there is no comparison.

Outside of encompassment, asymmetry becomes inequality: there persons (or objects) are definitively compared.

This two-levels configuration should be elaborated further where men versus women relations are concerned (cf. Tcherkezoff forthcoming a, b). We can add here a few analogous transformations concerning other holistic relations mentioned earlier as so many instances or derivatives of *feagaiga*, in order to enlarge the understanding of this two-levels logic. However, even if we did not possess these complements, we would still need to find a configuration that takes account of the actions which may occur between the same persons during the same day and which do not fail to surprise recently arrived observers. For instance, the same young man who slaps his younger sister with violence because she was seen talking to another young man on the path near her home will act as a perfect servant to her and the others in their home – preparing food, laying the table (garnishing fibre platters which he places at his sister's feet, everyone being seated on the floor), getting up to fetch water, and so forth. What is more, far from being restricted to a few domestic contexts (in which we have already observed a reversal of the situation that is frequently observed or at least reported: the woman only becomes dominant within the secondary home sphere), this second attitude epitomizes their whole relationship and involves their whole existence. Thus it can become a matter of life and death: suicide by young men who have been rebuffed by a sister is not unknown (apparently when they felt their reprimand had been unfair or when their quarrel had had too many witnesses thus giving rise to 'shame', *ma*).[13]

DIFFERENT EXAMPLES; SAME QUESTIONS

Let us add a few analogous examples. We may recall that our criticism of the procedural method of establishing analogies between distinctive pairs had led us to grouping by analogy relations between two levels (Tcherkezoff 1983: 74–6). Analogy becomes useful again once the elements involved are relationships and not terms, and the analogy is effected between two relations of relations: in other words, between two transformations. This type of grouping is, given the present stage of the holistic-structural method, the best means of revealing the layers of value in a particular society.

We began by citing the relationship between the pastor, the 'sister' of the village, and the village itself (in the sense of *fono*, the circle of family title-holders who together constitute the village).

At the first level, the village serves the pastor, constantly bringing him the things a brother brings his sister (food, money and, in the present case, dwelling and entire upkeep). Thus, in the large villages of several thousand inhabitants, a pastor can be a very rich man in Western terms (and thus he is one who is expected to provide substantial gifts in the exchanges). At this level, the pastor brings God-given sacredness (*mana*) to the village. The village is encompassed, in the sense that the detention of power *pule* and the capacity to exercise it through the decisions of the *fono* depend in the last resort on the will of God, according to the Samoan representation. At another level, however, the village affirms itself as distinct from God: the pastor is excluded from the *pule*. In fact, he is the only man in the village (and in all other villages where he has kinship ties) who is forbidden from aspiring to a title. Although candidature for titles is wholly open in the Samoan system, all that is required is some sort of kinship tie with the ancestral name and previous participation, in the form of service, in the group's ceremonial activities and in supporting the previous title-holder. Thus, the pastor cannot take a place in the *fono* to contribute 'politically' to its decisions (if he is invited, it is to provide a blessing). Consequently, he, as an inhabitant of the village, is subject by his office to the decisions of the *fono*.

Thus two levels are apparent. Furthermore, it is interesting to observe that, in the last resort, it is possible for the pastor to counteract the decision of the *fono* council. This comes down to bringing things back to the first level, and indeed such cases have been known to occur and are often commented on. It has happened several times, fifteen years ago, then six years ago, and quite recently in November 1990. When an inhabitant, whether a title-holder and thus member of the village council called *fono* or not, openly and repeatedly defies the council's decisions by refusing to submit to them (refusing to recognize a neighbourhood right and/or to pay a fine for a misdeed committed by a member of his family, persisting when the fine is doubled and staying put, pretending to ignore what is going on when they come to banish him), and if he fails, whether due to naïvety or bad judgement, to find enough support among his peers, he will be threatened with 'being burnt alive and cooked in an oven' (with hot stones). Samoan informants say that he would very likely be killed and that this would be perfectly admissible.[14] As it was, in the cases mentioned above, an enormous oven was prepared, the culprit was tied to a stake like a stuck pig and brought by some men to be roasted. In the latest case, according to an unverified rumour, the man was set down and began to howl, upon which his devastated wife dropped down dead from a heart attack (they were an old couple). The man, however, was saved, as in the previous cases, because the pastor intervened by throwing himself over the culprit or by publicly threatening to do just that. At this point, the proceedings were halted and the guilty man was banished.

According to our hypothesis, by covering the body of the culprit, the pastor was equating himself with the fine mat (the first of the objects of ceremonial giving, an attribute above all of the 'sister' and manufactured by women), similar to the mat that the perpetrator of a murder (or his head of family, a title-holder) covers himself with when he comes to offer peace and compensation to his victims. The culprit, too, or his representative, is covered in this way, holding oven stones and presenting himself as a pig about to be roasted (the latter traditional act is nowadays no longer present in the rite of murder price). Here, the change of level is effected in the reverse direction, through a procedure which can be said in passing to be characteristic of ritual logic (Tcherkezoff 1983: Conclusion, 1986a, 1986b, 1989, forthcoming d): that of encompassment by the sacred, which often consists in Samoa, as well as the whole of Polynesia, of wrapping something up in a fine mat.

Whatever the nature of this other ritual transformation from level two to level one, it is notable that we find here in a wholly different context a priest versus chief(s) relationship which is set on two levels, as was the case in India, where Dumont long ago considered this kind of relationship (Dumont 1966) and inaugurated the search for a holistic methodology about hierarchies. As in the Indian case, we see here that the question involves something quite different from identifying a context of religious power and a different 'political' power context, and then saying that precedence between the persons representing these contexts reverses when one of them passes from one to the other.[15] The central fact, for a methodologically holistic consideration of the social system, is that one level depends on the other, and that we have to expose this hierarchy (order between the relations). In India, royal power (on earth) to which the priest himself is subject, depends on it being possible for the king to be in a caste relationship (and thus to be ritually purified when necessary), and this latter relationship pertains to a system that is represented by the priest. In Samoa, it is apparent, beyond the division between priest and village council, that while one can turn things back (to return to the relationship in which the pastor is superior), the other cannot; any observer present for long enough would be able to note that no circumstance exists whereby the council could counter a decision by the pastor or the Church in matters relating to the Church.

A second and, for the time being, final example is provided by the two kinds of title-holder. They are all heads of family invested with holding their ancestral name. However, some of them are names of *alii* ('sitting chiefs' I shall say) and others names of *tulafale* ('standing chiefs'). The sitting chief (the term has no known etymology, and is the pan-Austronesian term for chief) is the one who is expected to be 'in place, sitting, immobile', *nofo*; for he is 'close to the divine' and 'the origin'. The standing chief, who is 'the base (or the stake), *tula*, of the house, *fale*',[16] is also called 'he who makes the speeches' or *failauga*. It is he who speaks in a strong voice (whereas the *alii* always speaks in measured tones, audible in a gathering but without raising his voice), declaims publicly the sacred words, the genealogies and the ornate speeches filled with mythological allusions, and who also engages in the rites and the verbal sparring matches that occur during exchanges.

The relationship of the *tufale*, or orator in short, to the *alii*, the chief in short, is respectful and involves paying him the prestations due to a superior (gifts of cooked food; in return, the chief gives him mats), especially when each of them is linked by their respective title within the framework of a family or a whole village. Nevertheless, it comes as a surprise to find that every category of Samoan shares a whole way of talking and a common attitude, whereby the orators are the people 'who really do things', who 'make village policy', because they can 'move' and 'go here and there', whereas the chief 'stays still'. The latter attribute (*nofo*), which is a sign of 'dignity' or *mamalu* at the first level, somehow becomes a sign of weakness at the second level; Samoans in general, and title-holders of both categories in particular, joke about the subject when explaining things to strangers. They happily cite the instance of the ceremonial food which is shared out during feasts. The chief receives the small share, with more bones than meat (the pig's back, the fish-head), but this share happens to be 'the most dignified' or *mamalu* part of the animal's body. At this level, we find ourselves back in the world of 'positions' (*tulaga*, the place as sign of rank, the position on a whole, e.g. the ceremonial circle of title-holders sitting in council or the body of the cooked animal) and, in the gift of food, what counts here is also position. Nevertheless, at the same time but at another level, one compares quantities. Hence the laughter and joking at the stranger's surprise: 'Yes, we are there at the feast, keen to get lots to eat, greedy as dogs, and the *alii* will get almost nothing . . .' (said by an orator). The informant laughs at the stranger's surprise at what appears to be a system with double values, one of which, however, makes sense to him: 'This is how it's always been'.

In short, one could say that the more dignified the part, the less there is of it to eat. Here, the coherence has nothing to do with a division into sacred versus power, any more than it has in the case of the brother–sister relation, since in neither case is a theory of this type formulated or set in action. It may simply be noted that one level (receiving more or less: the distinction is made and joked about) is explained by another one (more or less 'dignified'), and that its reciprocal does not exist. The first level is not explained by the second, nor by anything at all, unless it be by general notions of 'dignity' and 'position' which refer directly to the titles system. This ambivalence characterizes the encompassed term (the orator, see *infra*); for he is the one they refer to in order to show that political activity is going on behind the dignity, and consequently that the chief is stipulated as inept because he is immobile. This ambivalence is brought to bear on the 'mobility' of the orator. He eats more 'because he moves' and 'makes things move', but he is less dignified because 'moving' is 'less dignified' than 'sitting still'. However, plenty of food 'makes you stronger' and 'moving' is 'stronger' than 'staying', etc. This talk becomes clearer once one has understood that two relationships are involved, two oppositions, and that the first – strong versus weak: moving around versus staying and not moving – is at a level encompassed by the second – sitting versus standing and talking: sitting in the sacred circle and communicating with the divine (*tapuai*) versus stepping out of the circle to carry out and do the actions decided in the circle. One would then have to add that the second relation is holistic (all title-holders can be called *alii*, more precisely *tamalii*; if necessary a chief can do the work of an orator), whereas the first is a distinctive opposition. Which is why 'orator' is the term we designate as 'encompassed'. We would rediscover the form and even the content of the relation of relations which answers our question about the sex difference.

Samoan society is after all truly dualist, but in the way every society is: a dual system of relations (and not a dichotomy of cultural contents). On the one side there are 'relationships' in the sense of the *feagaiga*; on the other there are oppositions of substance. And the former are accompanied (ineluctably?) by the latter, but although the latter are open to the universal, they are nevertheless a product derived from the former and subordinated with regard to their application. The hierarchical partition of the ceremonial pig or fish ('positions' which differ in 'dignity', that is to say which differ in their capacity to represent more or less of the whole body) also defines a second level, that of eating more or less. However, the latter does not define the system according to which the animal is carved up; in fact it defines nothing, and even interested parties say 'that's the way it is' and laugh when it happens. This is one brief but enlightening example of the recognizable empirical concomitants of a particular ideology. These have to be pinpointed so as to flesh out, so to speak, the global ideology. To a greater or lesser extent, the latter always represents and orders a set of 'positions' (even in societies without statutory social scales; *viz.* the positions held in a cycle of ceremonial exchanges). Without this 'flesh', the ideology would remain totally 'other' in the eyes of anthropologists. On the other hand, if we are content simply to observe the inequalities, like the one between those who 'eat more or less meat', we would be left with what we already know about inequality, and we would miss the whole Samoan specificity of an inequality which touches on, but from below, the hierarchy of positions (status) and which transforms it somehow. Thus, in the anthropological model, the hierarchy of relations (considering the two levels as a unit) is then to be expected in empirical terms and necessary in methodological terms.

CONCLUSION

Although this chapter is more of an introduction to the study of 'gender' in Samoa, it may be possible to reach a provisional conclusion.

Generally speaking, the observation of a society as a whole requires that its holistic relations and their transformations be classified. This is how we obtain two levels. In Samoa, the first level is a relation, *tapuai* versus *fai*, in which the 'doer', *fai*, exists only through him or those who, properly speaking, represent the sacred in the circle, by doing *tapuaiga*. The second level is a transformation of the first and reveals inequalities of 'strength' in the action of 'doing' – that is, in the agricultural-familial-political 'work' which occupies each 'family' and its title-holder or holders, formerly also in war, and formerly and today in shared sexuality, in which the same 'strong'/'weak' vocabulary appears.

Once we had exposed this hierarchical structure, a precondition to any line of questioning that could constitute a comparison centred on ourselves, we could then attempt to recognize the place of 'gender' in it.

If we were to consider that every man–woman relationship observed by us has something to tell us about 'gender', which means in fact that we avoid having with Samoans a real dialogue which would include the essence of our question, we could then undoubtedly conclude that gender is ordered above all as a brother–sister and not a husband(lover)–wife(woman) opposition, quite unlike many other societies in which the married or simply heterosexual couple is seen as the model for the gender classifications that those societies apply to the rest of the world. However, we would then be obliged to include statements in our answer which would be totally incomprehensible in Samoan and which would be pronounced 'wrong' by any Samoan who could read our language (the wife is 'male'; the sitting chief is 'female'; the man who through his title is in the position of 'sister' is 'female' as is the pastor, etc.). For our part, we consider it essential to retain a translation with *two meanings*. Although our interpretation certainly does not have to consist of a discourse that has already been formulated by Samoan society, whether universally or through a few specialists (Samoa is not necessarily what its philosophers say of it; India is not just what Brahmin literature tells us, etc.), it must be such that, when expressed in Samoan or to Samoans who speak our language, they themselves recognize their society through our own ideology. We must try to find a double translation for isolated relations and, more especially, for the order of their mutual determination. This can be done; at least that was the impression I got during some discussions with certain Samoans.

We could also say that the configuration of gender is a symmetrical reversal. At one level, female is superior, and at another, the opposite is the case. We would, however, have a problem establishing which level explains the other. So we would have to be content with a complementarity (religion as female, politics as male) which reflects no more than our own history of ideas. In which case, neither our journey nor the imposition of our presence on another would be necessary.

We could note, furthermore, that the opposition between different practices focusing on the bodies of women constitutes the limit of our levels. It could even be added that the boys have no concept of virginity as a limit and that prohibitions of pre-marital sexuality are either absent or weak for them (Samoa, Tuvalu, Tokelau; personal observations; Rotuma, cf. Howard 1970). In reality, however, the question about the sexual disposition of the female body is itself a consequence of the fact that this body is 'sacred-forbidden', *sa*, which should in turn be interpreted in relation to a central fact, that of the regeneration of the family title (*supra* note 7).

However, these questions apart, we are left with a single massive fact: this female body, which constitutes the limit or the matrix of the social system, is subjected by men to the rules that regulate its practice; to wit, the agent of its ritual deflowering at marriage used to be a title-holding man, an orator from the betrothed man's group. This leads us back to the concept of a system that is defined or retained by title-holders, the majority of whom are men. However, title-holders are not forcibly male (and title-holding is not defined primarily as pertaining to the male world, but as part of what the sister represents); and indeed Samoan history features some famous title-holding women (Gunson 1987; Schoeffel 1987). Thus, we have mentioned the fact that our informants (of both sexes) insist on the idea that the woman who becomes a title-holder somehow sacrifices her position as *feagaiga* because her family needs her to do the 'chief's work'. We also know that the sister could retain supreme authority in politics, through the decisions which are announced by the brother but which follow the sister's sacred counsel (Schoeffel 1987). Finally, and above all, although the female body is indeed attributed to the service of titles, the latter are not simply men (♂) nor are they simply an object of male power. The link with the ancestors to which the titles testify, while remaining 'in life', is the result of the 'brother–sister' relationship, in which the sister is the encompassing pole.

To sum up, we have a methodological choice: either we submit the society under examination to our imported question or we submit the latter to the former. In the second case, I would say that in Samoa, 'gender' and its distinctions begin where status ceases to operate ('status' sums up the whole system of titles and its reproduction); because these distinctions are immediately connoted and even defined within the sexual relationship and because this 'connection' (our term) 'reverses' the relationship which is at the centre of status, namely the sister»brother one (» is our symbol for holistic relationships). *A 'gender' difference is understood in Samoa as a difference of enacted sexuality* that pertains to the connections that occur between two 'agents'. This substantive comparison then presents the possibility of inequality, such as that of 'strong' versus 'weak'. Such connections are the opposite of relations which give meaning and existence to 'the action' (*tapuai/fai*). One major example of these latter relationships is the brother»sister encompassment. One sign of this orientated contrarity is the way men behave towards women, which seems to meet double standards: 'service' to sisters and 'violence', whether expressed or potential, towards a *fafine*.

It is significant that Samoan vocabulary of 'gender' is lacking; *fafine* has a limited meaning and its complement, *tane* (male) is a word used almost solely in the sense of 'my husband', or for universal maleness (the two sexes in humanity, beyond society, or a gender classification of objects;[17] and the usual word for man when referring to an empirical individual and not to the category as a whole is *tamaloa*, which implies that the man is, or is of an age to be, married). This lacuna in their vocabulary recurs in the particular case of terms relating to homosexuality. Such men are called 'like women', and *fafine* is the only word employed: *faafafine* (*faa* 'like'). As it is, we do not have a complementary word for lesbians such as *faatane* (which would mean 'like men') and the language has adopted a foreign word: '*tomboy*'. We find in this case one consequence of the fact that womanhood requires a dichotomous appellation, either 'sister' or 'sexual female'. This is not the case, or less so, on the male side, and such asymmetry is obviously significant given that, at this level, the distinction is controlled by male ideology. We must also know that both *faafafines* and *tomboys* are at first individuals who have been identified by their public behaviour; it does not necessarily indicate that a particular individual engages in homosexual activity. However, the available vocabulary is only *fafine*, 'sexualized women'. The fact that *faafafine* boys wander on paths and streets prevents them from being compared to *teine*, even if people thought that they had no sexual activity whatsoever (we know that the *teine* 'stays put', 'inside', *nofo*). At an individual level, in the case of a young boy, the parents or older siblings would joke at him, or scold him when he behaves in an 'effeminate' way, by saying: 'don't play to be like a girl'. Hence the way Samoans are led commonly to represent *faafafine* practices, according to which they would be really 'like sexual women' in their homosexuality, offering fellatio to non-*faafafine* men (especially unmarried ones). Indeed, this does seem to be what happens in a certain number of cases (although my information is derived from non-*faafafine* boys who were propositioned or sisters of *faafafine* who overheard private conversations). We can observe that, anyway, this is how non-*faafafine* Samoans represent to themselves the supposed sexual activity that some *faafafine* are thought to have. As though 'to be effeminate' (our word), but designated as *faafafine*, immediately meant to adopt a 'female sexual' position within a male homosexual context.

It is also significant that Samoans do not seem to possess a dominant or established representation of the *tomboys*' intimate practices, for which they do not even have a word (although *faatane* is a linguistic complement of *faafafine*, the expression is curiously enough not understood). Furthermore, *faafafine* form groups which are recognized in the villages (and even in the capital, where they put on dressing-up competitions to which everyone is invited), although there is nothing of the kind for the *tomboys*. The very notion of a socially recognized grouping for women who behave like men seems ridiculous or indecent.

Thus, the most particular feature of Samoan gender is the way it 'sexualizes' women, and only women, both from the male and *the overall point of view*; women are, however, placed at a precise level of the overall configuration which we must try to take account of. It is not enough to record the *feagaiga* versus *fafine* opposition (sister versus sexually active woman) as though it were simply a distinctive opposition, the product of a male view and practice. This dichotomy becomes a hierarchy of relations – sister»brother versus man♂»woman-female – even though it is very significant that, for men, the limit (in terms of virginity for instance) is a non-socialized and not very significant fact which emerges only very faintly in their vocabulary compared with the vocabulary for women. And even if male homosexuality does manage to be expressed and represented as a social fact, by means of a symmetrical reference to the idea of *fafine*, the female version is enclosed from the start in the non-spoken (the term *tane* avoids male sexuality and is limited to designating the 'husband';[18] the very notion of a '*faatane*' sexuality for women cannot be expressed).

We can conclude that, at a second level, women are enclosed into a limited ('sexual') definition that enables men to be dominant, but we must also conclude that this level is itself the encompassed result of an ideology of *alofa*, a-sexual and sister»brother orientated, which is no more and no less the result of male dominance than the title-system could be said to be or not to be male-dominated. There, the debate becomes different: shall we give precedence to the fact that most title-holders are male, that the word title-holder, *alii*, can receive a modern semantic extension to mean 'gentlemen' (see note 17), or to the fact that the reproduction of the relationship here called 'title' requires a 'sister and brother' pairing and is reluctant to recognize a world of 'males and females'? At this point, the debate is methodological, and, according to the initial question (universal study of male dominance versus comparison of societies considered as concrete wholes), the answer will be different. This chapter aimed at suggesting that there is indeed such a choice, by showing that, in Samoa, gender is not an overall organizing principle. The choice is the one between the kind of question we begin with. If it is universal study of male dominance, we shall relate all gendered relations we meet to the symbolic position of Male in the Male–Female dichotomy. If the question is how a society considered as *whole* answers to *our* question on gender, we do not need to restrict ourselves to a dichotomy (and we must avoid referring relations to one pole predefined by a dichotomy); but we have to find ways of ordering 'in relation to the whole' all the relations we meet, by placing first those which do indicate wholeness through their 'holistic' form, and by investigating how these relations can be transformed at some secondary level into more dichotomic relations, where distinctive opposition is then at work.

NOTES

1 On one level, A is a whole (whether global or partial in relation to the whole society) and thus includes one or some B parts (see *infra*: the sister with regard to the brother). At a second level, B and A are in distinctive opposition to each other (which can be specified as an unequal relationship; see *infra* male versus female); they have become contradictory. When this pattern is considered from the first level, it reveals that B is sometimes identical to (but included within) A and sometimes contrary to A. In the latter case, when considered from the second level, A no longer has a totalizing role; it is merely the complement to B.

2 All these male practices belong to the second level of the configuration (see *infra*). However, it is not in relation to these but to female practices that the contradiction with the first level is presented by their society (in the speeches and practices of *both* sexes). It is significant that the terminological divide between 'brother' and 'man' (the second word in the Western sense of the male sex $\male$) is less clear than that between 'sister' and 'woman' $\female$ (see below and note 5).

3 Free sex and non-free sex apply to women. However, most people say that it concerns free sex versus non-free sex as a whole ('it must be

done this way . . .', without stipulating the sexual category), even if, as we observed above, the vocabulary of kinship and the sexes can reveal an asymmetry ('man' encompasses more of the various terms that apply to men than 'woman' does the terms applying to women). This asymmetry extends to the sphere of responsibility incumbent on each person in relation to his own body: virgin girls are called 'she who bears the/a responsibility' *tausala*, a term which does not occur in connection with men; men's bodies are not 'responsible' for any social group, while 'the body of a family' (*tino o le aiga*) is 'the body of the girls of the family'.

4 Schoeffel (1979) had already produced a list of *feagaiga* relations, but by enclosing this list to some extent in a binary opposition of sacred versus profane.

5 'Man' (♂) is called *tamaloa* fairly often when married, but the term for 'boy' is the same: *tama* (the suffix *loa* merely indicates an extension). The field seems to correspond to our own. However, the '*fafine*' woman is not the whole woman (♀); she is merely 'female' in the French sense (*une femelle*) or else a woman is considered a *teine* (in which case she is presumed a virgin, or if married, considered by her family to be 'our daughter', solely from the kinship angle) and she is not a *fafine*.

6 She is simply *fafine* (her husband does not hold a title), *faletua* or *tausi* (the husband is a title-holder, belonging to the categories of *alii* sitting chief (our term) and *tulafale* standing chief (our term) or 'orator' (one of the Samoan designations) respectively). And/or she is *nofotane* ('she who lives in her husband's home'), meaning 'in the village of her husband'. The opposite case, whereby the husband comes to live in his wife's home, is designated by a term which no longer defines the wife but the man, 'he who makes a wife' *faiava*, in which case the wife retains her designation as 'daughter of the village', at least if her marriage has not transgressed the various prohibitions defining this status – pre-marital virginity, etc. . . .

7 It is here that the prohibitions concerning virginity are seated. The sisters' bodes are 'responsible' for the family. Their blood, if virginal, if not spilled in the bush, can, with the help of a man's semen that comes from 'outside' (outside the family and the village; if not, there is incest, the 'blood' of the woman 'comes out as a clot of blood' – miscarriage – which itself becomes a mighty spirit), produce 'sacred chidren', that is, children who can be 'true heirs' to the ancestor's name (for my own observations, see Tcherkezoff (forthcoming a, b) re. the ceremonial and institutional preponderance of sisters; see also Schoeffel (1979), Aiono (1984a, 1986), Weiner (1985, 1987, 1989) and Kamu (1988)).

8 See Needham (1960) in Needham (1973); Tcherkezoff (1983); Needham's reply, rejecting our criticism (1987: Chapter 8 *passim*) and Tcherkezoff (forthcoming c) for a survey of the whole debate.

9 A contradictory debate has already begun. See Love (1983), Shore (1983, 1984, 1985), Aiono (1984b), Freeman (1984, 1985) and Mageo (1989).

10 Others have already noted that the relationship between the contexts of violence and peace in Oceanic societies 'is not binary' but constitutes

a 'transformation' (White 1984: 6–7). See White (1985) and Kirkpatrick and White's (1985) Introduction, as well as some articles in Kirkpatrick and White's (1985) collection, especially those by White, E. Gerber and J. Kirkpatrick.

11 Thus Shore (1982) is mistaken in thinking that the term *amio* definitely has a pejorative connotation because it also designates the sex act, especially when illicit. The sex act, which is certainly always 'nocturnal – hidden – and has no place in the world of Day' *faapo(uliuli)*, is always referred to by an expression beginning with the verb *fai* followed (or not) by something more precise, even when the contest renders the sex act licit. Thus one can have *fai amio*, among other expressions.

12 The distinction defined here has already been the object of debate; see Tcherkezoff (1985) and the other articles of the symposium *Contexts and Levels* (Barnes *et al.* 1985).

13 Two cases of this type have occurred over the last five years even within the anthropologist's 'familial' surroundings (the few families in which he is kin by adoption *tama fai*). Generally speaking, suicide (which affects adolescents and young adults most) seems to result from a violent contradiction felt within a statutory relationship; the sister›› brother relationship appears to hold an eminent place within the set of these statutory asymmetries.

14 However, the law courts in the capital would then institute proceedings for murder, since the legal system operates according to a European code of law while attempting to intervene as little as possible in regulatory affairs with villages. Punishments are slight when such questions are judged in the villages, whether it be the case under discussion here or when ceremonial compensation has been paid following an actual murder.

15 See Needham (1987) for his criticism directed at Dumont in Chapter 7 and at myself in Chapter 8; see the works mentioned *supra* relating to Samoa, re. the sister: brother :: sacred (or 'formal' control): power ('instrumental').

16 The word *tula* is applied to the wooden base in which the mast of the traditional great boats (nowadays no longer used) is embedded, and to the little stakes with curved tops serving as perches for the tame birds which acted as companions to high-ranking title-holders (A. Krämer 1902; E. Schultz 1911).

17 Examples of such objects include the sides of a house or of a district, or the two washrooms in a European-oriented context, like in American Samoa international airport. Very significantly, the words written on the doors of the public washrooms located on the public and ceremonial central place of the capital of Western Samoa are different: *alii* (honorific term for men) and *tamaitai* (honorific word for *teine*, the non-sexualized woman). When Samoans are faced with applying a gender dichotomy in a public and Samoan context, they avoid the words of the level 2 (*tamaloa* and, more especially avoided, *fafine*) and assimilate with the pairs of level 1: *alii* represents the title-holders, the brothers, and *tamaitai* is the polite word for sisters (when not married) and for married sisters and mothers, used precisely when it would be totally injurious to use *fafine*. But it is the gender situation that borrows from

the title vocabulary, and not a sign of a generalized gender classification of all terms. This appears clearly when one sees the vocabulary about the village groups: if asked to dichotomize into 'men and women' (and the question has then to be put in English), the informant will group together the title-holders and the 'boys' *tama* (grouped in what is called 'the strength of the village') on one side, and the girls of the village and in-marrying wives on the other side. But if he explains spontaneously the composition of the village, he would always indicate the *alii*, the 'chiefs' as he would say in English, and the *tamaitai*, 'the daughters of the village', the 'sisters and daughters of the chiefs'. Only then would he talk of the boys who serve these two groups, with their 'strength', sometimes saying that this is it, and, at other times, mentioning the in-marrying wives.

18 See note 16. *Fafine* designates the universal sexual female. The word applies to humans as well as to animals. Significantly, this is not the case for the word *tane*. If one tries to use it for animals, the expression is not understood, just as it is not understood if used with *faa* in trying to designate women's 'masculine' behaviour and/or women's homosexuality. There is another specific word used to designate male animals, and significantly there is no expression using this word as a base followed by some suffix which could designate female animals. It should be noted, more generally, that there are no grammatical ways of denoting gender in Samoan; there is no system for nouns, such as a base with suffixes that would be masculine or feminine, there are no gender distinctions in adjectives, personal pronouns (there is no 'he' and 'she'), etc. Thus, there is never any complementary word, in terms of gender, to a given word. Humans are paired differently, as suggested above in note 16. *1st pairing* – sisters-and-brothers, not as the two sexes but as two complementary ways of reproducing titles ('ladies of the village' and 'chiefs', identity with the past and the spiritual world plus the human (and then somehow male) agency). It is striking that within a given village, even without genealogical ties, people are supposed to behave 'like brothers and sisters' (not to have sex and not to marry between themselves). And *2nd pairing* – where men in general – and women – are considered able to have (or to be 'forced' to have) sex. This 'forcing' that I evoke is the same word that as the male 'strength', *faamalosi* or *malosi*, is often invoked in stories of pre-marital sex. It is rarely a 'rape' in the sense of a knife being put at the throat, but more than often includes a strong psychological 'forcing': girls 'know that if they come out of their house' and accept meeting a boyfriend secretly and always without witness, they put themselves in a position of facing a 'strong side' and 'will not be able to stop it'; this *a priori* acceptance of their 'weakness' – if and only if they have entered such a context (meeting a boyfriend in the dark) where there is no more status and only sexual distinction – has the consequence that boys are always, in a way, 'forcing' a girl for her first sexual rapport; and this is true even if it is the bridal night after a 'respectful' marriage. Ortner has rightfully noted this ethos of 'stealing' characteristic of Polynesia (Ortner 1981) (at least in Western Polynesia).

4 Blood, sperm, soul and the mountain

Gender relations, kinship and cosmovision among the Khumbo (N.E. Nepal)

Hildegard Diemberger

Anthropological studies of women's life and status often have tended to dissociate themselves from the overall analysis of culture and society (McDonald 1990). Focusing research on various implications of the single category 'woman' can thus easily overlook the dense network of relations between individual, structure and cosmovision. In this network, the female body attains particular importance for the social construction and interpretation of gender identity.

The following chapter[1] explores this relation and concepts referring to the female body by an analysis of ethnographic and philological data from north-eastern Nepal and Tibet.

PROLOGUE – 'LUCKY STARS IN THE SKY, THE SUN SHINES WARM UPON THE EARTH'

It is a beautiful day during a period of plenty here in Sepa in the Nepalese Himalaya, in the late autumn of 1988. This bright sunshine in the 'month of the Pleiades' (*Mindrug dawa [sMin-drug zla-ba]*) evokes the propitious beginning of every ritual speech: 'Lucky stars in the sky, the sun shines warm upon the earth.' Caili, an energetic and sensual woman, is playing with her youngest son, Migmar. I enter the house. Caili offers me a cup of barley beer and then continues to play with Migmar who does not really want to be disturbed. He drinks some milk from the breast and plays with his erect little penis. He offers it to his mother who sucks it tenderly and then continues to chat with me. Migmar is five years old.

When I came back to Sepa, one year later, Migmar was there, but he was about to leave to look after the goats and sheep of his uncle. He was wearing a minimal strip of cloth to cover his genitals, the so-called *pishorok* (literally leaf, peel). He was cheerful as usual but he was also somehow different: he 'knew shame (*ngotsha [ngo-tsha]²*)'. A little piece of cloth and the shame had separated him for ever from intimacy with his mother.

Later, Migmar will rediscover desire, initiated by an older and more experienced girl. Like most boys and girls from Sepa, he will experience it in a playful game of transgression, using words of transgression in one of the little huts in the forest and on the high pastures. But by that time he will already know the transgressible and the non-transgressible. He will know the limit of the incest taboo towards all the women of his patrilineal clan and the more differentiated restrictions towards the girls of his matrilineal kin group. He will also know how far he can push the games of desire against prohibitions and what kind of sanctions he can risk.

Caili, when she was herself a little girl, learned about shame from her mother, her father, and her relatives, usually by hearing the reproachful '*ngotsha me te?*' – aren't you ashamed? – which for every child sets the limits of socially accepted behaviour and the different degrees of tolerance according to the context. It is 'shame' which tells every Khumbo that his or her body is part of a cosmos full of signs and values. Like every Khumbo girl, Caili 'knew shame' at about the same age as her playmates. This was expressed by the skirt covered by a specific multicoloured woollen blanket character-istic of women's dress among the Tibetan-speaking groups. Like all Khumbo children, she worked hard in the pastures and led her own life far away from the control of her parents. At night she enjoyed secret meetings, unbothered by any thoughts of virginity for which there is no name in the Khumbo dialect. But when 'the blood' appeared, she learned that a woman has to reckon with more risks than her partners. If 'something happens', she is the one who has to directly face wanted or unwanted consequences.

A shadow marks the adolescence of a Khumbo woman beyond the risk of an unwanted pregnancy. The blood of her menses is also the sign of the blood she will transmit to her children. Together with the basic social rules – such as the incest taboo – every Khumbo woman learns that she transmits blood and not bones. Only sperm can create bones and thereby pass on the clan (*rü [rus]*). This is why only sons keep the *phayul [pha-yul]*, the 'father-land': if a girl has brothers, she will have to leave her home and be a daughter-in-law in somebody else's house. It is the language of the body which irrevocably tells her what society expects from her.

THE KHUMBO

The Khumbo are Tibetan-speakers living in the Nepalese Himalaya. Khumbo is the self-designation of an originally rather heterogeneous people made up of different clans who came to Sepa (Nepali Shedua) from Tibet at different times and from various directions (Diemberger and Schicklgruber forthcoming b). Nowadays, they are farmers and animal keepers inhabiting the steep slopes of the Arun Valley and the high pastures at the foot of Mount Makalu in Nepal.

At present, the Khumbo community living in Sepa is made up of twelve scattered settlements. A loose and flexible network of relationships connects the households (*drongpa [grong-pa]*), the basic socio-economic unit of this society. The exogamous patrilineal clans, though relevant from a certain political and religious point of view, do not constitute corporate groups nor own clan land. It is rather the affiliation to the Khumbo community of Sepa as such which grants access to common land (pastures and forest).

There has never been any structure of institutionalized central power: the exercise of informal power is based on the concept of *uphang [dbu-phang]* (literally order of the head, exalted head, high head),[3] which may be glossed as 'prestige'. *Uphang* and *wangthang [dBang-thang]* (literally 'power'), ideally bestowed by clan and mountain deities, define the status of the 'great people' (*Mi che che [Mi che che]*) who determine internal politics. These are mainly religious specialists: the Buddhist *lama [Bla-ma]*, the *lhaven [lha-bon]* whose religion is centred upon the local clan and mountain deities and the *lhakama [lah-bka'-ma]*, the female oracle (see Diemberger 1991 and 1992). Yet there is no social stratification; social hierarchy is quite flexible and 'great people' are also peasants like everybody else.

Superimposed on the power of the 'great people' there is the external power structure of state administration, which may coincide with or oppose the interest of the local community. This kind of double power has been a long-lasting issue characteristic of societies at the edge of the state, such as the Khumbo. They have held a relatively autonomous position *vis-à-vis* Tibet, Sikkim and, more recently, Nepal.

Though of diverse origins, the people of Sepa managed to form a coherent community. Marriage alliances, the creation of common myths founding a social order based upon clan affiliation, and the adjustment to a common ceremony with the worship of all the clan deities and centred on the mountain gods, were all basic elements in this ethnogenetic process. Religion and kin ties succeeded in homogenizing a complicated heterogeneity. The result is the divine order of 'one's own land' (*dagpe lungba [bdag-pa'i lung-ba]*) and of 'one's own people' (*dagpe mi [bdag-pa'i mi]*) in Sepa. Thus the Khumbo developed their shared identity in the name of the gods who inhabit their sacred landscape: the mountain gods of Beyul Khenbalung. The mountains are considered the abode of the ancestors of the community. The ancient clan ancestors are transcended by common ancestors of the whole community related to these common mountain deities. In spite of the different political and historical origins of each clan, these ancestors affirm a common spiritual descent beyond the clans.

For the Khumbo, as in most areas of Tibetan culture, pre-Buddhist conceptions concerning the religious and political dimensions of mountains overlap with Buddhist theories (Stein 1972: 47; Uray 1978: 556–7). Sacred mountains are considered the protector of Buddhist teachings. Buddhist *lama* are socially seen as the greatest of the great people. A religious syncretism exists between the local cults of pre-Buddhist origin and the Tantric Buddhism typical for Tibet. The Khumbo were never well integrated into the state, nor were they under significant monastic influence. They seemingly continue to present archaic features which recall pre-Buddhist beliefs and the period of the early Tibetan Kings.

Elements of this history and of social relations made up of different overlapping perspectives, or echoes of them, are articulated in the conceptualization of the female and male body.

KINSHIP IN SOCIETY AND COSMOS

As in most Tibetan societies, Khumbo kinship is conceptualized in terms of 'flesh' and 'bone', categories referring to the components of the human body (Lévi-Strauss 1969). Flesh is created by the mother and bones by the father. Among the Khumbo, there are five main patrilineal clans, referred to by the word for 'bone', *rü [rus]*,[4] whereas matrilineal kin ties are considerd ties by 'blood' (*thak [khrag]*), 'flesh' (*sha [sha]*) or 'milk' (*oma [o-ma]*).[5]

I briefly present the connection between kinship terminology and the 'flesh and bone' ties (see Figure 1). Since parallel cousins are equated to siblings, and parallel uncles and aunts – though less directly[6] – to parents, the system stresses the closeness of kin ties through people of the same gender.[7] On the other hand, it radically distances kin ties through people of the opposite gender (mother's brother, father's sister, cross-cousins, children of siblings of the opposite gender, etc.). The system also includes an asymmetry which recalls the Omaha skewing rule, yet is flexible according to the context.[8] Thus the terms for mother's brother (*azhang*) and mother's sister (*ushu*) are extended to matrilineal cross-cousins and even to their children, and the category *tshaphiuk* and *tshaphiukma*[9] (children of the ego's sibling of the opposite gender) to the patrilineal cross-cousins. These features emphasize the closeness and the prestige of the ties with the maternal clan, radically distancing the 'blood' ties of the father. The category of *azhang (a-zhang)* (mother's brother) defines bride-givers, that is, those who give the women who become mothers. It implies a high position towards bride-takers, shapes the relations within the Khumbo ranking system and has a long-lasting political effect. Inherited in the following generations, it records marriage alliances for at least three generations.[10] The kin ties by blood include the clan of the mother as well as a kind of weak bilineal counterpart to the patrilineal clan, that is, classificatory aunts and sisters through the mother's own 'blood' ties.

The 'bones' of the ancestors inherited patrilineally make up the 'bone-line' (*rü gyipa [rus brgyud pa]*). A specific clan name allocates every Khumbo, man and woman, to the clan of his or her father. According to this line, land is handed down from father to son. Besides the house, the main part of the herds and agricultural utensils are transmitted in this way. They make up the *phonor [pho-nor]*, 'male wealth'. The ties by 'blood' form a much more hybrid category entailing elements of complementary filiation (Fortes 1953: 33–4; Levine 1988: 54) as well as cognatic and bilineal features (after Godelier 1989: 1142).[11] Female goods, such as jewellery, clothing, household utensils and sometimes money, comprise 'female wealth' (*monor [mo-nor]*) which is transmitted in a female line. Particularly for girls, the strong tie to matrilateral kin can be crucial: in cases of divorce, boys are allocated to their father and girls to their mother. The girl who belongs both to the clan of her father and to the 'blood' of her mother becomes defined by the latter. The absence of a name and of deities from this female line, however, drastically reduces its genealogical depth.

Post-nuptial patrilocal and neo-patrilocal residence spreads the links by 'blood' throughout the area following the pattern of marriage alliances. This renders women visibly mobile.

Marriage is usually monogamous. Marriage alliances entail

Figure 1 Khumbo kinship terminology

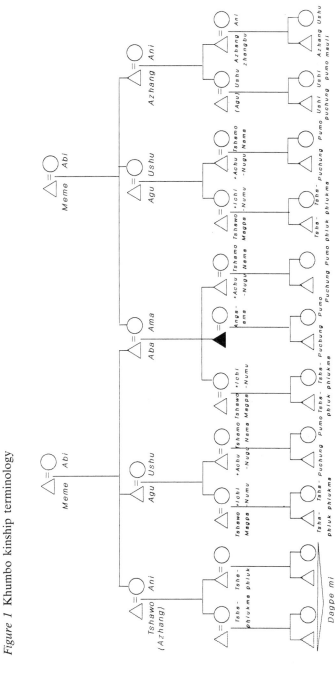

Figure 1a From the viewpoint of a male ego

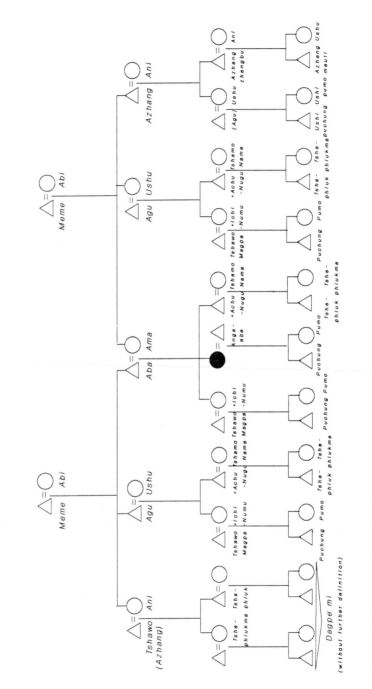

Figure 1b From the viewpoint of a female ego

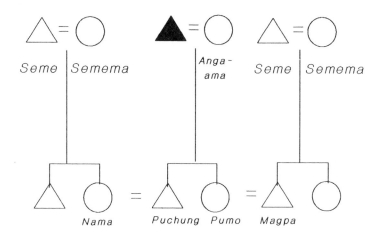

Figure 1c The Seme relation

prescribing clan exogamous marriage and prohibiting marriage to matrilateral cross-cousins and to women of the maternal clan and their daughters. Thus Khumbo cannot reproduce the marriage of their fathers and have to look for new alliances in each generation.[12] In its own way, this system is extremely flexible, allowing the easy and quick integration of different groups but without the constitution of fixed bride-givers and bride-takers as is the case in generalized exchange (Lévi-Strauss 1969). It thus emphasizes alliance not between kin groups, but rather between households. This relation is expressed by the term *seme [sras-mes]*, literally 'ancestors of the descendants', reciprocally used by the two households involved. This kind of marriage alliance favours the dissolution of larger kin groups within an overall integrating unity. Here, institutions other than kinship (such as those based on religion and politics), with their own potentiality for stratification, take over the integrative function of society.

The logic of kinship resembles the weaving of a cloth: the warp is made up óf, to my mind, ties by 'bone', the weft of ties by 'blood'. In the framework of this imaginary loom, the affinal *seme* become 'bone' and 'blood' ties in the following generations. Then they are woven into ancestors, *meme [mes-mes]* and *abi [a-phy]*.[13] The ties by bone persist in the clan names which transcend the genealogical memory, whereas ties by blood disappear and make way for new alliances. With the category of *azhang* and its derivatives, it is the bone tie within the blood which persists over the generations, together with the prestige and political role linked to this position. Memory of the blood ties, as such, remains embodied in the abstract idea of the ancestral mothers of the clan. Yet the male ancestors of the clan also lose their genealogical identity, and eventually all the ancestors return to the sacred mountains. These are the sacred mountains of Beyul Khenbalung which, in transcending the clan and the clan deities imported from the old 'home', give identity to the whole.

The place of kinship within society: descent versus residence

Blood ties seem to constitute a kind of latent principle which is activated according to social context and practice. Furthermore, for many Khumbo women, their kin group of origin is more than a strong but distant support. In spite of the patrilocal rule (residence in or close to the household of the husband's father), 20 per cent of the Khumbo women reside close to their paternal house. They are considered as belonging to the group with whom they reside, although their household notionally belongs to their husband's clan. The role of the residential unit is strongly political and can override principles of patrilocality and of patrilineal descent (Diemberger and Schicklgruber forthcoming a). Such may be the case where households remain without sons or have sons who are too young to supersede their sister, or in households with strong political influence and an economic basis which allows a woman to stay 'at home', provided she can convince her husband. Practice, then, is co-determined by factors other than kinship. It is not just the kinship system but the place kinship has in society which affects its impact on women's lives. Khumbo society is structured along principles which transcend kinship and kin groups, and in which these are embedded. The numerous transgressions against patrilocality, the dissolution of clans as corporate groups in favour of an idea of the community as a whole, and the hierarchical relations between 'great people' and others, all stress the role of the *drongpa [grongpa]* (household) as the basic unit in marriage alliances, in the competition for social status and in the economy. The autonomy of the *drongpa* in turn emphasizes the position of *drongpa ama* and *drongpa aba*, the household mother and father, the heads of the household. The strategies of each *drongpa* are pragmatic and determined by a complex of factors. The exchange of daughters (and occasionally of sons)[14] between households throughout the society is one of the main concerns of the *drongpa*. The bride-taker household has to cover the ceremonial expenses and to provide labour to the bride-giver household during the engagement period. The bride-giver household provides a dowry of jewellery, household items and occasionally a few animals to be given to the bride.

The political and economic purposes of marriage alliances go beyond kinship, even though they may be expressed and exercised through kinship. They may involve putting herds together or co-operating in diverse agricultural activities, perhaps establishing a partnership in trade or a politico-religious alliance between religious specialists, or may involve a *lama* who marries his son to the daughter of a paper producer. Household strategies are thus determined by principles other than kinship and on occasion oppose and transcend the clan systems. This generates a structural contradiction between descent (clan), residential groups (household, village) and ethnic groups ('one's own people'). Yet, insofar as other social relations are expressed in a kinship idiom, they shape both the way kinship is dealt with and the practice of gender relations.

A comparison will facilitate a deeper understanding. Kharta is a valley north of the Khumbo which belonged to the Tibetan state for several centuries (Diemberger forthcoming). The Tibetans of Kharta are trading partners of the Khumbo and occasionally enter into marriage alliances with them. Their kinship system and terminology are similar to the Khumbo, yet there are also certain radical differences, parallel features nowadays widespread in central Tibet (Aziz 1978: 117*ff*; Guigo 1986: 78*ff*). These include there being no named clans and no terminological differences between cross- and parallel-cousins; the spouses of aunts and uncles not being equated to consanguinual relatives; people defining themselves as belonging to a household and a village (rather than to a clan). However, 'bone' indicates patrilineal filiation and descent and 'flesh' matrilateral kin ties. But the *pholha* (who represents the clan deity for the Khumbo) is a mere household and personal deity and is often confused with the local mountain deities. Buddhified mountain gods are the religious focus of the community, side-by-side with the deities of the local Buddhist tradition. This comparison suggests that 'flesh and bones' kinship entails both cognatic and partilineal elements and these were continuously reshaped over the course of social changes in Tibetan history.

In ancient times, Khumbo clans seem to have been kin groups linked to specific ancestral territories and gathered in clan confederations. Women were a means of political alliances between groups, and retained a strong tie to their natal group. Stein reports: 'In those days "there was no distinction between people and ruler", and so these twelve (chieftains) worshipped the holy mountain, and welcomed him who descended from it in order to have a king' (Stein 1972: 47). This was the legendary origin of the first Tibetan king (see Bacot *et al.* 1940; Lalou 1959; Pelliot 1963). With the shift from clan confederations to the early state, a territorial military and civil organization was implemented and the *stong-sde* (the 'group of a thousand' or 'thousand-district') became the 'fundamental units of the ancient Tibetan empire' (Uray 1982: 545).[15] This administrative structure redefined the function of the clans.

With the fall of the kingdom and the emergence of religious centres as social and political foci, from the twelfth century onwards, clans and clan names largely disappeared.[16] Since then, people have been defined by place of birth and residence and/or religious affiliation. The kinship system tended to place even greater emphasis on the residential unit,[17] while the weakening importance of descent allowed cognatic elements to become visible in specific contexts: a redefined patrilineality remained a distinguishing mark of the dominant aristocracy and priesthood with their clear genealogies (Aziz 1978: 119*ff*). Furthermore, the introduction of the system of reincarnation allowed the political sphere to transcend kinship for its reproduction with the institution of lines of hierophanies,[18] a feature which had first appeared where no particular family line had been dominant (Snellgrove and Richardson 1980: 136–7).

Women, though possibly made prominent by the cognatic aspects of the kinship system, were less influential in the political and religious institutions which dominated the destiny of society. None the less, Tibetan women enjoy considerable economic powers as managers of households, a remarkable autonomy in all spheres of their activities, strong ties to their natal group, the high status accorded to motherhood and a religion open to toleration (Szerb-Mantl forthcoming). This has formed the well-known image of strong and independent Tibetan women which has fascinated travellers coming from Islamic and Hindu countries.

Gender in Tibetan 'flesh and bone' kinship: co-existence and contradictions

Tibetan 'flesh/blood and bone' systems present a broad variety of interpretations on a common theme. They can emphasize either cognatic or patrilineal aspects and can support different forms of gender relations – from explicit female subordination to more or less egalitarian tendencies with various forms of strong female power. The conceptual oppositions between patrilineal and cognatic aspects in Tibetan flesh/blood and bone systems are mostly, but not always, resolved in favour of patrilineality.[19]

The potential conflict entailed in the sphere of marriage alliance and inheritance – and its expected solution – is explained in a myth of the Tibetan Bon religion contained in a text for marriage rituals.[20] This myth relates the first marriage alliance between human beings and gods. It presents a father and mother and a son and daughter pair in the realms of gods and the same configuration in the realm of human beings. The human father asks for the daughter of the gods and proposes an alliance: human beings will worship the gods and the gods will protect the human beings. The god father agrees. A discussion within the family of the gods follows, presided over by the *lha-bon* priest. The daugher does not really want to go to an unknown country, the 'land of the people' (*mi-yul*). Her mother supports her but the father explains that though the Ha-la plant is beautiful, it contains poison and its sprouts have to be burnt in the fire, just as salt (which is good) needs food to be eatable. Thus she is sent to the 'land of the people'.

A discussion about the partition of the goods follows. The daughter points out that father and mother are like the heart, brother and sister are like the eyes. If son and daughter have no right to the goods, it is as if they were without water; thus she asks for equal shares. The *lha-bon* replies to her: you descend from the penis of your father and from the matrix of your mother, thus you are born from parents. But from the beginning of the world you are born as a woman and people told your mother that she gave birth to a girl. On that occasion there was no worship of the gods, no roasted flower was thrown up to the sky. If a girl is born she will leave as the possession of a man. There has never been a woman who kept her *pha-yul* ('paternal land'); if the daughter goes to the bad she can become a kind of demoness. It is not possible to sleep next to a demoness. You are going to go to the 'land of the people', your brother is going to keep the paternal land.

The partition is decided by throwing the dice (a system used also in archaic forms of elective government) (cf. Walsh 1906: 305), whereupon the daughter receives one-third and the son two-thirds. The daughter plays with the protection of her *mo-lha*, the deity of the maternal side, and the witness of the *dgra-lha*, the defending deity. The son plays with the protection of *pho-lha* (the male deity), *dgra-lha, srog-lha* (the deity of life) and *yul-lha* (the deity of the country). He plays for the *pha-yul*. At the end of the unequal division, the *lha-bon* invites the daughter to prostrate herself three times in front of the gods who gave her life, in front of the father who gave the bones, in front of the mother who gave the shape and the beauty, and in front of the brother who gave fame and prestige.

It is the incest taboo and the difference between the brother and sister affirmed in the name of religion which make her leave and become a daughter-in-law. Similarly, the Khumbo legitimation of patrilocality is also based on the relative weakness of the tie between the girls and their paternal clan and its deities. At the same time, the 'great people' – among them many *lhaven (lha-bon)* – are responsible for seeing that this sacred social order of kinship is respected and adjudicate over tolerable exceptions. It is the sacred social order, then, which defines the patrilinear 'skeleton' of the society, the weakness of the daughters-in-law and the power of the household mothers and thus shapes gender relations.

GENDER IN KHUMBO SOCIETY

There are no distinct female and male worlds for the Khumbo. Therefore, when discussing the position of women and men in general, one must always specify exactly which women and which men, in which social position and in which context of life. The following lists general tendencies in gender relations across diverse life contexts.

1 *Division of labour by gender*. Within a weakly defined social division of labour, there is a weak division of labour by gender too. Differentiation is mainly restricted to handicrafts – weaving is a female activity, wood-working a male activity. The male members of the household participate significantly in childrearing. The division of labour by gender is found mainly in the social role of household mother and father. The household father represents the household in political and religious terms, but has no specific activities linked to his role. The household mother has, and this primarily involves taking charge of the household management: she distributes tasks, decides the timing of agricultural activities, administers the stores, chooses what will be eaten and worn by the household members (she is the one who weaves), decides what has to be bought and sold and keeps a (mental) account of the household finances. In the case of major deals

(e.g. cattle or land), the grown-up members of the household decide together. Slaughtering is the only exclusively male activity of importance today.[21] Warfare and defence have been of minor importance in Khumbo life for centuries, though find some expression in religion and in the classification of weapons, particularly of the knife as male. Although a woman does not carry a knife, however, she can make use of one.

2 *Ownership of land, cattle, instruments, products and finances.* Everything that is not the common property of the Khumbo is owned and managed by the household heads. As mentioned above, land is generally passed on from father to son: a woman can inherit land only in the event that she has no brothers. All other goods can be owned by both men and women.

3 *Kinship.* It has been shown that kinship entails cognatic as well as patrilineal principles. Men have the 'bones' and transmit the patriclan whereas women usually play the mobile part in the kinship alliance, and in that sense bear the impact of marriage alliances. Being the ones who know the kinship network best, they are also the protagonists in the spinning of new marriage alliances.

4 *Politics and traditional law.* This is considered the concern of men and mostly of religious men. Yet powerful household mothers exert very strong influence. Since politics does not imply a separate institution, its course is determined in the houses of the 'great people' or of the people involved in/concerned with a specific issue. Here, wise women can be important mediators and even set the co-ordinates of the discourse. Since the ranking system focuses primarily upon men, women who are considered 'great people' because of their intelligence and knowledge enjoy their position with greater flexibility.

5 *Religion.* The Buddhist *lama* and the *lhaven* are always men. They are the ones who possess the knowledge for performing the rituals for the community and for the events in the life-cycle of every Khumbo. Yet there is a religious role which is performed only by women, namely that of the *lhakama [Lha-bka'-ma]*, the oracle. She is a woman who (in trance) gives voice to the dead spirits and to the mountain deities. This role is transmitted from mother to daughter and it is the only existing 'female line' in this society. Presumably it is no mere coincidence that although honoured and powerful, the *lhakama* stands outside the rules of commensality which shape normal social interaction. She expresses the things which nobody dares to say and thus have to

be said by the gods: the origin of diseases and conflicts. Her religious power extends into the political sphere although in a different way from the power of the *lama* and the *lhaven*.

I would like to make a final remark about the power of knowledge. Religious and ritual knowledge, together with skill and intelligence, make up the determinant part of the power of male religious specialists. Knowledge involving practical calculations, the organization of time, information on kinship, and on biological and physiological events related to motherhood and human psychology, are all a determinant part of women's power. This is respected and pragmatic knowledge accumulated over a lifetime; it usually sees a woman leave her parental household, become a mother and attain a powerful position as household mother. The obstacles a woman has to overcome contribute to the knowledge she is regarded as deriving from experience. And knowledge generally becomes a source of prestige and power for both men and women as soon as it can be socially implemented. Among the 'great people' there are always some who are considered 'great' because of their knowledge: they are called *mi sheba [mi shes-pa]* ('people who know'). They can be priests but their power is independent from any religious role. Often these are clever persons who have travelled widely, have different types of experience and are thus considered to be able to provide reasonable advice for any community or personal issue.

What it means to be a Khumbo woman

Girls grow up in a very similar way to their male playmates. No initiation marks the passage to adulthood and children of both genders grow up in a very independent way. Marriage and parenthood are central events in a common Khumbo life.

It is a path which sees a woman pass through the roles of: *pumo [bu-mo]*, daughter; *nama [mna'-ma]*, daughter-in-law (this term seems linked to *mna'*, 'oath' (Benedict 1942: 322), and underlines the position of daughters-in-law as the links of alliances); *ama [a-ma]*, mother (this term semantically denotes generation in every sense, from the warp of a woven cloth to the original of a text from which copies are taken); *abi [a-phyi]*, grandmother, female ancestor (the grandmother is also a mother and as such becomes part of the ancestors, *phama [pha-ma]*, literally 'father-mother', a title also attached to several Tibetan deities).

Sexuality as a natural function, the reproduction of life and the need for manpower, are the basic elements which determine time and mode of marriage alliances. While sexuality and manpower do not, in practice, present a significant difference between men and women, the reproduction of life does. It is in the womb of a woman that children are conceived; it is with her breast that she feeds them; it is she who, notwithstanding the usually co-operative Khumbo fathers, is primarily responsible for this human *proles inepta* who is unable to care for itself for such a long time. For a man, fatherhood is a choice he takes and/or the social system has taken for him (if he is already married). A woman can either decide to leave the child she has given birth to in the forest or to take it home.

Children are often, in fact, taken by the high child mortality. Dysentry, bronchitis, pneumonia or an epidemic of measles can destroy all the labour and efforts involved in rearing the child. Confronted with numerous mothers who had lost their children, I sensed an equivocation, which finally makes Khumbo women accept again and again a system which ties the fathers to their children. Where a better level of nutrition, of clothing, of housing, often means a better chance of survival, at the same time it is a system which makes women pay for the service they render to society. Female subordination can be addressed in terms of this equivocation which renders the woman dependent of others for periods of her life. Subjective practical problems and needs blend with ideological categories: a woman does not only need the father of her child, but also his kin group and his clan deities. She needs a priest who will integrate her and her children into the sacred order of the patriclan – the 'bones' of society. She accepts that her brothers have the exclusive rights to the paternal land and to the best share of the family wealth and that she has to marry outside and to 'go to the people'.

The daughter-in-law is in a totally subordinate position in the household of 'strangers' she has married into, facing a lot of work, and lack of control, often even over her own food. It is true that an uxorilocally married man is also in a subordinate position. But he has contractually decided to accept the disadvantage of uxorilocality in exchange for other advantages. In the case of a normal, patrilocally married *nama*, the system has already decided for her, although she has a veto right concerning the specific person she is going to marry. Even the great *drongpa ama*, who can possess a power significantly superior to their own husbands and male relatives, have mostly had a hard part as a *nama* and recall that period of their life with bitterness.

Only as a mother and (usually later) in taking over management of a household, that is, as *drongpa ama*, does a woman change her position. Her power is linked to this title which describes her as *ama* (mother) of the *drongpa* (household), the basic unit of society. Once she has attained this position, she cannot be removed by anybody. However, she cannot transmit this power to her daughters. They have to follow the same path: from strangers to 'landladies', from object dealt with in the alliances, to producer of alliance strategies.[22]

In this context, it is the language of the body which makes clear to a Khumbo girl what society expects from her. For the Khumbo woman, motherhood, symbolized by her blood, simultaneously indicates her weakness and her power.

THE GENERATION OF A HUMAN BEING: THE HUMAN BODY AS LANGUAGE AND ORDER

The conceptualization of the human body and of the physiological events related to the conception of a human being is inscribed in the whole cognitive system. Their categories of interpretation enable the Khumbo to act upon the concreteness of the event and thus provide it with a cognitive and social framework. Herewith the body expresses meanings and is linked to the 'moving horizon' of (hermeneutic) abstractions in which the relations of the Khumbo have developed throughout history. Beyond the words are the images and beyond the images is the body. The identity of a new human being and the framework of his or her social interaction is shaped – via emotional relations that precede systematic intellectual conceptualization.

What is a human being, where does it come from and where does it go to?

The Khumbo baby is considered as made up from the blood (*tak [khrag]*) of his/her mother which forms the flesh, the blood and the shape of the child's body; from the sperm (*da [zla]*) of his/her father which produces the bones and the brain; and from a kind of 'soul' (*namshe [rnam-shes]* or *la [bla]*) which is linked to the cycle of reincarnation according to the Buddhist perspective and to the sacred mountains of Khenbalung in the local conceptions of pre-Buddhist origin. At the same time, as we have seen, ties by 'blood' comprise matrilateral kin relations, while ties by 'bone' comprise patrilineal clan relations. The local mountains to which the 'soul' is related compose the sacred 'land-owners' (*sadag [sabdag]*) and protectors of the territory inhabited by the Khumbo.

The Khumbo belong to the Khumbo community by virtue of being born under the protection of the local mountain deities, and are Nyingmapa Buddhists in the name of the Buddhist protecting deities of the local tradition. They belong to the clan of their fathers by virtue of the ancestral bones they received from them. They are linked to their mothers and the matrilateral kin ties by virtue of their blood, flesh and the maternal milk. Yet, since the maternal substances are transmitted in a cognatic way, there is no female line to belong to. Thus already, at the time of conception, a child is appropriated by a socially and historically shaped interpretation of anatomic elements and physiological processes.

The mountain deities who act as the 'gods of birth' (*kye-lha [skyes-lha]*) first bestow identity as Khumbo. The mountains are the abode of the common ancestors of the community and they are the common point of reference for peoples of different origin. As such, they preside over the Khumbo territory and its geographical, social and symbolic border. In this context, ritual commensality, together with kinship alliances, acts as the main cohesive factor for society. The collective ceremonies have been a determinant moment for social integration and still mark the main event in the agricultural and pastoral year – the departure to and the arrival from the high pastures. On these occasions, food and *chang*, fermented drink, are offered to the god and to the people. This expresses the unity of 'one's own people' who share the same cup and worship the same gods[23] (cf. Figure 2).

In opposition to the prosperity, power and prestige bestowed by the mountain gods when they have good relations with the human beings, lies *ḍip [grib]*, defilement. Like *uphang* – 'high head', prestige – it can be applied to humans, gods, and environment. *Ḍip* originally means 'shadow' and, in an extended sense, everything which darkens or interrupts a relationship – man and gods, man and man, man with himself. In a derived sense, it is applied to everything which lies beyond or is against the social order. A myth lies behind this concept associating shadow with incest, the lack of kinship terminology and namelessness, birth, death and conflicts (Diemberger *et al.* 1989: 326*ff*). Each event or behaviour considered to be *ḍip* evokes shame, *ngotsha* – the 'hot-face' – and if not

Figure 2 Khumbo 'household mothers' ritually sharing the cup of *chang* during a ceremony

properly dealt with means a loss of *uphang* and, in the most serious cases, social marginalization.

In Sepa, life moves between shadow on the one hand and the order granted by household, clan and mountain deities on the other. A Khumbo enters this order at the name-giving ceremony and comes into *ḍip* whenever he or she has contact with death, birth or conflicts, with moral sins (in a Buddhist perspective) and with any *ḍip*-carrying thing or person. At death, when he or she leaves this society definitively, the personal name is burnt and the spirit has to detach itself from relatives, friends and belongings. In a Buddhist perspective, the 'spirit' as *namshe [rnam-shes]* ('principle of consciousness') either reaches enlightenment and *Nirvāṇa* or continues to be reincarnated in the *Saṃsāra*, the eternal cycle of rebirth. In an originally pre-Buddhist local perspective, the spirit, as *la [bla]*, goes back to the sacred mountains of Khenbalung.

The generation of a human being: sexual relations

Sex and the birth of a child transforms Khumbo partners to parents. This creates the issue of the responsibility towards the new baby, provides new members of the group and can seal an alliance. Interpretations of the female, the male and the child's body are part of a discourse which shapes the social relations between the sexes and the attribution of the child to a social group (Godelier 1982, 1990: 33). It is a language of the body whose words and gestures appear as natural rules informing the ideological background of gender relations.

In general, sexual relations take place among 'one's own people' and always with people with whom one can share the cup (Sherpa, Tibetans, sometimes Tamang, and nowadays Westerners). They can occur within the framework of an organized marriage alliance or as an adventure in the forest, but they always respect the strict rules of clan exogamy and the rules of commensality.

Food, sex and alliances are intimately linked. Food, and particularly fermented drink, *chang*, are protagonists of human and divine links: by 'asking *chang*' (*longchang [slong-chang]*) one asks for a woman, with a 'medicine *chang*' (*menchang [sman-chang]*) one feeds the mother of a new baby, with the 'name-binding *chang*' (*mindachang [min-gdag-chang]*) one gives a name to a child. Marriage itself is seen as a main occasion where one offers food and *chang* to the whole community and to the gods and thus establishes and renews the network of alliances through commensality. Conversely, the generation of a child is considered the best way for sealing alliances.

Sex itself is like an act of commensality. It both satisfies basic human needs and is a means of communcation. Sex is spoken of in terms of 'hunger', of 'good taste' and so forth, and intercourse should satisfy the appetite of both partners. This is why old Khumbo men suggest to the younger men that they should take time and play with the clitoris in order to satisfy the hunger of the female partner. This hunger is taken as natural for both sexes, and girls do not have to worry about virginity. In informal meetings, a first offering of food can mean an invitation. Usually, the woman offers food and the man satisfies her appetite, but it can work in both ways. A man can say to a woman 'I have a nice straw (*pipa*) but I lack a *chang* pot. Have you got a nice *chang* pot? Let's go and drink *chang* together'. In this case, *chang* stands for both pleasures since they both 'give water' (*chu tenje*).

The female womb is seen by the Khumbo as a red flower which blooms every month. It closes if no sperm comes into it within twelve days following the end of menstruation (cf. Meyer 1980: 110). If sperm gets inside while the flower is open, an embryo starts to develop and the flower closes around it. This flower is called either *mendok [me-thog]* (literally *'flower'*) or *'kyedok [skyes-dog]'* (literally 'receptacle of generation').[24]

The woman's breasts are regarded as full of grain which, like squeezed ears of corn, give milk, the food of the baby.[25] This comes from the food the mother eats and from sperm, a kind of metaphorical food. A young girl is 'like a field' and sperm 'the manure' which allows the grain of her breast to grow and the 'flower' to blossom in her body. And for the Khumbo, 'manure' is the 'fodder' of the earth and it is designated with the same term, *cha [cag]*.

Thus the theory of food and sex of the Khumbo is linked with the ancient Tibetan perspective which associates sexual intercourse with agricultural activities, and the female body with the fields. In the texts of Tun-huang, we find the term *'so-nam bu-srid'* to define human sexual intercourse which literally means 'to make agriculture and children extension' (Bacot *et al.* 1940: 115). And the Khumbo often use the term *'leka [las-ka]'* ('work'), the common term for agricultural activities, to refer to a man delivering sexual services to his female partner.

Sex and food are thus linked to the cosmic interplay of sacred meanings. It is a cosmos dominated by sexual relations: mother sun and father moon sleep together at the new moon. She is red and warm and makes things grow. He is the lord of time and of the white element (*da [zla]* = sperm, moon). The meteorites in the night are the star lovers looking for their beloved; male and female sacred mountains join and have children, and so on. This is a world full of mothers and fathers, where the very conception of human life seems to be a cosmic act. On the one hand, it seems to present complementarity and equality between the sexes. On the other hand, it can include a sharp asymmetry. Fecundation does not imply subordination or any kind of relation of power between the sexes, but it can do so through the association of man/above/sky versus woman/below/earth.

Khumbo-oriented space is endowed with an opposition of above and below,[26] which leads to a cosmogonic interplay of analogies. Although there are male and female deities at every level, we generally find men associated with the above, with the sky, and women associated with the below, with the earth, water of the underground and the chthonic deities. From the sky came the religion of the Khumbo forefathers (and the social order), while everything living comes from the Sashi Ama *[Sa-gzhi ama]* – the 'Earth-foundation mother' – and to her it returns. Conversely, every mother is considered an emanation of the 'Sashi Ama'. So, on the one hand, the earth itself is conceived as a female body with earth as flesh and stones as bones. On the other hand, woman is interpreted as fertile land which gives children and food and is dealt with within the framework of the rules of commensality.

The space in which the encounters take place, then, is an orientated space, dense with analogies which can be perceived in the language of the body itself. When the Khumbo make love, the woman usually lies below and the man above, or they lie side-by-side if they have to disguise the sexual act (in the presence of other people in the houses which have only one room).[27] Women should never step over the body of a man since this would badly effect his *uphang* – his 'high head', i.e. his prosperity and prestige bestowed on him by the clan and mountain deities. Conversely, the common Khumbo love position does not imply that the man directly steps over his partner: rather he sits on his heels in front of her. Thus the time of love reflects an all-pervading above/below opposition which prevents anyone from stepping over anything respected (people, food, religious items, fire), or from wearing or using as a pillow clothing used for the lower part of the body, and prescribes the sleeping position in the house with the head towards the altar and the mountains and the feet towards the door and the valley.

Aside from the traditional associations, a continuous production of new metaphors shapes and reshapes the concrete reality of the body language. One evening in a tourist area close to Mount Everest, a girl invited a Sepa boy by singing: 'I have a nice camera but I haven't got a film. Have you got a nice film? If you give me your film we can make nice photos'. The boy, who did not have a film and did not look as if he was likely to have one, was rather confused and surprised by the question. Then the girl made it clear to him that he *did* have the nice film . . .

Conception – body interpretation and social affiliation

According to the Khumbo, when a man and a woman make love and the woman conceives, they are both likely to feel weak and slightly indisposed afterwards (*tene*). If the man is attentive and has a good relationship with his partner, he will know in advance about the conception by the feeling in his testicles, the 'house of sperm' (*da'i khampa [zla'i khang-pa]*). Thus, from the beginning, a father is considered to be physically and emotionally involved in the creation of the new human life, never separated from the physiological events

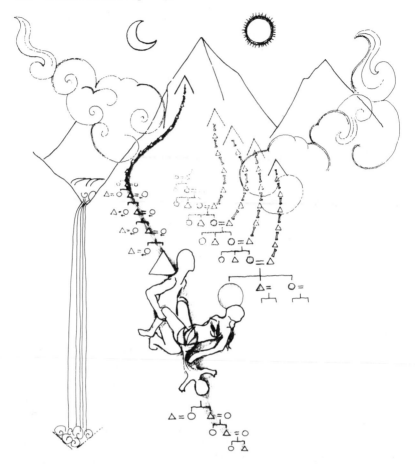

Figure 3 The female womb is seen by the Khumbo as a red flower, the woman's breasts as full of grain. A Khumbo baby is considered as made up from the blood of his or her mother which forms the flesh; from the sperm of his or her father which produces the bones; and from a kind of 'soul' linked to the cycle of rebirth (in a Buddhist perspective) and to the sacred mountains of the Khumbo. At the same time, ties by 'blood' constitute matrilateral kin ties and ties by 'bone' the patrlineal clan. The bones of the ancestors of the clans are transmitted to the descendents through the sperm of the male clan members, whereas blood is transmitted cognatically. The mountain deities are the sacred 'land-owner' (*sadag [sa-bdag]*) of the present Khumbo territory and they are the abode of the common ancestors of the group. (The interpretation of the human body is part of a discourse which shapes social relations between sexes and the attribution of a child to a social group.)
Source: Drawing by Karen Diemberger

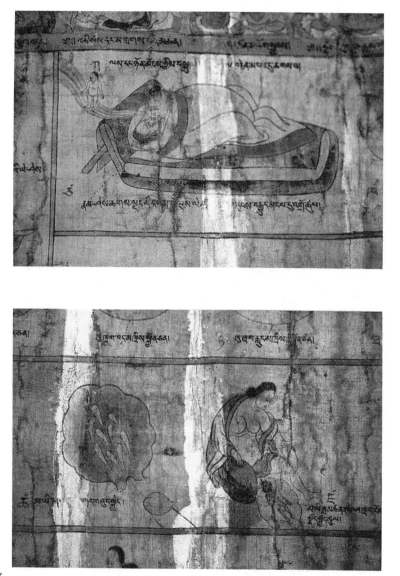

Figure 4 Tibetan embryology as represented on a Thanka painting of the 17th century. At the moment of conception, the soul arrives from the 'interspace' (*bardo*) of the cycle of rebirth and enters the mother's womb (Figure 4a). As the text explains, the bones are generated from the sperm, the blood, the flesh and the shape of the body from the mother's menses (Figure 4b)

Source: Institute of Medicine and Astrology – sMan-rtsis-khang – in Lhasa

of the mother. This emotional participation is the first act of a role which assigns to Khumbo fathers the task of helping the mother, at the child's birth as well as through a significant contribution to its rearing.

Once the sperm has come and the flower has closed, the embryo starts to develop. The sperm of the father forms the bones and the brain of the child. The sperm needs the blood to become bone as the blood needs the sperm to become flesh. But the bones are the hard part which is transmitted over generations in the clan name. Bones produce sperm, sperm produces bones. 'Bone' is the patrilineal clan which gives the bones of the ancestors to sons and daughters of the clan and these are passed on with the sperm of its sons. The 'bone line' (*rü gyipa [rus brgyud-pa]*) is related to the male clan deity, the *pholha* which dwells on a person's right shoulder. This deity has its own clan-specific name, is worshipped by all the members of one clan and was once taken from the sacred ancestral mountains in Tibet along with the migrations of the clan. Nowadays, however, clan and *pholha* are *de facto* reduced to a principle of sacred social order and clan names can be created or clan deities may be borrowed. The link between clan and ancestors is transcended by the 'new ancestors' of the group dwelling on the common holy mountains of the new home, the mountains of Beyul Khenbalung.

The blood, which forms the flesh and the shape of the body, is transmitted cognatically. The blood and vaginal secretions of the mother are produced by the sperm of her father and by the blood of her own mother. Blood has to combine with sperm in order to be transmitted, and is transmitted cognatically. As the maternal blood gives the flesh and the shape to the baby, so relations by blood shape its social life. Spread throughout the area according to the alliances which generated them, they are a network on which everyone can count but inside of which one cannot marry. Due to the extremely high position of the bride-giver, her family of origin and her kin group represent strong ties, particularly for the woman herself, which protect her position within the contracted alliances. These relations are perpetuated by her children through their relationship to the mother's brother's household. Ritually, these kin ties are associated with the deities *molha [mo-lha]* (the female god) and *zhanglha [zhang-lha]* (the god of the maternal uncle) who dwell on any person's left shoulder and are invoked in the text for the Lhabsang ceremony: '*molha* on the left and *zhanglha* supporting her'. However, these deities are much less emphasized than the *pholha* and are merely named during the rituals. While clan brother-hood is a stable and often behaviour-regulating element, matri-lateral kin ties represent the dynamic part of kin relations and bear a significant political dimension (particularly expressed in the role of mother's brother). In the genealogies, one is likely to find all the basic clans of the group united by the 'blood' of their alliances after three or four generations (see Figure 3).

To summarize the specific ambivalence concerning women's part in conception with regard to kinship: on the one hand, and starting from a female ego, one finds women-to-women relations independent of their respective paternal clans and thus denoting an autonomy of 'blood' relations. The acknowledgement of bilaterality in everyone's make-up means that it is not possible in this system to deny or reduce the maternal part. The bones need the blood to be transmitted, the clans need the mothers of the clan. Yet, on the other hand, 'blood' is often used as a mere negative to 'bone': the daughters and the sisters are the offspring which cannot transmit 'bones' and thus have to move away and produce children for the clan of their husband. As such, it legitimizes the general rule of patrilocality and the subordinated position of the daughter-in-law.

Life and identity as a Khumbo and as a Buddhist come to the child with a kind of 'soul', indicated by the Buddhist term *namshe [rnam-shes]* (literally 'principle of consciousness').[28] As such, it is related to the cycle of rebirth. According to *The Tibetan Book of the Dead*, when a *namshe* is pushed by its *karma* (past actions) to a human rebirth, it becomes encapsulated in the originating embryo. If the *namshe* feels attraction towards the mother and repulsion towards the father, it is going to be a male. It the opposite occurs, it is going to be a female (Freemantle and Trungpa 1975: 84). As a principle, it is related to the religious message of Buddhism which refers to human beings as such and thus has a universal character.[29]

The *la [bla]* which is often used as a synonym for *namshe* is less precise. A common Tibetan notion, for the Khumbo it is related to the mountain deities of Khenbalung to which it returns at death. These mountains act as the abode of the ancestors of the community as a whole and as *Kye-lha [skyes-lha]*, the 'gods of birth' of the child (cf. MacDonald 1971: 300–1). They are the *la-ri [bla-ri]* of the area, the abode of the collective 'soul' of the community (Karmay 1987: 100–1) whose prosperity is directly linked to the integrity and religious worship of these holy sites. *La-ri*, the 'soul mountains', and *la-tsho [bla-mtsho]*, the 'soul lakes', are seen as the protecting fathers and mothers of the area. They bestow fertility to fields, herds and women. As *yullha* (literally 'gods of the country'), these deities dwell on the head of every Khumbo.[30]

In the past, however, the notion of *la [bla]* could have been part of a complex of beliefs which related clan territory to its sacred mountain and ancestors – a unity dissolved by processes of migration, ethnogenesis and centralization. The survival of this connection between 'soul' and bones could be seen in the role bones fulfil in funerals – a role which led Tucci to define the bones as an ancient abode of the soul (Tucci and Heissig 1970: 219).

This ambivalent category of 'soul' shows how the religious integration of the human being can be rooted in the conception of the embryo. *La [bla]* can be seen (a) as related to the local mountains according to the local Khumbo perspectives, (b) as having the nature of light and being related to the sky according to the systematized Bon religion (Karmay 1987: 100), and (c) as a 'principle of consciousness' associated with *karma* and rebirth according to Buddhist perspectives. Constantly redefined as a cognitive category, the 'soul' links religion, kinship and politics.

Pregnancy – a critical period for the 'soul'

During pregnancy, the Khumbo women continue their normal life. They work hard and only avoid lifting heavy loads in order to prevent miscarriage.

At the same time, pregnancy is considered to be a special time for the body and for the 'soul'. The Khumbo term *'sugu nyiba'* *[gzugs-sku gnyis-pa]*, meaning 'the double body', indicates that this state changes the one body into two. It is a time of danger for the *la [bla]* of the mother and the *la* of the baby. The mountain deities might steal the *la* and this would cause illness and death. This can happen to human beings at any time, but pregnancy is considered particularly critical. Thus a ritual for 'calling the soul' (*langu [bla-'gugs]*) has to be performed during pregnancy. The *lhaven* priest makes little dough statues (*torma [gtor-ma]*) as provisional bodies for clan and mountain deities. Then he offers a goat as ransom to the most important and wrathful mountain deity of Beyul Khenbalung, Chekyong Surra Rakye *[Chos-skyong Zur-ra rva-skyes]*. In a ritual speech, he offers 'the root of bones, the root of flesh, the root of life, the root of the vital breath' to the god in order to appease him and to divert him from taking the *la* of the humans.

Sexual intercourse continues throughout pregnancy. Food from

Figure 5 Khumbo children are usually born at the pasturage huts. The father usually assists the mother at childbirth and afterwards

the ground and metaphorical 'food' from the father, feed the mother. The mother feeds the baby from her body.

Birth – a natural birth in the 'shadow' beyond society

Birth takes place outside the house lest the deities dwelling there would be defiled (see Figure 5). As a consequence, they would withdraw their protection and this would invite hail and diseases. Birth usually takes place in the pasturage huts. The mother bears the child in a squatting position. The father is usually the one who helps at birth. He sits behind her, holding his hands round her waist and helps in pressing down the baby. Once the baby is born onto a clean cloth laid in front of the mother, he cuts the umbilical cord (*lhe [lte]*) at three fingers' length with a knife sterilized in fire. He buries the placenta (*shama*) in the forest. Then he offers a special *chang* (*menchang [sman-chang]*), prepared for the occasion in advance, to the mother and prepares a chicken soup in order to help her produce milk.

For three days the whole family is in a condition of defilement (*dip*) and is cut off from every social contact. The people of the village whisper the news of the event to each other and avoid going to the '*min ma taba [min ma btags-pa]*', 'the not name-bound'. The mother especially cannot share the cup with anybody, nor can she serve food. She is outside the rules of commensality.

The baby is not yet born socially. If it dies at this point, no burial is performed; it is simply buried in the forest in a hole filled with flowers. The baby is still part of the mother earth and returns whence it came. After three days (or at any propitious day after that), the baby is brought to the house and a name-giving ceremony eliminates the *ḍip*.

Name giving – a social birth

With the *mindachang [min-gdag-chang]* 'the name binding *chang*', mother, child and the family return to the community. The name marks the entrance of the new human being into society. Since natural birth is *ḍip* and lies outside the symbolic border of society, there has to be a ceremony to remove the baby, its parents and the whole family from this state. It is a social birth in which the child is presented to the clan and mountain deities as their child and as the continuation of their 'human root' (*mi tsa [mi-rtsa]*).[31]

The child's mother has already been brought under the protection of her husband's *pholha*, the clan deity, through the marriage ceremony (or in urgent cases by means of a short engagement). Her child first of all belongs to the clan she has married into and whose bones it shares. A child needs a father to be socially born. A mother needs a social father for her child to re-enter society.[32] Boys usually receive a more elaborate name-giving ceremony than the girls since the latter 'are going to leave' and they are not going to transmit bones.

A *lama* or a *lhaven* purifies the birth *ḍip* with dew, 'the water of the sky' (*namkhai thu [gnam-kha'i khrus]*). Afterwards he puts butter-marks on the head of the child in blessing (*gyen [rgyan]*) and bestows a name (see Figure 6). If this is the first child, the name-giving ritual is more than a *rite de passage* for the baby. The parents and the whole household undergo a definitive change underlined by the use of a technonym. In the community, everybody is known by the name of their first living child, boy or girl. From now on it would be a bad offence to call the new parents with their own personal name. They define themselves in relation to their first living child. This passage underlines the leap to a new generation of alliances and at the same time the leap for a man and a woman into adulthood – from partner to parent.

Figure 6 A Khumbo *lhaven* makes dough figures as provisional bodies for clan and mountain deities and presents the new child to them

The social process of birth, therefore, reveals that Khumbo women are more closely associated to *ḍip* than men and that they have more difficult access to the sacred forces of religious life. Women, apart from the oracle, are separated from religion not only by virtue of the bones they do not transmit but also by virtue of their blood. Ritual offerings are performed with the fourth finger, the most pure since in the mother's womb the baby keeps it inside the nose. Menstruation, though evoking no taboos in practical life, is a reason to avoid entering the altar area during ceremonies. For the Khumbo, blood seems to be the main symbol for a creative potential which has to be tamed and integrated in the sacred social order of the patrician in order not to be *ḍip*. Outside of the context of the sacred social order and its kinship rules, it would bring about chaos and potential incest.

According to Khumbo myths (Diemberger *et al.* 1989: 325–39), *ḍip* is the name for the unnameable, the undefined, the 'shadow'. It associates birth with death, with a mythic time pre-dating the social order, and with conflicts that are potentially disruptive of social relations. It is the name which separates human beings from animals. But the separation between society and *ḍip* is not definitive. At death, those 'born from a womb' return to the mother-earth, a final incest for the undefined returning to the undefined, to a pool of ancestors without names lying between the 'shadow' of death and the 'light' of the social order they themselves grant. Those ancestors thus rest where shadow and light melt: on the mountains they are intermediaries between earth and sky, and are providers of fields, cattle and human fertility, and of peace and prosperity in 'one's own people' of Sepa.

Summary: the human body as language and order for gender identity

Khumbo gender identity is defined both by men's and women's position within a kinship system centred on the residential unit of the household and by the religious concepts of birth and life associated with this context. Kinship and religious life both privilege the patriclan. Accordingly, the control of female fertility, symbolized by blood, is limited to the legitimization of patrilocal rule and to the appropriation of the child by the paternal household and clan. Social paternity is indispensable for a child, but the blood relations on the maternal side facilitate considerable freedom of action and some social mobility for women. Moreover, the blood ties of a household, introduced into the alliance system and shaped by the higher position of the bride-giver household, represent lasting links for a woman that can be mobilized for her protection at any time.

This is the context in which the body expresses to every man and woman its message of blood and sperm, of flesh and bones, of soul, holy mountains and Buddhism. For the Khumbo, male and female bodies certainly carry 'natural meaning' (Douglas 1970), in the profound sense that shapes their cognition of gender identity. At the same time, this social construction of gender yields a principal social identity. The language of the body legitimates social rules and gender relations. Blood does not speak the strong taboo as it does in other more male-dominated societies, nor does it speak of a separation of female and male worlds or of a hostile attitude towards female body and sex. None the less, this is a social order which grants to the brother over his sister the privilege of keeping the *phayul*, the paternal land. This not only implies an economic resource but also the religious and the political power linked with it. A woman may have more power than her husband but she can never have more power than her brother. He is the *azhang* of her children.

THE LANGUAGE OF THE BODY, OF SOCIAL ORDER AND OF TRANSGRESSION

According to common Tibetan Buddhist perspectives, women are a 'lower' form of rebirth,[33] with a stronger link to *Saṃsāra* and more closely caught up in the unstable stream of passions than men. Women generally are separated from many essential aspects of religious life, although among the Khumbo as well as in Tibet there is a whole range of religious women who transcend this rule.

In Tibet, religious women lean upon Tantric philosophy, which gives a sacred dimension to the female principle. Furthermore, they are inspired by the concept of potential Buddhahood innate in all 'sentient beings' (Paul 1979; Allione 1984). Apart from nuns and religious lay women subordinated to their institutions, there also exist mystic ladies who transcend the rules and by inverting them may use powerful social and religious conceptions to achieve a liberating awareness (Dowman 1980). Emotions such as fear, desire and the very language of the body which is hidden and repressed by society, are the main field of reference for these women.

Sacred ladies dwelling in Beyul Khenbalung and belonging to different traditions (oracles, Tantric mystics and even Hindu renunciates) make concrete this potential of women by achieving mystical insight into, and transcending, the language of power of their society (see Figure 7) (Diemberger 1991). They, as well as the mystics, continuously exercised a radical criticism of society and its conventions. These ladies, however, have never been numerous and they are generally marginal to the politico-religious establishments. Except for a few famous cases, they usually are quickly forgotten. Most other women remain caught up in the social and symbolic bondage of their 'Samsaric blood'. In practice, the mystic path to religion and transcendence presents more obstacles for women than for men.[34]

It has been shown that 'blood', in both the metaphoric and metonymic senses, stands for 'ordinary' Khumbo women's existence in kinship and life cycle. For the mystic 'exceptional' ladies, 'blood' is an aspect of transcendence, of criticism and of their potential (spiritual) power. Finally, it must be added that 'blood' also is an essential element of the most important 'great man'. It is part of the secret offerings on the altar of the Khumbo *lama*. The *Rakta* (Sanskrit, 'blood') ritually represents the principle of rebirth in the *Saṃsāra* and the root of transcendental wisdom. As such, it links

Figure 7 This 84-year-old Tibetan woman is a contemporary
representative of the mystic traditions which flourished throughout the
area of Beyul Khenbalung. Following the destruction of the temples and
monasteries during the cultural revolution, she takes care of the
reconstruction of the Kuye Labrang monastery in Kharta. At present,
she celebrates the ceremonies for the community and she passes on her
initiations to the little girl considered a reincarnation of the old lady's
own mother, a Tantric mystic lady

the Khumbo *lama* to the Tibetan Tantric traditions and their philosophy of liberating awareness (Tsuda 1978; Snellgrove 1987; cf.
Kvaerne 1975). In the context of Khumbo *lama*, however, 'blood'
is a sacred symbol part of the ritual knowledge which represents

the root of his political and religious power within the social order of his society.

The social and ritual meanings of blood bear witness to the way in which the same symbols can be part of different yet interrelated discourses. Religion shaping the cognitive and social framework of society can at once legitimate and emancipate through one and the same language.

The language of the body expresses a discourse which reaches far beyond conscious categories of understanding – which is why it is so powerful. It is a language, and yet it is more than that since it is rooted in the concrete perceptions and functions of one's own body. Its categories become part of what Erdheim (1988) calls 'the social production of unconsciousness'. It is the subtle but powerful tie which links every individual to the social relations by which it is shaped. It is a kind of 'orcus' which swallows everything that could jeopardize the stability of social relations. The body is one of those privileged media through which society speaks, to the female Ego as well as to others. And this language, too, is polysemic – it may articulate either order or transgression in women's life. Transgression can be expressed in many different modes: through a sacred or opposed world which can confirm and/or transcend the present situation;[35] through movements of emancipatory awareness; or in new forms of art and knowledge.

EPILOGUE – HOW LADY KHANDRO YESHE TSOGYAL ESCAPED HER SUITORS AND DEDICATED HERSELF TO THE TANTRA AND THE ACHIEVEMENT OF MYSTIC INSIGHT

From the biography of Khandro Yeshe Tsogyal, the most famous mystic Tibetan lady and Tantric partner of Guru Rinpoche,[36] in the translation of Dowman (1984) (explanatory notes are mine):

When the hordes of suitors descended upon Kharchen, my parents and their officials held council upon the question of my marriage . . . 'I will go with neither of them' I insisted. 'If I was to go I would be guilty of incarcerating myself within the dungeon of worldly existence. Freedom is so very hard to obtain. I beg you my parents to consider this.' Although I begged them earnestly, my parents were adamant. 'There are no finer places in the known world than the residence of these two princes', my father told me. 'You are totally lacking in filial affection. I would be unable to give away such a savage as you in either China or Hor. I will give you to one of these princes' . . .

(Dowman 1984: 15)

After a complicated struggle she managed to escape. 'I fled, fled faster than the wind. Crossing many passes and valleys, I travelled to the south. The following morning my former captors were angry and shamefaced . . .' (Dowman 1984: 17).

Free from the obligations of the common lay life, she met Guru Rinpoche and dedicated herself to the mystic experience. She practised the Tantric union of 'Skilful Means' and 'Perfect Insight'[37] with her Guru and her Tantric partners and became a female Bodhisattva. On her path to mystical insight she encountered goddesses and blood as sacred principle. I quote:

Then I had a vision of a red woman, naked, lacking even the covering bone ornaments, who thrust her *bhaga* (Sanskrit vagina) against my mouth, and I drank deeply from her copious flow of blood. My entire being was filled with health and well being. I felt as strong as a snow-lion, and I realised . . . inexpressible truth. I decided that the time was ripe to go naked, depending upon air for sustenance . . .

(Dowman 1984: 71)

Offering her body in a Tantric initiation she sang:

In the intimate Maṇḍala[38] of pure pleasure.
The body's tactile sense is the sacred Mountain[39]
my four limbs and head are its four satellite continents
and the 'Lotus'[40] of pure pleasure is the source of
both Saṃsāra and Nirvāṇa, accept it for
the sake of all sentient beings.

(Dowman 1984: 38)

NOTES

1 The present chapter is based on data collected during several fieldwork projects in eastern Nepal and southern Tibet (31 months, 1982–90). From 1983 onwards, they were continuously financed by the Austrian Federal Ministry of Science and Research, and in 1989 and 1990 also by 'Professor Ardito Desio's Ev-K2-CNR' project.

   I wish to thank Andre Gingrich, Christian Schicklgruber (both from the Vienna Institut für Volkerkunde) and Maria Antonia Sironi for their supervision and critical remarks. Maurice Godelier and the members of his seminar (EHESS, Paris) provided the first inspiration for the topic of this chapter as well as valuable suggestions and critical remarks thereafter. Geza Uray offered his precious assistance in dealing with historical material.

Furthermore, I thank Walter Dostal and Ernst Steinkellner for their constant support during my research. I also thank Samten Karmay, Philippe Sagant, Charles Rambles, Kalden N. Lama, Namgyal Ronge, Barbara Aziz, Fernand Meyer, Helmut Lukas and all the colleagues and the Tibetan, Khumbo and Sherpa friends who contributed to the data and to the discussion concerning the topic of this chapter. I thank Michael Gingrich and Sophie Kidd for the supervision of the English text, Adriano Sandri and Davide Bressan for the computer graphics and Karen Diemberger for the drawings. Finally, I thank my father, Kurt Diemberger, for his support and my daughter Jana Diemberger, who shared the emotions and the difficulties of fieldwork and writing, for her participation and understanding.

The Khumbo and Tibetan terms are written as they are pronounced. The transcription of the Tibetan written form – if available – follows in brackets. As far as quotations from manuscripts are concerned, I mention only the written form.

2 *Ngotsa* (*ngo-tsha*) – literally 'hot-face' – is the Khumbo and Tibetan term for shame.

3 *Uphang* seems to be an archaic Tibetan notion which occurs among Tibetan and Tibeto-Burmese groups of Nepal. A detailed discussion of its significance among the Limbu (who incidentally translate their expression for it into Nepali by '*sir uthaune*') is to be found in Sagant (1985).

4 This notion is reported in the earliest Tibetan documents (seventh–ninth century AD). '[T]he full name (of a person) . . . consists of three components in a fixed order, notably a clan name and two individual names labelled in Tibetan by the term *rus*, "bone-clan", *mkhan* (original meaning unknown) and *mying*, "name, word" ' (Uray forthcoming).

5 The category of 'blood' and/or 'flesh' ties places the Khumbo in the Tibetan context (Stein 1972: 94; Levine 1988: 53). The category of 'milk' is probably linked to the neighbouring Tibeto-Burmese Rai, with whom the Khumbo share some elements of the kinship system (McDougal 1979: 91–3).

6 From Godelier (1990):

> *Les rapports de consanguinité sont donc par essence et dans leur fond des* rapports cognatiques, *i.e. des rapports qui additionment et combinent aussi bien ceux qui passent par les hommes (rapports agnatiques) que par les femmes (rapports utérins).*
>
> *Ces rapports cognatiques constituent la matière première des rapports de parenté, le* matériau de base *sur lequel éventuellement d'autres principes peuvent intervenir, qui, en privilégiant certains rapports de filiation au détriment des autres, restructurent l'ensemble des rapports de consanguinité en leur donnant une courbure et des formes nouvelles. Ces principes concernent la manière dont est établie la descendance d'un individu quelconque, homme ou femme, au sein d'un système de parenté déterminé.*

(p. 36)

Further:

> . . . *des réalités qui n'ont rien à voir directement avec la parenté et encore moins avec la sexualité* structurent *les rapports de parenté et se métamorphosant en aspects, en éléments de la parenté. Mais la métamorphose ne s'arrête pas là, car tout ce qui est parenté se retrouve finalement investi dans la sexualité, puisque tout ce qui est parenté se redistribue entre les individus selon leur sexe et leur âge et se métamorphose en* attributs *de leur* personne, *i.e. finalement de leur sexe.*
>
> *Voyons d'un peu plus près comment le jeu de la parenté métamorphose en éléments de sa propre substance des réalités qui la débordent. Et pour cela examinons l'effet sur le jeu de la parenté de l'intervention d'un mode de descendance. Cette intervention à le double effet, sur le plan des structures des systèmes de parenté, de privilégier certains rapports de filiation et de les pousser sur le devant de la scène dans la mesure ou ils sont investis de fonctions sociales importantes. Les autres rapports, sans cesser d'exister, sont refoulés au second plan ou dépourvus de poids social, ils s'effacent jusqu'à devenir des ombres de rapports qui cependant peuvent reprendre vie et forme dans certaines circonstances. C'est ainsi que les systèmes linéaires refoulent, sans les faire disparaître, les structures cognatiques de la consanguinité. Les systèmes cognatiques, au contraire, accordent une importance secondaire aux relations de filiation linéaire passant par un seul sexe à l'exclusion de l'autre.*

(p. 38)

According to Godelier's argument, 'blood' seems to stand here for that part of kinship which lies in the shade and in certain circumstances can come to the fore.

7 Mother's sister (*ushu*) and father's brother (*agu*) are considered as 'little mother' and 'little father', terms also used to define further father's wives and mother's husbands.

8 For example, the children of same-sex siblings or of parallel cousins are considered as one's own children, etc.

9 There are alternative terms for those relatives whose designation determines the difference between a bilaterial symmetric system and a system with Omaha features. The first case recalls what Clarke (1980) describes for the Sherpa of Helambu. The second case is similar to what can be found among the Sherpa of Solu and Khumbu (Oppiz 1968; Allen 1976).

10 This term is derived from *tsha*, meaning grandchild, nephew and possibly son-in-law (Benedict 1942: 321; Uebach 1980: 301–9; Guigo 1986: 99–103).

11 *Azhang* is a widespread term for maternal uncle. *Zhang-tsha* designates the mother's brother–sister's son relation which is endowed with a strong political relevance. *Zhang* in the early Tibetan kingdom designates the male members of the clans which provided the queens, mothers of kings, and became a hereditary aristocratic title (Rona-tas 1955; Stein 1972: 132; Uray, personal communication).

12 The direct exchange of daughters between households and the fact that marriage of a man to a patrilateral cross-cousin is tolerated tends to enclose the alliances in short cycles (Schicklgruber forthcoming). The result is a system which does not venture on what Lévi-Strauss calls the 'big adventure' of generalized exchange based on matrilateral cross-cousin marriage (Lévi-Strauss 1969), which seems to be quite common among Tibeto-Burmese groups (Oppiz 1988).

13 These terms are derived from the ancient Tibetan *myes* and *phyi* which designate grand-father and grand-mother as well as ancestors. They are reported in the Tun-huang documents (Bacot *et al.* 1940: 13, 20; Uebach 1980: 301). Remarkably, *myes* is used for the early kings. According to Benedict, *phyi* is related to the Tibeto-Burmese root **p'i*, 'grandmother' (Benedict 1942: 315). At present, in Central Tibet, grand-father and grand-mother are often designated by *mo* (*rmo*) and *po* (*spo*) (Guigo 1986: 79; Goldstein 1986: 189).

14 Labour is a critical factor in the local economy. Thus boys can sometimes be 'given away' instead of a girl if required by the constellation of the households involved.

15 Tibet proper was divided into four *ru* 'horns' or 'wings', each consisting of eight *ston-sde*, 'thousand districts' (Uray 1960: 31). One 'thousand-district' could include more than one clan and one clan could be spread within more of these units. Yet clans persisted and descent and residence acted as different co-existing structuring principles during the royal period as is shown by documents which report the name of clan as well as of the thousand-district (Uray, personal communication). In this context, the term for mother's brother became the aristocratic hereditary title *zhang* which defines the member of the clans who provided the mothers of kings. The term *zhang-blon* (literally 'uncles and ministers') referred to the political leadership which surrounded the king.

16 Uray points out that, 'The Tibetan mode of forming personal names was radically altered by the profound social change that took place following the decline and the fall of the kingdom. It entailed various religious, political and ethnic consequences, namely the rise of Buddhism to the status of established religion, its subsequent persecution and final victory; the collapse of the unified state . . . and a great decrease in the role of clans' (Uray forthcoming).

17 'In modern times, the clan has disappeared or rather been replaced by the name of a territory or house, while among nomads the name of the tribe is added to the personal name' (Stein 1972: 107). B. Aziz (1978: 117–33) notices the pre-eminence of the residential unit as a determinant element in the social structure of Dingri in southern Tibet.

18 '[R]eligious heads, abbots and spiritual masters – who occupy their positions either by heredity, or through pupillary succession within a magisterial or preceptorial line, or again in virtue of being regarded as a link in a line of hierophanies (*sprul sku*) – are regularly invested with temporalities that are frequently considerable and sometimes indeed truly princely; very often, therefore, they are in effect abbot-princes in hierocratic lines' (Seyfort Ruegg 1988: 1249).

19 The only exception I know of is represented by a Tibetan society in Yünnan where land is inherited matrilineally (Corlin 1978: 75–89).

20 The title of the text is 'The dividing of the wealth between the brother and the sister and the entrustment to the gods' (from a collection of Bon texts, *'gTo-phran*, published by the Tibetan Bonpo Monastic Centre, Himachal Pradesh, 1973). I am very grateful to Samten Karmay, who refers to it elsewhere (1975: 207*ff*) for drawing my attention to and patiently discussing the original with me.

21 The evaluation of slaughtering is rather ambivalent: from a Buddhist point of view, it is a sinful activity and *lama* do not slaughter, yet is also a field of power and among other reasons, women are prevented from becoming *lhaven* priests because they cannot perform animal sacrifice.

22 Yet a household mother will try to find a good place for her daughter, often represented by the household of her own brother. This is the psychological and social background of the frequent and tolerated patrilateral cross-cousin marriage (Schicklgruber forthcoming).

23 This is simultaneously a symbol for social integration and for social differentiation. It differentiates between the people with a good mouth with whom it is suitable to have marriage alliances, and the people with a bad mouth (who belong to other ethnic groups or who are socially non-acceptable, with whom marriages are impossible). For an analysis of the role of *chang* in a culturally related context, see for example March (1987: 351–87).

24 *Dog* means receptacle and also fertile soil. It is an ancient Tibetan notion and can refer to the fertile soil also as a place of cosmogonic union between sky and earth (Tucci 1966: 64*ff*; Bacot *et al.* 1940: 81; Hazod 1991).

25 Sometimes the 'grain' is also compared to the fermented wheat, barley or maize which when squeezed produce the whitish *chang*.

26 The Khumbo follow the common Tibetan conceptions: the above is inhabited by the gods of the sky, the below by deities of the underground, the space in between by the spirits of the intermediate level, and by human beings. Life on this intermediate level is always tensed between the above and the below and mountains are a kind of *trait d'union* (Stein 1972: 202*ff*).

27 The position of the woman above the loins of her male partner is transgressive and as such is reserved to Tantrists or gods (as can be seen in the icongraphy of Tantric Buddhism) in a sacred world beyond the conventions which rule the common use of the body (cf. Prince Peter of Greece and Denmark 1963: 542).

28 The concrete use of this ambiguous term gives a substance to the principle of consciousness that flatly contradicts the Buddhist theory which denies the existence of a 'soul'. It is the contradiction noted by Tucci when he describes the concept of 'soul' in the Tibetan religion (Tucci and Heissig 1970: 219).

29 As such it is independent from the elements transmitted by the parents. When Buddhist religion became a dominant influence in Tibet, the reincarnation of the 'principle of consciousness' became the conceptual

basis for the transmission of leading politico-religious roles (cf. note 17).

30 This is a widespread Tibetan concept (Stein 1972: 222). It directly links the human body to political power and prestige, *uphang* – 'order of the head, high head' – and to the mountain deities who bestow it.

31 The individual (and natural) birth is ritually denied while the blessing of the ancestors and the deities which give identity to the group is transmitted to the new human being with the name-giving ceremony. Since the child carries the 'eternal' bones of the ancestors and the 'eternal' soul of the community, the new individual is a mere link in a timeless mythic dimension of the social group. This link between descent groups, time perception and ritual presents analogies to Bloch's discussion for Merina (Bloch 1986: 167*ff*).

32 Theoretically, a fatherless child cannot leave the *dip* of birth: this defilement would upset the deities who would send hail, diseases and misfortunes to the whole community. In practice, however, many solutions are possible, from 'buying a father' to ascribing a child to a mother's sister's husband (his *agu*).

33 The common term for woman in Tibet is *kyemen [skye-dman]* meaning literally 'low birth' (Jäschke 1975: 28).

34 Snellgrove underlines that in spite of the praise of the female principle, most texts merely refer to ritual practice from the point of view of a male practitioner (Snellgrove 1987: 287–8). Yet historical mystic ladies like Machig Labdronma who founded the *gcod* tradition in the twelfth century are witnesses for the tough yet possible path towards mystical realization of women.

35 To show the genitals is considered a bad offence and corresponds to an open declaration of conflict. As such it can be used by both men and women. One who does this is in *Khon Dip [khon grib]*, in the 'conflict shadow', together with the offended person or group. The open gesture is restricted to a few very serious occasions. There are, however, common mitigated versions, for example a woman turns and lifts her apron towards the one she wishes to offend. There is historical record of analogous behaviour in the old Tibetan documents. The Tun-huang chronicle reports the case of a powerful lady who broke an alliance by showing her genitals as intentional offence (Bacot *et al.*, 1940: 103).

36 Alias Padmasambhava, the Buddhist Tantric saint and magician considered one of the main founders and patrons of Tibetan Buddhism in the eighth century.

37 This expression refers to ritual sexual union and its mystic aspects.

38 Maṇḍala (Sanskrit 'circle'), as concept for sacred space or enclosure is a basic element of Tantric rituals (Snellgrove 1987: 198*ff*).

39 I.e. Mount Meru, according to Indian and Tibetan cosmogony the centre of the universe surrounded by four continents.

40 The Tantric symbol for vagina.

5 Home decoration as popular culture

Constructing homes, genders and classes in Norway[1]

Marianne Gullestad

At the present stage of the comparative study of constructions of gender, I see five main challenges. The first is to put aside the axiom that women are everywhere subordinated to men (Ortner and Whitehead 1981). This assumption may be perfectly justifiable on an abstract level of analysis and from a specific social and historical vantage point. The main question, however, is not whether the assumption of global subordination is tenable or not, but whether it is a fruitful guideline for empirical investigations. In my view, the axiom of global subordination assumes what should be examined, and reduces the ability of the analyst to uncover the subtleties, complexities, contradictions and ambiguities of gender relations in different contexts. The relations between the genders have dimensions other than power and prestige – such as love, sexuality, spiritual communion, dependency – and the analyst should constantly be open to new experiences, new vantage points and new research questions to be asked.

The second challenge is to design investigations of gender in such a way that not only the differences but also the sameness, the similarities and the commonalities of the genders are made explicit. The problem often is that studies are in different ways continuous with folk models of gender: gender is either invisible (in most scholarly work) or too visible (in some gender studies). The latter examines gender in terms of conflicts and contrasts, while the shared concerns of women and men are taken for granted and left unexamined.

Since cultural ideas of masculinity and femininity are mutually constituted, the third challenge is not to examine constructions of gender in isolation, but rather as relational constructs. The fourth challenge is related to the third: constructions of gender are neither natural nor static. Gender studies could therefore be designed in such a way that it is possible to study changes of cultural categories, symbolic expressions and activity systems. When, for instance, Western women attempt to change their roles and definitions of themselves, these changes have profound implications for the definitions of masculinity as well.

The fifth and last challenge is to study how constructions of gender interact with other kinds of social differentiation, such as those based on age, generation, kinship, race, ethnicity, religion, region and social class. Students of gender tend only to see gender; class analysts tend only to see social classes. The research questions are often crudely put as being questions of gender *or* class instead of asking how gender and class interact in the lives of historically situated social groups.

THE HOUSE AS AN OBJECT OF STUDY

With these five challenges in mind, I want to approach constructions of gender and class through an examination of some of the cultural practices of the house. This substantive field has been analysed from a variety of perspectives within anthropology. One such perspective is the study of households. In the analysis of household and local organization, it has become common to distinguish between household functions and family relations (e.g. Bender 1967; Rudie 1969/70; Grønhaug 1974). Making and tending the house is a central household function. In Western contexts living together is often emically central for deciding who belongs and who does not belong to the household.

Another perspective on the house focuses on its symbolic and cosmological aspects (Griaule and Dieterlen 1954; Cunningham 1965; Bourdieu 1977a, b; Wright 1980; Tambiah 1985; Moore 1986). A house has generally many aspects and meanings. It is a tool with practical utility, and with economic, social, aesthetic, cosmological and symbolic aspects. A place to live in is created by people and functions as a framework for their lives. The house and the inhabitants are in this way mutually constituted. The study of houses, therefore, offers rich comparative data for the study of culture (Cunningham 1965). Indeed, in many cultures the house can be seen as a microcosm of important cognitive categories (Bourdieu 1977a). Such categories are stored in walls, doors, room divisions and objects, and may indicate what is assumed to be good and bad, beautiful and ugly, sacred and secular, male and female. For the researcher, it thus becomes important to look at the following: (a) the physical structures of the house and the environment; (b) the objects found in the house and in its surroundings; (c) how these objects are arranged and grouped; and (d) the use of the objects, the house and the surroundings.

However, Bourdieu (1977a) emphasizes that it does not suffice just to look at the objects: one must also study who uses them, and how and when they are used. The meaning which materializes in the organization of objects in space can only be discovered through associated social practices which may be expected to reveal the same cognitive schemes as the objects in space.

Because the house embodies cultural categories, it is an important element in the socialization of children. Sometimes small children learn their culture too well; for instance, when a modern three-year-old girl strongly opposes drinking water from the taps of the bathroom. She has learned that water in the bathroom and water in the kitchen are used for different purposes, but she has not yet learned that it is the same water only in different taps. Children learn their culture through the body in space. Indeed, the arrangement of space 'talks' directly through the body: our use of space has therefore been called a silent language (Hall 1973).

In modern houses, the number and variety of artefacts is greater than ever before. Many artefacts are mass-produced consumer items. Recently there has been a new scholarly interest in the study of material artefacts (Csikszentmihalyi and Rochberg-Halton 1981; Appadurai 1986) and mass consumption. Miller (1987) argues that mass produced goods represent culture, not because they are merely part of the environment in which people in industrial society operate but because they are an integral part of the process of objectification by which both persons and society are created. He rejects the approach to goods predicated on reducing consumption to the nature of the commodity item, and the consumer to the process by which the commodity is obtained. Instead, he gives the consumer a much more active role, by emphasizing the recontextualization that takes place following the purchase or allocation of each item.

THE HOUSE AS A KEY SYMBOL FOR MODERN INTIMACY

Building on these works, I want in this chapter to contribute theoretically to the study of the constructions of gender and class through an investigation of some aspects of meanings of Norwegian homes.[2] Western family-households have not only lost several functions in the process of modernization, they have also taken on new functions. The most important, in my view, is to provide a setting for modern intimacy. This function is so central that the modern family-household can be described primarily as a moral community. Intimacy is created and expressed by the way other household activities are performed. It is simultaneously a household function and an intrinsic part of family relations.

In modern Norway, the home is a key context for intimacy. Like other Northern Europeans, and also the North Americans, Norwegians do not only have houses, they have homes. The word *hjem* (home) brings together in one notion both the idea of a place and the idea of a social togetherness associated with this place. The notion has both material and less tangible social, emotional, moral and spiritual connotations.

According to the famous functionalist and modernist architect Le Corbusier, the house is a machine to live in. I cannot imagine a more inappropriate statement for how most Norwegians feel about their homes. I will argue that Norwegian culture is home-centred, and that the symbolic value of the concrete and physical aspects of the home is in the process of becoming more important. Norwegians use the home to create and express their specific ideas of identity and intimacy. The home thus serves as a key symbol, suggesting and justifying a complex set of cultural categories, values and relations. Through the arrangements of their homes, Norwegians express themselves as gendered human beings belonging to specific social classes and reference groups. Home decoration and home improvement is thus a part of the construction and reconstruction of social groups. Simultaneously the home is both highly gendered and highly shared as a cultural symbol and a focus of attention for women and men.

The analysis is based on two periods of fieldwork among urban working-class families in Bergen,[3] on written autobiographies from all over Norway,[4] and on comparisons with materials collected by other researchers.

HISTORICAL OUTLINE

Within Norway there exist regional variations. Along the coast, social life was egalitarian. Peasant adaptation often comprised a combination of farming, with a few cows, sheep and goats, and of fishing and economic activities in the home, like making nets, slippers and so on for the market. Farms were usually small, and survival depended on a variety of resources and on continuous hard work. The division of labour was one where the wife tended the farm while the husband went fishing. Women were accustomed to rough work, and to being alone for long periods with total or major responsibility for the household and for the farm. Economic differences often depended on personal ability and luck, and gave less foundation for social stratification than in the broad valleys in the eastern parts of the country where one found, relative to Norwegian conditions, both rich owners of farmland and forests and a landless proletariat of some size. The North Sea coast (in the west and part of the south) is sometimes humorously called 'the dark coastal strip', because traditionally it has been characterized by strong adherence to pietist religion, to total temperance and to missionary work.

Urbanization on a major scale was late in coming. Many rural people migrated to the cities in the second half of the last century and also today quite a few are first generation inhabitants. The late urbanization is reflected in the way the flexibility of the old combinations of resources is carried on in new circumstances. Even when they are wage-workers, many Norwegians still to some extent think and act as if they were self-employed, self-employment actually being sought in occupations such as taxi-driving and trucking (see Brox 1984; also Højrup 1983a, b about self-employment in Denmark). Norwegians, like many other Northern Europeans since the Romantic period, have relatively few positive images of large-scale urban life. In their ideas of the good life, many look back in time to the supposed qualities of the local rural community (Gullestad 1985; 1992).

According to the historians, life in the Norwegian upper class is more different from its counterparts in Europe than life in the working class (Dahl and Vaa 1980). The Norwegian upper class have been less wealthy and more divided between themselves than (for instance) the upper class in either Denmark or the southern part of Sweden. There has never been, in the European sense of the word, a landed aristocracy in Norway, and economic class differences are smaller than in many other European countries. Part of the picture is, however, that Norwegians like to think that class differences are small, and this is supported by an egalitarian interactional style that de-emphasizes difference. A dominant cultural category in Norway is equality defined as sameness (Gullestad 1984b, 1985, 1986a, b, 1992).

The welfare state in Norway, developed mainly after World War II, is based on the ideas of solidarity, security (*trygghet*) and equality defined as sameness (*likhet*). The government has made considerable efforts in the sectors of housing, social policy, health care and state insurance funds for the old, the disabled, the unemployed, and unmarried and divorced mothers. Like the other Scandinavian social democracies, Norway developed a characteristic blend of a capitalist economy and strong state institutions. Among other things, a state bank for housing (*Husbanken*) gave cheap loans in order for every family to be able to own their own dwelling; in the larger cities, housing co-operatives were established. The welfare state was developed under considerable political consensus, although this consensus seems to be dissolving in the 1980s and 1990s.

Over the last twenty years, more married women than before have started working outside the home. Highly educated women as well as women with relatively little schooling are employed at different levels in the welfare state and in private companies. There have been considerable changes in the relationships between spouses, first and foremost of an ideological kind. The ideals of equality as sameness are increasingly being used *within* households. Not only highly educated feminists but also the women with no more than nine years of obligatory schooling now define their marriages in terms of equality as sameness. In many Norwegian homes, spouses more and more *negotiate* their division of tasks, and the legitimacy accepted by both spouses is that of sameness. Arguments such as 'I work full time just as much as you do, and therefore . . .' or 'I have been home with the children all day and that's work too, so therefore . . .' are forceful in negotiations about who is going to do particular tasks (Gullestad 1984b).

Some might interpret these changes as feminist ideas having 'filtered down' to women who do not identify themselves with feminism. I believe rather that both milieus are influenced by the forceful representation of equality as sameness in Norway. Once this is applied to a new context, the process acquires a dynamic of its own. Together with these changes, marriage is increasingly defined in terms of romantic love, togetherness and the sharing of tasks.

The rise in paid female employment has led to a general fear that the amount of care in the home and among relatives, neighbours and friends is diminishing, because women are no longer there all the time to perform their traditional tasks. Divorce figures have been rising, and most divorces are initiated by women. This diversification of family life implies that there are more female-headed households and more one-person households than before.

Old people now generally live alone, as do young people before cohabitation and marriage, and middle-aged people after marriage or between marriages.

The paradigmatic home in Norway comprises a single family house. More than half of the population live in such houses, although in the largest cities, only a small fraction of the population can afford it. The municipal (rented) housing sector is restricted, whereas the co-operative housing sector is considerable, providing both semi-detached houses and apartments in housing estates.

In the cities, people usually change housing when they can afford it, either by remodelling what they already have or by moving to a superior apartment or house. Because of this, a house is generally not transmitted from one generation to the next. When it does happen, other considerations are often more important than family feelings. In the rural areas, the house is transmitted together with the farm. In urban areas, it may happen if the younger couple is not yet established and the parental house compares favourably to what the younger couple can get on the market. However, even if housing generally is neo-local, both rural and urban couples sometimes establish themselves close to the parents of one of them. Parents may be able to help a young couple to establish a home in different ways (by providing a site for house-building, membership in a building co-operation, important knowledge and relationships).

Because urbanization is recent, many urban families are connected to the rural areas by kinship ties. It is common to own a cottage or an old farmhouse in the rural areas. This can be seen as a second home 'out in nature', and is often a focus for kinship ties. The family may have some of its 'roots' in just these rural areas, the summer house may be inherited, or it may function as a focus for kinship reunions during vacations.

HOMES IN NORWAY

To Norwegians, the home is an important setting not only for family life but also for social life. It is a setting for interactions both within the family and with relatives, and extending outside of the family, with friends. There is not much of a pub or restaurant culture in Scandinavia and in the neighbourhoods there are few neutral and informal settings for meeting other people. Becoming friends often means being allowed to pass through the doorway. In many neighbourhoods, a line is drawn between the people one visits (*går inn til*) and others.

The most important opposition inherent in the form and use of the home is that between the home itself and the outside world (*hjemme/ute*). The doorway is the main boundary between the inside and the outside. The front door, locks, name-plate, door mat and door bell can be seen as practical and symbolic markings of this important boundary. The doorway can be seen as both a protection of the values of the home and a barrier against the outside world.

In the opposition between the home and the outside (*hjemme/ute*), 'home' stands for warmth, security, cosiness (and perhaps a little boredom). 'Out' stands for excitement but also some danger. One talks about 'going out' to a restaurant or a party, 'going out to work', and 'going out for a walk in nature'. The home-centredness in Norway can only be understood in relation to the central notion of nature, on the one hand, and on the other hand the notion of the city (which is often considered to be unnatural and artificial). Nature and the city are in different ways considered to be dangerous and exciting places.[5]

The boundary between the inside and the outside is restated both outside and inside the house. Within each house there are rooms which are more or less private. The hall and the living room are the most public rooms. The parents' bedroom is considered the most private room for outsiders. This is often expressed when someone shows off a new apartment or a new house. Guests walk into most of the rooms except the master bedroom where they often stand at the threshold just peeking in respectfully. If the parents' bedroom is considered to be the most private room of the house, it is not entirely because sexuality is felt to be the most intimate part of life. Probably it has to do also with the fact that sexuality in Norway, as in the rest of Scandinavia, is perceived as especially natural.

The boundary between *the public and the private* does not only vary with place but also with time. Some parts of the day are more suitable for visits than others, and then the living room is more public than at other parts of the day or night.

There is also a division between *nature and culture*. Preparing meals, sleeping, sexual relations and going to the toilet are seen as being more closely associated with nature than is entertaining friends. The living room is the cultural main stage of the house, while the other activities are associated with smaller stages and back rooms. In other words, the activities are organized in a hierarchical order, evident in the inhabitants' decoration of the different rooms as well as in state regulations for houses.

Another opposition inherent in contemporary arrangements of the house is the division between *generations*. In the Norwegian countryside, one can still find old and middle-aged people who as children slept first in the same bed as a grandparent, and later in the same bed as a sibling (Thorsen 1989). But today a division between the generations is prevalent. Grandparents seldom live in the same house as their grandchildren (although they may live not far from them), and children get their own rooms, separate from their parents, at a quite early age. When they are older, and if the family has a single family house, an extra living room (*peisestue*) is often set up in the basement.

'ORDINARY PEOPLE' IN BERGEN

As already noted, my ideas about the Norwegian home derive from fieldwork experiences as well as from autobiographic materials. However, the second fieldwork, conducted among young urban working-class families with small children,[6] has been particularly important. A few glimpses from it will provide an empirical foundation for the discussion which follows. The husbands had jobs as labourers, craftsmen, salesmen and lower-level clerks. All of them were wage-workers, although one, a hairdresser, was planning to set up his own business. The wives worked as self-employed childminders (*dagmammaer*), as cleaning assistants, shop assistants and office personnel. Husbands and wives alike had relatively little education beyond the nine years of obligatory schooling. They used the expression 'ordinary people' (*vanlige folk*) as a designation for themselves.

The couples were young, at a stage in the life cycle where they had little money and many needs. Most lived in three-room apartments with a kitchen and a bathroom. The apartments were located in large co-operative housing estates in different satellite towns of Bergen. This meant that the home-making activities were mainly concentrated upon the interiors of the houses. In addition, the car was, as we shall see, an object of improvement and decoration.

The young couples were also at a stage of life where home-making is important. At any one point in time, most had a project planned. 'Last year we did the bathroom and next year we plan to panel the hall', was a typical refrain. Within the apartment, the different rooms were decorated according to different rules. The living room is the main room for display and has a higher priority than all the other rooms. It is the most public room, where guests are received, as well as the room where the family 'relaxes' in the evenings. To 'relax' (*slappe av*) and to have a good time (*kose seg*) means to sit idly, maybe watching television, chatting and eating some snacks.

Since the living room is a room of display, it usually contains the best furniture, lamps, pictures and ornaments. The arrangement of objects shows a desire for a polished and almost sumptuous comfort. This impression was created by shining surfaces, for example leather, glass, painted wood and an abundance of plants and ornaments made of glass, porcelain, brass, alabaster and onyx, and by maintaining a spotless order.

Furniture was dark and voluminous, and together with lamps, plants, pictures and ornaments, arranged in a set of compositions or zones. The couch ensemble with soft chairs and a coffee table, often close to the TV and the wall unit is one zone. Other zones may be a dining table, a bar, or a stereo unit. Some people have a dining table and chairs, but many prefer instead to create an extra zone around the TV by adding a couple of soft comfortable chairs and a coffee table. This kind of furniture fits well with serving cream cakes and open-faced sandwiches. If guests are invited for dinner, it is also served on the coffee table. In this way, a balance is ideally struck between a polished and spotless display and a soft and easy comfort.

Few old things are found in these homes. The young couples see no charm in buying furniture at a flea market as many students do. Neither is it relevant to obtain a prestige-filled past by going to auctions as many well-off, educated people do. They would rather be modern and follow the fashions in the furniture catalogues which arrive in the mail. The young women are the consumer experts, study the pictures and comment upon who in their circle of friends already has this bedroom set or that living room set. This explicit interest for novelty and fashion appears to have some connection with a childhood in which they lived in close quarters and could not afford things: old things are associated with a past one wants to leave behind, not with a past one looks back on with nostalgia.

The furniture making up the different zones is co-ordinated with lamps, pictures and ornaments. The wall unit, preferably with glass doors, is the frame for several of the decorations (*pynte-tingene*). Having baby Vaseline or similar items of use in the wall unit is quite clearly not right – such things just do not belong there. In some cases, the decorations are bought from the wife's earnings, to symbolize her paid work in a special way. 'I buy one ornament every month when I get my wages', a young woman says, 'just to know that I am working'. Such ornaments may be grouped in twos and threes in the wall unit, on the TV set or on the window sills. The principle behind each of these smaller compositions is some kind of likeness of, for instance, colour and material, combined with an interesting contrast of shape. Sometimes small crocheted doilies, placed underneath an object or a group of objects, mediate between the different small compositions. The principle behind the total arrangement of decorations seems to be symmetry: each little ornament or group of ornaments is placed at a fair distance from the others.

In this way, smaller compositions make up larger compositions or zones which again make up the 'wholeness' (*helheten*) or 'style' (*stilen*) of the living room. In the desire to be able to display a spotless and shining living room 'in case someone should drop by', we can sense a certain continuity with the parlours of earlier peasant and working-class generations. Signs of activity, for example children's toys on the carpet or newspapers on the coffee table, damage the general representative impression. In order to keep the living room spotless, small children are seldom allowed to play there. They play in their own room (the smallest of the two bedrooms), in the kitchen and in the narrow hallway. The door to the living room is very often locked in the morning, being first unlocked to the children for the daily ritual of children's evening television and for the time that parents and children spend there together. Then the parents are also present and make sure the children do not break anything.

The kitchens of these apartments are generally rather small and narrow, and from the functionalist middle-class architect's point of view, apparently intended just for cooking and doing the dishes. The young families, however, turn it into a much more central, multi-purpose room. The family takes most of the daily meals around a small Formica table in the kitchen. Often the young women have their purses sitting in a regular place in the kitchen. Many families also have important papers, such as bills and bank books, in the kitchen, which therefore also functions as an office.

In one of the drawers, cosmetics, hair brushes and combs are found. There is a mirror on one of the counters which is brought out when needed. Women often sit in the kitchen when they make themselves up and do their hair. In other words, nature is converted to culture in the kitchen, not only through the preparation of food, but also to a certain degree through the decoration of the human body.

In addition, the kitchen is a second room for receiving guests. It is the more intimate, smaller stage of the apartment. Close women friends who come for a visit in the morning are invited into the kitchen for a cup of coffee. Then they sit around the kitchen table and chat while the children play.[7] In the afternoons and evenings, when the husband is at home, the kitchen is an extra place to be. If a woman comes to visit, the two women can gather in the kitchen while the husband watches television in the living room; or he can listen to the sports news in the kitchen while they occupy the living room. If a couple come for a visit, the women often go together to the kitchen to prepare food or drinks. Those sitting in the living room may note the door to the kitchen being closed carefully: the conversation behind the kitchen door is then confidential.

Being shown into the living room can be either a way of honouring the guest or a way of creating distance. There is a degree of creative ambiguity in this. With two places to choose between, there is a greater opportunity for juggling the definition of the situation. When many people choose not to have a kitchen which opens directly into the living room, it is not only because they dislike the cooking odours, but also because a separate kitchen offers the opportunity of having two separate rooms for social interaction.

Even if the kitchens are small and narrow, the inhabitants carry on more activities there than the planners of the estates had intended. This use has its roots back in the farm kitchen where, for example, one had a barber's mirror and a wash-basin. While the planners intended a separation of functions (applying make-up in the bathroom/bedroom, playing in the children's room, receiving guests in the living room, etc.), their inhabitants thus put some of these activities back together in more complex ways.

The picture the inhabitants hold of a good kitchen is neither the functionalist laboratory nor the romanticized farm kitchen with a lot of cooking smells and tastes. The working-class town kitchen is the pivotal place in the house. It is similar to the farm kitchen by virtue of the many functions that are collected there, but different from the romanticized notion of the farm kitchen which parts of the Norwegian middle class now entertain.

While the living room is the most public and most representative room, the bedrooms are considered the most private rooms. The rules for their decoration are therefore less strict. At this stage of young family life, the living rooms had been renovated, but not all the bedrooms. Most used the bedrooms just as the architect had imagined: the big bedroom for the parents and the little one for the children.

In principle, the home as a whole is a gender-neutral universe. In practice, it is largely a female universe. Especially for husbands engaged in physical work, there may be a contrast between the living room's ideal polished comfort and their own appearance. There is a somewhat greater contrast between men and women in this social class than, for instance, in much of the Norwegian academic middle-class. A 'real man' is strongly built and handy when it comes to building things and making repairs. Parts of the home are associated more with one gender than with the other. To a large degree, the kitchen is the domain of women, while the men have the cellar, the garage, or the car. But as these apartments do not have cellars, garages or other typical masculine places, the men turn to the car as the most masculine place to be and to do things. The car is, so to speak, the apartment's male annexe. Small wonder, then, that the cars in these social circles are in very good condition.

That the home is very much the woman's domain is discursively expressed in many ways. When talking about their parental home, young adults say 'at my mother's' (*hos min mor og de*). Also, the young women commonly used the expression 'my carpets' and 'my floors' in discussions about housework with women friends. Having the main responsibility for housework gives a degree of control over the placing of people and objects. These observations say something about both the women's creative activity as well as their controlling influence in the small and close contexts of the home. This influence, however, is often paired with a corresponding impotence in other social contexts.

Since the husbands were in lower-level jobs where they received low pay, worked hard and generally did not exert much influence over their own work situation, there was no great difference in power and prestige between husbands and wives. In many ways, some of these wives had a more varied and autonomous round of life than their husbands. This was especially the case with those wives who managed the family income. Management of the money is a key function of the household and gives the person who performs it both a variety of experiences and influence over important family matters. In this respect, the middle-class idea that working-class women are doubly oppressed, first as working-class and then as women, does not quite fit this situation (Gullestad 1978).

As for me, I was left with an image of the husband sitting heavily with his legs a little apart at one end of the couch, his body language and facial expression suggesting that he was slightly bored and out of place. At times, when there is no renovating work to be done, a man is not completely at home in his own home. This is expressed even more clearly in divorces: it is most often the man who has to leave the family home. He moves 'home to the mother' (*hjem til moren*).

This image of the vulnerability and marginality of the husband and father in relation to the home is elaborated in two studies exploring the interconnections of family life and work life, one of sailors (Borchgrevink and Melhuus 1985) and another of employees in the offshore oil industry (Solheim *et al.* 1986). The families of sailors and offshore workers are extreme cases, but the extreme case may be used to magnify and render visible a more general tendency. In both kinds of families, the husband's periods at home are as challenging to the other family members as the periods when he is at sea. The wife's main dilemma consists in being fully independent and competent, while at the same time constantly keeping a place ready for the husband and father.

HOME DECORATION AS A CONTINUOUS PROJECT

Norwegian men and women have for several generations prioritized a good house (or apartment) over other kinds of consumption, such as visits to cafés, restaurants and bars. This may be related to the cold climate and to an underlying value of religious pietism that explains the relative dearth of public meeting places. However, there are today some striking new tendencies which require analysis. Over the last generation, many kinds of home production have been reduced, while one kind has become considerably more important. There is an increasing emphasis placed upon renovating and furnishing the home. Most people use less time on such things as making juice and jams and sewing their own clothes, while at the same time they spend more time, money and love on decorating their homes.

Beate's and Nils' home is a good illustration of how home decoration has become an ongoing concern. These are people admired by friends and acquaintances for their nice home. As soon as they moved in, they started decorating their apartment. When they completed decoration, they started all over again, so parts of the apartment were decorated more than once during the two years of my fieldwork. First they did the living room and the hall. The living room has two different wallpapers in patterned red and green, and contains a dark leather couch ensemble, dark brown tables and a white cupboard with drawers and shelves. There is a white bench for the stereo equipment, brown velvet curtains, and an abundance of lamps and ornaments. An old kerosene lamp from the husband's childhood home at a farm near Bergen, with a pot of green plants where the kerosene used to be, hangs over the coffee table. An Italian reproduction of a crying boy hangs over the couch, in addition to a 'real painting', made in Japan from a photograph of Beate's son (obtained from a door-to-door salesman who came to everybody in the block).

When the living room was done, the kitchen was redecorated. Walls and cupboards were panelled with different kinds of laminated panelling; every cupboard and drawer was covered and framed by wooden mouldings and given new knobs. A dish-washer was installed, and the room was equipped with new curtains and a new dining table. Then the bathroom walls were covered with Formica, and a new mirror, hooks and towel-racks were installed. The walls and ceiling in the toilet were painted. In the boy's room they put up two kinds of 'boyish' wallpaper (with cars and airplanes), as well as curtains, shelves, a table and a bed. Lastly they did up their own bedroom. They sold the beds that Beate's father, a carpenter, had made for them (nobody in the family wanted them) and bought new fashionable beds. New wallpaper and a soft wall-to-wall carpet was installed. In all the rooms in the apartment they had installed new covering on the floors, either carpet made of artificial materials or vinyl.

In the meantime, the furniture in the living room was rearranged many times. Beate's father made them an original bar in the form of a small open wagon arranged as a man lying over a woman. The bar-wagon is about 1½m long and stands on the floor with glasses and bottles. They bought stereo equipment in a vertical rack, acquired second-hand from someone who needed the money. The stereo bench they had before was given to Beate's brother: since her father had made it, she did not like the idea of selling it to him.

Beate lost her liking for the dark patterned wallpaper in the hall and she wanted lighter colours which became more fashionable in 1980–1. They plastered and textured the walls in white, and changed the frames around the doors, the door sills and the floor covering to a dark-brown shade. The fashion was inspired by the architecture of holiday hotels in Spain. They also changed the floor covering to imitation tiles to go with the white walls and dark brown frames. The next project was to treat one of the walls in the living room with the same white plaster. There, too, Beate became tired of the two dark, patterned wallpapers. But she did not want more than two white walls; four white walls would have been too uniform in her opinion. They subsequently changed the couch ensemble to a still more fashionable one, covered with oxblood-coloured leather and filling the whole corner.

Whenever I asked Beate about the division of work between her and her husband Nils, she answered, 'We do it together. We share it'. After a while I learned what this means: that it is a joint project, not that there is no division of tasks. For heavy reconstruction work 'doing it together' meant that she helps Nils, for instance by holding something, or handing tools to him if he works alone. She may also help him by making a good meal, and keeping him company while he works. He is an especially handy man, having been brought up on a farm close to Bergen. Beate, on the other hand, is a 'typical urban girl', and does not identify with rough kinds of work. She knows how to sew and knit, even though she does not practise this very much. She is proud of several silk lampshades that she has made for herself and for others. Both of them, and especially Nils, get help cheaply from relatives and friends. Because of his job, as a repairman in an automobile repair shop, Nils is able to offer other services in return. They may also occasionally use hired craftsmen, but that is uncommon. He often (alone or together with male friends) puts up the wallpaper or the panel, but she is responsible for choosing the equipment and often for finding the best buys and paying the bills. For larger items they always go shopping together. Both want to have a say and agree on what to buy, but she plans and directs most of the aesthetic and economic aspects of home-making, whereas he plans and carries out the more technical aspects. As she explains, 'He does not care whether there are one or ten pots of plants in the window. To me it means a lot'. She plans, but needs his consent and co-operation. 'Beate has such good taste', other women say, 'and she is so determined.'

In their social circles, this couple is particularly successful in the way they manage to equip and decorate their apartment. There are several reasons why Beate and Nils are so successful at this stage of their marital life, where many other families have economic problems. They receive income from two full-time jobs. In addition, he often works overtime and together they have a job of a few hours of cleaning every week in the neighbourhood. Because of his job, Nils is able to offer services to many friends and acquaintances and to get their services and help in return. There is much work and a complex economy behind their success.

Home improvement has generally become more important not only for working-class people, but also for other groups, and not only for the very young, but also for their parents who are now in their fifties, and not only for urban people, but also for people in the rural areas. Holtedahl (1986), for instance, describes the 'suburbanization' of patterns of life in northern Norway, while Thorsen (1989), in her study of three generations of farmer women in inland Norway, describes how the family and the home have become more important. All over Norway, Norwegians are thus buying furniture and gluing wallpaper like never before. Renovating and furnishing have in many ways become a continuous project. Home furnishing is not something done and finished with only to be redone when something wears out. Things are renewed for the sake of change.

This enhanced activity has given birth to businesses selling furniture, ornaments, plants, materials, tools and other things needed for home improvement, and is met with ambivalence by planners and representatives of state agencies. A state journal advising consumers (*Forbrukerrapporten*), for instance, complained that reasonably good kitchen furnishings which have fallen out of fashion are being taken out in favour of more modern ones. They state that 30,000 completely usable kitchen furnishings are removed annually at a consumer cost of approximately 500,000,000 kroner plus people's own labour. According to their estimates, this accounts for approximately half of all the changes. Instad of new paint or an extra cupboard, a complete new set of kitchen furnishings gets installed.

In this way, middle-class professionals seem to lament what they see as a waste of time and money. Their understanding of why people restructure the interiors of their houses and apartments is generally somewhat condescending: money to burn, psychological obsolescence, compensatory consumption, hunting for status, privatizing, materialism, egotism and manipulation by advertisers. Since the home is a rich and multi-faceted phenomenon, there may be something to several of these explanations. For example, when more time, money, love and care are put into the house, there may be less time, money and strength left for other things. Home improvement activities can therefore have unintended consequences. However, there is also evidence that house-building and home improvement are embedded in a social network exchange of goods and services (Gullestad 1978, 1979, 1985).[8]

The usual ways of looking at the phenomenon are in my view one-sided and negative. Before we have listened to the people themselves and participated in their daily rounds of life, we have not really understood why secularized Norwegians invest so much of their time and money this way.

In my view a whole set of reasons make the home an important symbol and focus of attention for Norwegians. Different aspects may explain the continuous preoccupation with its physical appearance, and I summarize them as follows: (a) a relatively cold climate; (b) secularized religious pietism; (c) creativity and expressivity – the home is an important locus for modern popular culture and mass consumption; (d) identity – many values which are important for the identities of both women and men as individuals and as families can be objectified through the home; (e) work patterns – women's participation in the paid workforce gives them a less direct and more sentimental relationship to the home; (f) egalitarian ideologies within the household – in an attempt to realize the new values of sameness, togetherness and sharing, traditional definitions of masculinity and femininity are to some extent also reinforced; (g) home improvement as a way of continuing a kind of 'self-employment' within the leisure sphere of late capitalist society – tinkering around the home may reconcile a nostalgia for the work ethic with the modern desire for intimacy; and (h) status – the home is a central part of very different lifestyles, and is therefore instrumental in the creation of social and cultural class differences.

HOME DECORATION AS CREATIVITY

Norwegians do not only use more time for renovating and furnishing the home. These activities have also received a new significance. 'The home' is also a creative and expressive statement and it is my theory that this has come more into the foreground. The advantage of the analysis that follows is that it takes into consideration the reasons people themselves give.

In order to develop this argument, let me first point out some striking contrasts between the outsides and the insides of co-operative estates. Planners are responsible for the outsides of apartment estates and residential areas, reflecting the functionalist architectural view for which the aforementioned Le Corbusier was the most prominent spokesman. The outsides of the houses are, therefore, often lacking in decorations, detail and any visual stimuli. These houses are, so to speak, almost 'mute' on the outside. They 'talk' very little and the message that emanates from them is relatively monotonous and dull.[9] By contrast, the *inside* of the houses is a great display of objects and ornaments. The interiors are decorated to what is almost an extreme.[10] These interiors 'talk' by constituting very rich and flexible representational forms.

When Norwegians receive visitors for the first time, they often say something like: 'Well, we do not care about how other people decorate their homes. We have chosen to do it our way'. First and foremost these utterances demonstrate the importance of independence and self-sufficiency as cultural values in Norway. But implied in such statements is also a request that each home be considered personal and unique. True, seen from a superficial point of view, such statements can appear to be a little off the mark as one home is usually not that much different from other homes in the same social group. But the fact that people themselves emphasize the unique and exceptional qualities of their homes is an important piece of information. Why do they do this?

One of the answers is that home improvement is a way to be creative. Many elements are involved in this creative process, including gifts, furniture bought at a store and self-made bookshelves. The decoration of the home is, therefore, a result of inheritance, exchange in social networks, tangible home productions and creative consumption. The objects are given new meanings through recontextualization, actively interpreted and arranged in new compositions. These compositions follow established patterns, but they are also in a certain sense unique. Each person or family creates its own representational form. I therefore see the home as an important part of modern popular culture in Norway.

The activities involved in interpreting and recontextualizing mass-produced goods are not necessarily less creative than the interpretation and recontextualization of objects of fine arts. There is, for instance, evidence that a whole series of cultural as well as personal meanings can be invested in very conventional mass-produced pictures (Reme 1988). The meanings of folk aesthetics do not derive from the objects in isolation, but from the relationship between persons and objects. Wallpaper, furniture and other elements are creatively selected and combined in compositions which can give subtle messages with many nuances, since the elements which make up these compositions are also involved in other contexts of meaning.

In this way, the interior of the home has not merely large utility value but also large symbolic value. Since the supply of mass-produced goods, and therefore the possibilities of choice, are greater than ever before, the expressive aspect has become more prominent and the home become more of an expressive manifestation. The homes emanate more subtle and more complicated messages in the creation of lifestyles in Norway.

THE HOME AS AN EXPRESSIVE STATEMENT

What values and ideas are made manifest through the home? One answer is that people create themselves as individuals and as families through the processes of objectification involved in creating a home. The home is a rich, flexible and ambiguous symbol; it can simultaneously signify individual identity, family solidarity and a whole range of other values. The following lists some elements in the symbolic value of a home: personal identity; the identity of the family; marital, filial and parental love; closeness (*nærhet*), sharing and togetherness (*deling og fellesskap*); a sense of wholeness (*helhet*), integration and unity in life; independence and self-sufficiency; safety, security (*trygghet*), control, order, 'peace and quiet', cosiness (*kos*) and comfort (*hygge*), and decency (*være skikkelig*); practical sense and a realistic outlook; control and mastering; direction in life; and social reference groups.

The connotations of the expression 'a good home' (*et godt hjem*) are moral, while the connotations of the expression 'a nice home' (*et pent hjem*) are of an aesthetic kind. However, through aesthetics a vision of a moral order is created and expressed. One of the worst things one can say about somebody's home is that it is impersonal (*upersonlig*) and without ambience (*uten atmosfære*). Impersonal interiors give off the connotations of institutions or public waiting rooms, and do not really qualify as homes. The centrality of the home in Norwegian culture is thus complemented by a fear of institutions.[11] A nice home should literally and figuratively be warm. The figurative meanings of warmth (*varme, lunhet, hygge, kos*) are, among other things, achieved through the arrangement of and care for objects. A home should be decorated (*pyntet, utsmykket*) in order not to give off an impression of impersonal emptiness. In addition, a nice home should, of course, be relatively clean and tidy, and thus bear witness that the inhabitants are decent (*skikke-lige, ordens*) people.

A home is a setting for relaxation (*å slappe av*) as well as for feelings of security (*trygghet*) and 'peace and quiet'. Two other important notions are *hygge* and *kos*, both used as substantives, verbs and adjectives. The word *hygge* is almost impossible to trans-late:[12] only some of its connotations are captured in the English word 'comfort'. The connotations of the adjective form of *kos, koselig*, is close to but not quite the same as the English word with the same root, 'cosy'. Both notions imply ideas of beauty, warmth and emotional closeness, as well as feelings of solidarity and relax-ation from work. If we keep to the furnishings, a cosy home has a wealth of textiles, potted plants, souvenirs, pictures and photo-graphs.

When interviewing people about their house, one quickly dis-covers that talking about houses often involves telling a life story. The individual's life cycle and the family's development cycle are closely connected to moving house or forming and reforming a house. Improving the home is a lifetime project which gives mean-ing to life. It also expresses what social categories one belongs to, i.e. whom one would prefer to be compared with. For most cate-gories, and especially the elderly and the young, living alone is an important sign of independence. Being able to 'manage by oneself' (*rå seg sjøl*), is highly valued. It is important to be 'the master of the house' (*herre i eget hus*), and to preferably 'not need to take heed of others' (*ikke behøve å ta hensyn til andre*). In addition, using money on the home goes hand in hand with the Norwegian ideals of diligence, simplicity, and having a realistic outlook. Norwe-gians generally emphasize all those things that are practical and useful and place little direct and explicit emphasis on aesthetics and playful creativity.

This emphasis on practicality is illustrated by some of the particu-lar reasons that people usually give for redecorating their house or apartment. Most often, practical and functional reasons are given, even if the work of installing the improvements exceeds by far the time and work saved over a subsequent period of time. Economic reasons are also often given, for example, that the improvements will increase the value of the apartment or the house if it were to be sold in the future. Such reasons, which of course can be real enough, allow Norwegians to pursue contradictory values. On the one hand, they want their homes to be considered 'tasteful', 'per-sonal' and unique, but, on the other hand, they do not want to be accused of immoderation and status-hunting. As mentioned earlier, equality is defined as sameness, and sameness is emphasized in social interaction through a code of modesty (Gullestad 1986b, 1992). Emphasizing practicalities allows each person and family the opportunity to appear both modest and creative. Thus home improvement gives Norwegian men and women the opportunity to carry out creative and playful activities camouflaged as serious useful things which 'must' be done. Norwegians often play not out in the open but under the cover of doing something practical and reasonable.

THE SEARCH FOR 'WHOLENESS' AND 'CLOSENESS'

One of the most important values for identity formation is inherent in the idea of wholeness (*helhet*). 'Happiness is a difficult word. I think one is happy when one feels whole' (*lykke er et vanskelig ord. Jeg tror en er lykkelig når en føler seg hel*), are two revealing phrases from a written autobiography.[13] The idea of wholeness gets its value from the negative opposites of fragmentation, and sums up a reaction to modernity and a search for integration and unity on the part of the individual and the close circle of family members.

The idea of wholeness gives the home a potential healing function. The home is ideally not only a 'shelter in the storm' or a 'haven in a heartless world', but a hospital, capable of healing the wounds of social fragmentation and anomie. This healing potential is predicated upon the sharp ideological division between the home and the outside. Inside the ideal home the relationships are personal, defined in terms of love (*være glad i*), as opposed to the impersonal relationships of the market and of bureaucratic organizations. Many people experience a considerable gap between their personal lives and the overall structure in society, expressed in statements such as the following: 'There is so much misery in society as it is. You do not want all of that inside your home, do you?' Often the house is described as the 'last sane place in an insane society', or as a 'last defended bastion', where the evils of bureaucratization and monetarization have not yet reached.

Norwegians experience life fragmented and divided into different forums, roles and activities, and they attempt to tie these together through externalizing and objectifying the idea of wholeness in the creation of a home. The idea of wholeness is embodied in the physical arrangements of the home through the practices associated with notions of style (*stil, særpreg*) and taste. When Norwegians arrange objects in a space, it is important to them that these objects 'fit together' (*passer sammen, står i stil*) and thereby contribute to the creation of 'wholeness' (*helhet*), 'style' (*stil*) and a 'characteristic feature' (*særpreg*). In many popular contexts, the idea of having 'good taste' can be equated with the ability to make a convincing personal presentation of wholeness in terms of a specific style. In this way, Norwegians objectify these values of unity, independence and integration in the home.

Moreover, in the home and through the home a feeling of direction and meaning is created. Here people combine the various roles they play into the experience of *one* whole person, and in a household consisting of more persons, into the feeling of being a tightly-knit family. For households consisting of more than one person, the ideas of closeness (*nærhet*), sharing (*deling*) and togetherness (*fellesskap*) also apply. The notion of closeness (*nærhet*) is particularly important to the Norwegian idea of intimacy. Through anchoring the ideas of 'wholeness' and 'closeness' in the arrangement of objects in space, the interrelations of people in the home acquire an almost organic quality, reinforcing the cultural division between the inside and the outside.

Home furnishings create and express the family members' joint interests and emotional closeness, to themselves and to the rest of the world. Instead of the ritualistic middle-class Sunday dinner in the last century and the beginning of this century (Danielsen 1984), home decoration is today a ritual and symbol for large groups of the population. To a certain degree, the family members create themselves as a family by elaborating the physical home as a visible framework for their existence.

In pre-modern times, the Church to a large degree acted as a cognitive umbrella over life's different spheres and institutions. Religion offered integration and meaning through the belief in something which was not of this world. In the modern West, many people instead find much of life's meaning through intimacy and immediacy here on earth. For Norwegians, the home and the sphere of intimacy have become sources for deeper meanings and have, therefore, in a secularized sense, been made into something sacred.

Its organic quality is linked both to the idea that the family is not completely a social, but is also a biological or natural, phenomenon at the margins of society, and to the idea of the home as a point of balance (*balansepunkt*) in people's lives, as they move between different social spheres. Norwegians create their homes within a society with a very marked division between what has been glossed as domestic and public spheres (Rosaldo and Lamphere 1974) and where the domestic sphere is ideologically considered to be located, so to speak, on the margins of society. The home is, as already noted, defined in opposition to the impersonality of the market and of bureaucratic institutions. This means that, even if Norwegian homes embody many important social values, they do not directly embody the most central social divisions. Therefore, a Norwegian home could not be seen as a microcosm in the sense that might apply to a house in a society with a much less marked division between domestic and public spheres or where this division does not apply at all.

But the Norwegian home can be analysed as a microcosm in another and perhaps equally strong sense. It can be analysed as an *intentional* effort to *create* a whole and complete microcosm within a marginal social field. The Norwegian home can thus be seen as a form of *resistance* to fragmentation and anomie, and as with most forms of resistance it also embodies that which is resisted. In the way the Romantics emphasized the ability of the fine arts to over-come fragmentation by creating 'green spots' where the evils of modernity could be overcome, the Norwegian home can be seen as a romantic folk utopia. Through their homes, Norwegians con-tinuously objectify their specific visions of the good life.

CONSTRUCTING GENDERS

Until now I have emphasized some of the shared aspects to the cultural categories underlying the continuous home decoration pro-ject in Norway. Both women and men of different social categories create themselves as individuals and as families through their homes. I now want to problematize this analysis by discussing first gender and then social class. The home is a joint project for a husband and a wife, but they have different roles and are also differently located in relation to the division between the home and the outside.

I begin the discussion by spelling out some meanings of the shared cultural notion of 'a female hand' (*en kvinnelig hånd*), closely associated to notions such as good taste, *hygge* (comfort), *kos* (cosiness), *nærhet* (closeness) and care (*omsorg*). A female hand is needed to turn the house into a home: to create a good emotional ambience, to arrange the objects, as well as to clean, polish, tend and keep order. Even though particular men may be good home-makers, as they are defined in contemporary Norway, these abilities and activities are to a great extent a part of femininity. Men are expected to be handy and clever at construction work and repairs, while women are aesthetic and emotional specialists. In addition, by carrying the main responsibility for housework, the woman of the house tends the important boundaries around the home, a fact which, as already noted, implies certain forms of power and control within the household.

This means that the healing potential of the home is to a large extent something wives provide for their husbands. Since women embody the home values of love (*være glad i*) as against the abstract and impersonal values of the outside, husbands are dependent on their wives to find wholeness and a point of balance in relation to their paid jobs. Wives, on their part, have been dependent on their husbands for economic provisioning for themselves and the children. The interesting question is what happens to these dependencies when women take up paid work and it is no longer legitimate to be an authoritarian husband or father.

On the face of it, there is a contradiction between women's paid work and home improvement becoming more (and not less) important as a creative and expressive activity. Actually, there is no contradiction. These different trends are related in several ways of which I will explore a few.

Even if women continue to be left with the main responsibilities for cleaning, nurturing and care, and even if they mainly work part-time, women are now allowed legitimately to leave their homes. The general trend is that Norwegian women no longer have to justify all their actions away from home in terms of the needs of their families (Gullestad 1984a; Holtedal 1986; Thorsen 1989). However, as married women engage in paid work, they also have the daily strain of reconciling quite different fields of activity. The opportunities to leave the home give women a less direct and more sentimental relationship to the home than before. Like their husbands, they also need a 'point of balance' and a place of 'wholeness', and this is part of the background for the home as a shared sentimental concern.

There are other interconnections. The new ideals of 'sharing' (*deling*) and 'togetherness' (*fellesskap*) among family members are created and maintained through the kinds of co-operation they are able to achieve, and these feelings are objectified in the composition and arrangement of objects in space. As the household is a moral community, producing and reproducing human beings, *how* decisions are made and tasks are allocated is very important.

The new ideologies of sharing, togetherness and equality defined as sameness between spouses in marriage, imply that the division of tasks can no longer be taken for granted, but constantly has to be negotiated and renegotiated. Because many factors other than ideologies shape the division of tasks, ideological changes have relatively little impact. Yet there are some important changes, both direct and indirect. Men do more child-care and housework than before. But, by tradition, different tasks have accumulated symbolic value as belonging to one gender or the other, and this makes changing the division of tasks much more than simply a practical and organizational matter. Playing with the children does not threaten masculinity as much as, for instance, changing soiled diapers or cleaning the floors. Sports, overtime at the job, repairing the car and redecorating the home are some of the alternatives men prefer, and throw into the negotiations. Of these alternatives, home decoration is, for many reasons, most attractive to the wife. Husbands, when negotiating division of tasks, may trade installing new wallpaper for cleaning the floors, and thus expand some of the masculine tasks within the household.

This pattern of exchange seems to prevail in many different forms of organizing work. In my first study in Bergen, for instance, I found interesting differences between working-class families where both spouses had grown up in the countryside and families where both had grown up in the city. The rural men had fewer buddies than the urban men, and the rural women were less opposed to doing rough work than urban women. For these and other reasons, rural couples in the city acted more as a team compared with urban couples who were engaged in gender-segregated social networks for performing household tasks. There are also differences between these social circles and career-oriented couples who may be inclined to use hired help for some of the tasks. The heavy reconstruction work may therefore be done by the husband alone, by husband and wife as a team, by the husband and his buddies, or by paid craftsmen (Gullestad 1978).

In spite of such differences, making home improvements in most families is a joint creative project, with the husband fulfilling a male role and the wife fulfilling a female role – in a transformed traditional sense. Making home improvements is in a special way an expression of a man's love for his wife. He is doing something for her and shows her that he gives her and the family a high priority in relation to other activities outside the family. For couples, home decoration can therefore be said to be a project of love.

The idea of sameness, in fact, may indirectly contribute to a reinforcement of traditional masculinity and traditional femininity, through the associated ideas of sharing and togetherness. When spouses negotiate the division of tasks, sameness becomes the legitimate ideal for both. Accordingly, the spouses appear as a team of two similar and equal persons. However, otherwise submerged and less legitimate ideals of masculinity and femininity, in fact, influence the actual outcome. The differences between husband and wife are thus shaped and contained by the ideals of sameness. And in this process, home decoration gets a new value as a shared concern for both spouses: the home can be seen as an objectification of intimacy, a visible display of congealed love.

Because of their paid work, and because of the provisions from the welfare state, women have become somewhat less dependent on men as economic providers. Men, on their part, have probably become more dependent on the emotional and aesthetic intimacy provided by women. That men remarry more often and more quickly than women after divorce has been interpreted as a result of women's loss of value on the marriage market as they get older. In my view, it is equally reasonable to suggest that the reason is male dependence on a female hand.

Because of the frequency of divorce, all marriages appear more fragile. And as a consequence of divorce and remarriage, many families do not feel quite like 'real' families. But through continuous home decoration, they can attempt to create themselves as such. The more fragile the family's solidarity, the more important it probably is to stress symbolic unity. The symbolic flexibility of the home is so great, however, that after a divorce, when co-operation went manifestly wrong, it can equally symbolize the newly-found freedom and independence. This quotation from the written autobiography of a divorced woman is rather typical: 'I love my apartment. It is mine alone. Decorated by me, renovated by me, in *my* colours and *my* style'. In this way, the home functions as a symbol of intimacy for single persons, nuclear families, as well as other family forms.

CONSTRUCTING CLASSES

The question remains how valid it is to describe and analyse Norwegian or Northern European culture on the basis of fieldwork among the urban working-class. There are at least two different issues involved in discussing this question. The first is how reasonable it is to use working-class people as opposed to educated people to discuss new trends and tendencies. The second is to what extent it is reasonable to treat Norway, Scandinavia or Northern Europe as one culture area or as a variety of Western modernity.

Let us look at the second issue first. The population of Norway is less homogeneous than Norwegians usually think. Depending on region, religious affiliation and social class, people engage in various ways of life. With specific reference to Denmark, Højrup (1983a, b) has argued that the population can be divided into three main ways of life: the self-employed, the ordinary wage-worker and the educated career-oriented executive. The three ways of life are defined by mutual opposition and conflict. When people of different social origin use words like work, family and home, they mean something entirely different. According to Højrup, all they share are the linguistic expressions.

Contrary to Højrup, I would argue that, in spite of considerable differences, they share more than mere words. First, they share an assumption that such notions have some common meanings. Second, they share the ability to use the notions rhetorically in order to make themselves understood, and this necessitates that they to some extent share the implicit frameworks of meanings within which such notions are embedded. Most Norwegians would, for instance, invest the cultural categories of 'wholeness' and 'closeness' with similar abstract meanings. In my view, there exist in this region certain common cultural categories tying together and legitimating differences of social class and lifestyle. In addition to gender, I have therefore tried simultaneously to attend to at least three dimensions: (a) the specificity of certain urban working-class practices, (b) more general Norwegian (Scandinavian or Northern European) cultural categories and (c) those practices and categories seen as one specific variety of Western modernity.

Most Norwegians want to have a 'nice home', but different social classes have somewhat different ideas about what 'a nice home' should look like, and differential economic and other means to realize their ideas. The concrete ideas of a carpenter in a rural community differ from those of an architect in the capital. Young people do not have the same ideas as middle-aged and old people. Their particular objectives may differ, as well as the ways of organizing the tasks to be done. The variation is associated with a diverse set of factors: (a) way of life, associated with occupation, education, region, religion, age and generation; (b) type of ownership of the housing unit; (c) financial means; (d) knowledge and interest in doing things for oneself; (e) participation in exchanges of goods and services in social networks; and (f) alternatives for using one's time.

In a study of aged upper middle-class ladies with a 'bourgeois' lifestyle in Oslo, Danielsen (1984) has described how the old ladies continuously look back in time in order to present their superiority. It is important to be able to display a nice home with prestigious objects. But Danielsen also points out that when an object is worn out or broken, there is little change, just a replacement with a very similar object. A worn oriental rug gets replaced by one which looks as much as possible like the old one. In other words, these old ladies are not engaged in the cultural practices of continuous home improvement. This is probably a question of generation as well as a question of their very special class position. But even if their specific way of life is dying out with them, there may be other contemporary Norwegians for whom home decoration is less important as a continuous focus of attention.

Yet the upper class is small and culturally almost invisible in Norway. And since few families have been educated urbanites for several generations, there is also no large culturally-refined upper middle-class. For career-oriented families, the home can be a way to translate male power into visible status and, for many Norwegians, in working-class as well as in career-oriented occupations, home improvement exists as a way of carrying on elements of a self-employed lifestyle within the leisure sphere of post-industrial society.

The pattern underlying the decoration and use of working-class homes around 1980 was closer to that underlying the homes of the old or middle-aged business upper middle-class than to the homes of younger academics. The established upper middle-class (my informants called them 'directors' (*direktører*) and 'fine people' (*fine folk*) also want a comfortable and representative living room where everything is spotless. Their homes also give off an impression of polished comfort and fashion. Moreover, tradition is more important here than in the satellite towns. The most important contrast is thus not the overall pattern, but the price and quality of the buildings and objects. For example, whereas one type of home is equipped with wall-to-wall nylon carpets, the other has pure new wool or parquet. Where one home has a store picture of a rococo lady, the other home has paintings signed by known artists, though in both cases they may be in gold frames. The objects vary, but their arrangement is not so different.

In these respects, there is more of a contrast between my informants and the younger part of the educated middle-class. In the 1960s
and 1970s, many of those who benefited from the 'educational
explosion' after World War II found their livelihood in the service
of the expanding welfare state, as social planners, social workers,
teachers on all levels, and so on. There are obviously many differences concerning income, working conditions and lifestyle within
such a broad category. There is, however, a common ethos in this
part of the educated middle-class which justifies grouping them
together for certain purposes: they look for identity in the ways
of the traditional middle-class as well as in Norwegian peasant
traditions.

In these families, the husband may be interested in aesthetics as
much as his wife, but often he is not. The husband will generally
have a job with more autonomy and influence than the working-
class man. His wife may have a similar job, but since she often
works part-time, there will be some difference in power and prestige
between them.

Around 1980, the homes of many young educated people dis-
played a typical Scandinavian mixture of modernism (*funksjonal-
isme*) and a transformed rustic peasant tradition (*almuestil*). Walls
were often painted white or covered with pine wood; floors were
made of wood or covered with cork. Furniture was made of pine
wood, with wool covering the couch ensemble. Instead of the wall
unit, one would find simpler book-shelves filled with paperbacks
and original graphic arts or posters on the walls. This representational form objectified a political vision, containing ideas about
being close to nature by using 'natural' products, ecological awareness, a sense of quality, and so on. The rustic theme was evident
from the natural materials and craftsmanship. The living room did
not necessarily have to be spotless: signs of activities (the 'right'
pedagogical toys, musical instruments, periodicals, books) bore witness to an 'active' prestigious life. Tradition did not mean polished
mahogany, but rather antiques from Norwegian farms and objects
from other parts of the world – such as India and Afghanistan.

When choosing ornaments, these people favour the authenticity
and exclusivity of hand-made objects as opposed to what they consider cheap, mass-produced goods. Young educated people like to
think of themselves as uninterested in fashion and 'status symbols'.
While the satellite town families I studied would rather have the
latest colour television, many academics demonstrated that they did
not 'sit and passively watch television all the time', by having only

a black and white television set. In such ways, by setting up a contrast to the 'passiveness' of uneducated people, the educated middle-class usually construct themselves as 'active'. They implicitly present themselves as always eager to move on, in terms of social status as well as in terms of personal development.

At the time of my fieldwork, young educated people interpreted the polished and sumptuous living rooms of my informants in terms of notions such as 'passive', 'petty bourgeois', 'tasteless'. When my informants, on the other hand, interpreted the signs of multiple activities and the rustic quality of the living rooms of these young educated people, they applied notions such as 'shabby', 'disorderly', 'unfashionable'. Both tend to formulate an awareness of cultural class differences in moral terms. Since middle-class people define themselves in contrast to the working class, the working class to some extent influence what the middle class will or will not adopt. For instance, working-class people were the first to adopt video-recorders in Norway, while the middle class vigorously opposed it. But now, slowly, the meanings of video-recorders are reinterpreted from 'passive' to 'active'.[14]

CONCLUSION

In this chapter I have attempted discursively to spell out some of the very rich, flexible and ambiguous meanings of the Norwegian home as a representational form in Norway. The particular concern for the material and physical aspects of the home are connected to immaterial values and ideas. Or, to put it more precisely, values and identities are created and objectified in home decoration. Through explicating the meanings of cultural categories such as 'wholeness' and 'style' and their associated activities, I have demonstrated that the creative recontextualization of consumption (Miller 1987) is not only a question of a period of time following the purchase, but a question of a very complex interplay of ideas and practices. It is crucial to the development of modern, creative mass-consumption that individuals are organized in family-households, based on modern feelings of romantic love and intimacy, and with a gender-specific division of tasks.

The home can be seen as a shared cultural symbol as well as an instrument in the creation and maintenance of cultural class difference. The fact that the lifestyles of the classes are mutually constructed implies that the social science reduction of working-class styles to just a copying and an emulation of middle-class styles can itself be analysed as an extension of the common middle-class practice of constructing the working class as 'passive'. This goes for analyses of the 'embourgeoisement' of the working classes as well as for some applications of Gramsci's notion of hegemony (see Gullestad 1989b). It should no longer be possible to use educated middle-class people as the most typical representatives of modern Western cultures without reflection.

There is an interesting parallel between the construction of the working classes as passive and traditional constructions of women as passive. It seems as if the working classes are ideologically to the upper and middle classes as women are to men. However, looking at constructions of genders in the working class brings forth an aspect of dependency in the marriage relationships which is less pronounced but present nevertheless in the marriages of career-oriented people. This finding should inform our understanding of marriage. It has recently been argued that modern marital love is an arrangement which functions to mask an unequal power relationship where the woman is the loser (Haavind 1985). On the basis of the material presented here, I would hold that modern marital love can equally well be analysed as dependence masked as sharing. A man is in fundamental ways dependent on a woman for emotional sustenance and even for a coherent and 'whole' sense of the self. A woman, however, is no longer equally dependent on a man for economic provisioning. Even if marriage relationships have many other dimensions in addition to those discussed here, this asymmetry renders the definition of masculinity particularly problematic, a fact that should be taken into account in future studies.

The home objectifies both individual identity and family solidarity. It is shared concern for the spouses, as well as a female domain. It ties together the social classes, as well as being instrumental in the construction of the differences between them. These many contradictions constitute a span of ambiguity which demonstrates the very ambiguous and powerful location of the home in contemporary Norwegian culture: the home is privately central and publicly marginalized by being taken for granted. The values of the home are privately important and publicly neglected. And, to the extent that women are tied to the home, they may be privately strong and publicly powerless.

Because the modern desire for intimacy is particularly anchored in the home, it is possible to 'feel the pulse', so to speak, of modern Western civilization through an analysis of homes in Norway. The most seemingly trivial social fields may turn out to hold the greatest potential for cultural analysis.

NOTES

1 The ethnographic material presented in this chapter is taken from Gullestad (1984b). Earlier versions of some of the ideas have been published in Gullestad (1978, 1984a, 1986b, 1989a). I wish to thank Steve Borish, Anne Trine Kjørholt, Tora Korsvold and Gunvor Risa for constructive comments to the first draft.

2 There are indications that Norwegians are especially centred around the home, even in comparison to the other Scandinavians. For example, Norwegians on average buy considerably more furniture than the Swedish. Yet cultural boundaries are vague and fluctuating. Therefore, it may well be that Scandinavia, or Northern Europe, is just as feasible a framework for some of the phenomena which are described. But because I have carried out my research in Norway only, I use Norway as a provisional regional framework for the study of cultural themes in everyday life.

3 In 1972–3, I carried out one year of participant observation in an aged, central-city, working-class neighbourhood of Bergen, Norway (Gullestad 1979); in 1978–80, I engaged in two years of participant observation among young working-class mothers in several co-operative housing estates in satellite towns of Bergen (Gullestad 1984b).

4 In 1989, I organized a nationwide autobiography contest in co-operation with the Norwegian sociologist Reidar Almås. We received 630 autobiographies, and our analysis of this very rich material has just started.

5 The notions of 'nature' and 'naturalness' are discussed in Gullestad (1989c).

6 The term 'working-class' is used as a shorthand and not as an analytical concept.

7 This typical scene gave the book based on this fieldwork its title, *Kitchen-table Society* (Gullestad 1984b).

8 In a study of council housing in England, Miller (1988: 368) concludes that there is a link between people who seem lonely, depressed and isolated and a lack of decorative development.

9 The exception to this are a few owners of single homes who have not only decorated inside the house, but also the outside, with, for example, painted wheels, twisted roots, statues, running water and the like. In recent years, prefabricated houses have also become less functional, for example, the so-called Tyrol houses. In other words, there has been an expansion of decorating from inside to outside.

10 To many Americans, a typical Norwegian home appears as if an auction were about to take place, because of the staggering amount of furniture and decorations. However, both Americans and Norwegians have homes as opposed to just houses.

11 This is especially visible in child-care. Norway has fewer kindergartens and other day-care institutions than other welfare states.

12 *Hygge* as a cultural category and a set of associated practices has more

or less the same meanings in Norway as in Denmark. The notion is, however, more central in Denmark (see, among others, Borish 1991).

13 See note 4.

14 In the 10 years following my fieldwork, the fashions in both classes have changed. Educated middle-class homes have become either more sumptuous and polished or more high-tech; but with a slightly different vocabulary of objects, the mutual construction of contrasts is maintained.

6 Impure or fertile?

Two essays on the crossing of frontiers through anthropology and feminism

Translated by Michael Gingrich

The first part of this contribution is an essay by two female anthropologists on the experiences gained during several months' research in a traditionally oriented Sunni village in eastern Turkey. It tells of the sometimes painful crossing of personal and cultural frontiers by two European women on their way between male-dominated worlds of women. In the joint essay, which was written in 1988, the authors come to the conclusion that it is particularly the irritations of the first experiences which one tends to 'forget', or to distort beyond recognition with the help of scientific theory. The essay serves as a means of presenting – instead of covering up – developments in the dialogue between the problems and issues of concern to feminism and to scientific work.

The second essay is a reflection on the first from today's point of view, after one author (Sabine Strasser) returned to the same village a second time. This entails an outline of both changes and continuities concerning her personal situation, her relations to the people in the village, feminist discourse, political concerns in Austria and also the aims and results of the field research in Turkey.

I Women in the field – reflections on a never-ending journey[1]

Sabine Strasser and Ruth Kronsteiner

These notes were written shortly after our return from our first stay of several months in the so-called anthropological field – in our case, two villages in eastern Turkey. In the time following our return, we had feelings of uncertainty and alienation. It meant the renewed discussion of a framework of science in whose definition we had not taken part. We still lacked the necessary distance to reflect on our stay analytically. Still, in these notes we tried to give a transparent view of the process of our thoughts on research. No doubt, had we written this up a year later, through the distance gained, we would have been able to present the village in its wholeness and with more clarity, but then we might have swept away irritations more nimbly or 'forgotten' the confusion caused by these recent experiences.

It was not the results and the success which were our prime concerns in this essay, but the problems in dealing with fields of power. At the beginning of our journey stood the wish to be able to recognize what power really is and how it is exercised. It led us to *Ohnmacht* (fainting fits and feelings of impotence).[2] The journey is not over yet.

FIELDS OF POWER AND ANXIETY

The questions guiding our research resulted from an analysis of feminist approaches and many years of participation in an educational and social project for Turkish women in Austria.[3] This practical experience opened up a new dimension of anthropology for us. Observations in the literature concerning the relations between the sexes in Turkey are quite contradictory, and we wanted to form our own view of the cultural background to this relationship. We wanted the theory and experience gained to flow back into concrete work with the women from Turkey in Austria. In practical work with women originating in foreign countries, as well as in field research, we should recognize and grasp realities in order to find a way to improve on them in co-operation with the affected persons, changing practice through theory and vice versa.

The apparent consent of the women to their own submission led us to enquire into the causes for this collaboration. Which means of violence are being used to get women to give in to their own submission or even contribute to it? How is male dominance over women being justified, and how can it be kept up seemingly without recourse to explicit violence? Furthermore, the question arises whether this picture of male dominance is at all a correct one; or whether there is not some form of resistance or a subordinate, but nevertheless real, autonomous female sphere (Godelier 1982, 1984; Mathieu 1985; Marcus 1987).[4]

The literature concerning gender relations in Turkey is confusing. It suggests that women hardly own any means of production, cannot decide on the distribution of their products and have no direct influence on decisions affecting the village. Adultery is a much graver offence when committed by women than by men. It is the shame of the women which makes the honour of the men possible (Wiethold 1981; Abadan-Unat 1985; Petersen 1985; Marcus 1987). Yet this sinister image is somewhat brightened by reports of the emotional independence of women from their husbands and the advantage of segregation (Marcus 1987). The lesser importance of money and the sense of community among the women in Turkey, especially by comparison with the situation of migrants within Europe, is also described positively (Bennholdt-Thomsen *et al.* 1987).

> Women and their work suffer a loss of social participation, which they had previously controlled not in spite of, but because of an earlier segregation between women's socio-economic world and that of men. However, women had to abandon that world's subordinate antonomy not in spite of, but because of a postulated equality that was tied to the abstract (allegedly gender-neutral) standard of money.
>
> (Bennholdt-Thomsen *et al.* 1987: 28)[5]

In the Turkish village, patriarchal domination with its sharply defined forms of power, has not yet been replaced by the sexist rule.[6] The literature often depicts the solidarity of women who produce in accordance with the principle of the division of labour as a stronghold of self-realization. But one must not forget that this seclusion came into being under duress and is dictated by men (Schmitz 1985). Migration removes the village community, the king group and the community of women as emotional frames of reference, whereas conjugal love and maternal love gain in importance. In the village, more and more areas of work are subject to *Hausfrauisierung*[7] ('housewifization'), that is, defined as the work of women, which is for free. In Austria, these women gain access to money, which in turn constitutes a means of power. Thus they endanger the power of the men. The reaction is direct, haphazard violence, for the women have also lost the protection accruing to them in the patriarchal social order.

The examination of these statements was a second essential element of our field research in Turkey.

Power field – university

While Moore (1988) has already published a resume on feminist anthropology, it yet remains to be clarified whether such a thing as a feminist approach to research has any right to existence at the Vienna Institut für Völkerkunde (Institute of Social Anthropology). It was no big surprise that terms such as 'feminist tradition' had to be deleted as *frippery* and *a catchword* from our applications for a research scholarship. *Hausfrauisierung* had to be deleted because of its *ugliness*. Dependent on that money, we gave in – perhaps all too quickly. As there is no qualified female university lecturer for social anthropology in Austria, and since subject-specific powers of judgement are regarded as decisive and the viewpoint as *free* anyhow, there is neither a recognition of the need, nor the practical opportunity, to work with a woman as a second supervisor. A female lecturer of another faculty who is quite prepared to attend to our work is still being rejected. The question of methods is symptomatic of our discussions with the Institute. The joy over the discovery that feminists have not developed a method of their own seems huge. The lack of an explicitly feminist method is regarded as proof that there can be no such thing as a feminist anthropology. But that is quite wrong, because in feminist research,

> as in any other research, it must be decided which methods of research are commensurate with the respective formulation of the question. Thus 'Female Research' in itself is not a method, but a methodologically or politically autonomous approach to research. The actual preference for qualitative methods is a result of the political positions with regard to the contents and the interests of cognition, which nevertheless does not advance them to female methods.
>
> (Wildt 1987: 151)[8]

Our supervisor's cheering motto at the last meeting before our departure: 'My advice is, take in the material culture; you're not going to succeed with your intentions anyhow'.

Power field – research

Social anthropology, a branch without great prospects for the future, has always had a large percentage of women among its students. It is, therefore, not surprising that examples of women with field research go back to the 1920s (Warren 1988: 11) and that, especially since the early 1970s, publications relating to women in the field have presented an important arena for debating the category of gender in anthropological research.

While most scientists to this day are inclined to avoid reporting on their difficulties, fears and joys, or at least to separate them meticulously from their scientific work for reasons of seeming objectivity, many female anthropologists, influenced by the feminist movement, take a closer critical look at the effect their identity as a white woman from an industrial country has on their scientific endeavours. Apart from her age, class, ethnic identity, outward appearance, personal abilities and previous experience in life, gender is the constant companion of a woman and thus participates in the formulation of the questions, both in the process of field research and in the analysis of the materials gathered. Knowledge is not just political but also gendered (Warren 1988: 10). But gender gives no indication of the scientific approach. To be a woman neither implies feminist research nor choosing 'woman' or 'gender relations' as a topic, even though these subjects have been established both by women's and by feminist research (Moore 1988: 11). It is a principle of women's research,

> that in fact it always wants to be and can be understood as a politically motivated research, in which the central categories of research are not arbitrariness but experience, subjectivity and political interest.
>
> (Wildt 1987: 142)[9]

Science thus understood calls for the analysis of one's own person and cannot be restricted to an anthropological field or even certain subjects.

Preparation

Usually, a certain area, preferably not situated in Europe, is staked out, which a certain researcher then calls 'my' field or 'my' village or maybe even 'my' ethnos. The data gathered in 'My' supposedly serves to complete the knowledge of cultural forms. In former times, however, they supported colonial submission and rule; and today they support the tourist industry and the mutual adulations of regional specialists. Our time of preparation was thus marked by an agonizing discussion about the legitimacy of our field research, about responsibility and presumptuousness.

It was our intention to return from Turkey with 'useful' knowledge, useful for the women and children from Turkey who can or must live here in Austria. So we approached some of the women who attended the German classes and literacy courses of our Association, explaining our project. We told them that we wanted to make life in a Turkish village comprehensible to ourselves and to the people in Austria, in particular the life and work of women. We said that we wanted to write up the personal histories of some of the villagers and develop our final thesis for the university from all this. We did not quite succeed in making our intentions clear, but some of the women immediately offered us accommodation in their villages.

Up to this time, the relation with the women in the project had been characterized by our role as teachers and social workers. Now we traded roles – we became the ones who 'wanted' and the Turkish women became the ones who 'gave'. Though we remained unaware of this at the time, such a swap caused us problems. Often it took a real effort to probe the women on whether they had already sent the letter to their relatives or to beg them to spare the time to tell us something about their village. Henceforth, these women received preferential treatment. While we had previously declined invitations by the women in order to avoid any inequalities regarding our personal relations to them, now we had to intensify such contacts. Our relations with the women were functional; only in rare cases were they marked by friendship.

Already in this initial phase the first tensions appeared between us, Sabine and Ruth. We were not friends either. We knew each other through our work in the Association and felt attached to each other through our engagement. The decision to carry out field research jointly, to venture out into the world from which came the women with whom we were together daily, somewhat reduced the fear of the unknown, but brought along some new anxieties. In particular, there emerged a fear of inequality and of competition. For Ruth, who has a child, the preparation phase was dominated by her role as a mother. She had to leave her eight-year-old son behind in Austria in the knowledge that he was well taken care of and this care needed to be organized (she could not count on any support of her project by the child's father; indeed his desire to sabotage her intentions presented an additional burden for both of us). When the child was accommodated and the work in the Association had been delegated to the other women, we departed for the next 'field', equipped with literature to compensate for any lack of knowledge, and with presents, first aid box and contact lenses.[10]

The decision

After staying in Istanbul and Ankara for several days, we arrived in the provincial capital of Erzincan in the middle of the night. Without our knowledge, the taxi-driver took us to the best hotel in town. The next day we wanted to initiate contact with the village and right away made our first mistake. Due to problems with the local telephone system, we did not succeed in reaching our host in the village, so we asked the hotel porter for help, whereupon the director of the hotel took matters out of our hands. He spoke to our contact in the village and summond the old man into town. Even at the best of times, this would have meant an hour's bus-ride, but at this time of day the public transport had already stopped their service. Nevertheless, he came. While waiting, we worried lest we should already have presented ourselves as rich and spoilt Europeans.

In the village we were given a very friendly yet cool reception by our hosts. Our aim was to find a village where we could stay, i.e. rent a house, explain our plans to the people and count on their support. We wanted to build a rapport, establish friendships and create an atmosphere of rewarding work. But we soon realized that our host family were regarded as outsiders in the village community. We presented a burden for the family and we did not succeed in renting a house.

The village community consisted mainly of old people, women and children. Many families and most of the men had emigrated. We had to face the question whether a study of the mechanisms of power and violence was at all possible in a location without men, although rule by men was kept up in spite of their absence. The remarkable characteristics of this society are a language which is in danger of extinction (Zaza) and a suppressed religious branch – Alevi Islam – from which a special philosophy and a critical school of thought have emerged. But none of these factors played a primary role in the choice of a particular village. We sensed rejection, felt unwelcome and, most of all, we could not locate a house. Thus we decided to try another village in Trabzon province.

Again we faced the issue of establishing the first contact and our tension rose. This, and our agreement that neither of us must fall in love during that time, as this might lead to difficulties between ourselves and the villagers, caused an inflated fear of men. Nevertheless, we had to stand up to these men with apparent fearlessness:

they would decide our admission into the village and channel the flow of information to us.

The second village was completely different from the first. The deeply religious, conservative Sunni Muslims received us with exceptional friendliness. We tried to explain our intentions, as we had done with our female contacts in Vienna, by telling them about our interest in their lives, their work and about our doctoral thesis. Our intention to stay for a long time was appreciated. The intention to conduct research, on the other hand, was taken note of without much interest. A house was immediately put at our disposal. These comforts of traditional hospitality made us decide to stay on in this village.

YALNIZ MISINIZ? – ARE YOU ALONE?

The two of us – each one alone?

As we have mentioned earlier on, we knew each other from working together in Vienna. At the beginning of our 'field research' we were frequently preoccupied with our similar upbringing. From the age of ten we had both grown up in a female household. Both our fathers had ascended to the middle class, while our mothers had remained workers. We both work in a project for women and see ourselves as feminists. Our working conditions, the way we practise our work and the motivation to pursue this kind of work, but also our fears, are very similar. All this resulted in a 'mirror effect'. First one of us would get terribly outraged by a mistake the other one had made, then there would be a row and then a clearing discussion which often brought to light that each of us would notice in the other especially those mistakes which we ourselves found most problematic. Each would see her own mistakes reflected in the other. This similarity led to tensions and to an intensification of these qualities, all of which hampered the establishment of mutual trust. We both developed the fear that one would want to outdistance the other, withhold information and use her contacts to her own advantage. As soon as one felt and showed her strength, the other had the feeling of being suffocated by it. For months we were together day and night, even sleeping in the same bed. We often planned to work separately, but it hardly ever came to that.

The villagers regarded us as a unity, too. If one showed up anywhere alone, she was immediately asked where the other was.

The absent one had to feign illness to be excused. On the other hand, the girls and women tried to stir up rivalry between us. Knitting, dancing, clothing, being fat or slim, diligent or lazy – anything presented an occasion to point out differences or short-comings. We were constantly occupied with defining our differences and keeping up our individuality, while at the same time we jointly had to oppose the war of competition that was forced upon us.

But in spite of these tensions, our working relationship in the village was also a very creative one. We held long talks about new pieces of information, impressions and our thoughts concerning them. Often we understood and interpreted statements completely differently. This way, we discovered many contradictions which could be cleared up right away by following them up. Working in pairs, then, also considerably enlarges the mechanism of control.

Two women alone

Ever since we started working with Turkish women in Vienna, we have had problems concerning our self-presentation. Ruth is divorced, has a child and lives alone with him. Sabine is unmarried but still not a '*kiz*' (girl, virgin) any more. We concealed the divorce and the sex life. Our political views could be revealed carefully and diplomatically. But if a woman is not allowed to explain how she organizes her life, there is little she can give out of herself and there cannot be much discussion with the Turkish women, who, surely, do not tell everything either. More and more we suffered from the lies which seemed necessary.

Learning from experience, we had planned to be honest in the village, chancing a confrontation. But we could not do it! Not yet. In Vienna, much less depends on our honesty than in a Turkish village where our acceptance in the village rested on our reputation. We had to be classifiable in terms of indigenous standards and values. The restrictions applying to women are much stricter than those for men. Male anthropologists would not have had any prob-lems with being divorced or with a lack of virginity.

Thus Ruth presented herself as an independent, married woman. Sabine gave no further comments on her single status and was thus regarded as a virginal, independent girl. Again and again we tried to refer to the problems of our respective lives, but there was no way out of the estrangement we had chosen ourselves. Therefore, we mainly tried to present ourselves as working women, a picture which allows independence and thereby showed at least one side of our lives back in Austria. It was important for us to show that we, too, held moral concepts, standards and values. Young men often asked us whether European women really went to bed with every man. We knew of this prejudice, which was mainly created through tourism and the tales of migrants. To save our 'honour' we explained that in our country many couples live together without being married, not for reasons of 'promiscuity' but out of 'love'. We were extremely dissatisfied with our explanations. One of the reasons for this was the fact that we ourselves could not come to terms with the moral concepts, standards and values of our own society.

'*Yalniz misiniz?* – Are you alone?' was the question we were asked again and again. As we usually appeared together, this should have been superfluous, but it was not. The questions were getting at the men who should have accompanied and protected us. Yes, we are alone, we two women. People showed particular astonishment about the married woman. Again and again she was asked why her husband and her child had not come with her. Ruth explained that she was here to work. Her husband had a different line of work and, besides, he did not speak Turkish. The child had to attend school and therefore could not be with his mother. This answer was accepted, but with great astonishment over the fact that a married woman should be allowed to leave her family. We were women, but women who did not behave correctly, who could not be categorized.

At times, we really wanted to be alone. We had to work and we needed quiet to do so. Being alone because one wanted to was something unimaginable for the people of the village; work that required silence was unknown to them. Being alone means fear and loneliness. On the one hand, we were expected to look after their children, participate in the housework and in serving the men, thus ranging ourselves into the typically female work spheres. On the other hand, the villagers set hopes in us they would normally only have in men. For example, that we could help them to emigrate to Europe, give some sort of support to their relatives in Vienna or simply that we would be rich.

We were received as friends and as helpers of their female relatives in Vienna, and in this capacity served as a cause for prestige: the daughter or sister had integrated so well in Europe that she had even found rich European girl-friends. The personal relationship between us and the woman in question was exaggerated. We often tried to clear this up and explain that we had met the daughter/

sister through our work. The result was that we were made into little goddesses with lots of power and influence, who could surmount any obstacles for foreigners in Austria. People were convinced that we would offer their relatives an unlimited visa and work permit.

The 'virgin' is a potential marriage candidate. If she speaks Turkish on top of being *'temiz'* (clean, pure), she is a good match. Indeed, marriage often presents the only possibility for foreigners to stay in Austria for a longer period of time. In the beginning, Sabine was taken to be a future daughter-in-law as a matter of course and it was assumed that this was the real reason for our visit to the village. Again and again we had to explain that this was not so. Sabine said she had no intention to marry at all, at which our hosts remarked that she could get divorced again after their son had got his residence permit. The fact that divorced women have to fight lots of problems in our society, too, impressed them very little. Sometimes Sabine was not sure if all the friendliness she met with was not simply caused by her made-up virginity.

All those months we stood in the cross-fire of both the idealization of the existing standards and values in the village on the one hand, and of the European world on the other. Summing up, it can be said that the relation between 'ethnos' and 'female anthropologist' was marked by reciprocity. We wanted to find admittance and be given information; they wanted help for their relatives in Europe and ardently desired consumer goods from the West. We have not yet found any 'girl-friends'; the 'lies' are still standing between us.

BETWEEN ADJUSTMENT AND RESISTANCE

Not all female anthropologists have knowingly used this advantage (the access as a woman to the world of women) to the benefit of their field research. Some have succumbed to the temptation of playing a male role in male surroundings.

(Hauser-Schäublin 1985: 190)[11]

We did not give in to the attraction a male role holds, but we often asked ourselves if we really wanted to, or even could, voluntarily slip into the roles of the weak ones, the suppressed women. It had taken huge efforts to get one step away from the concepts of suppression in our own society. To find access to a foreign society, to earn its sympathy and consequently be able to gain scientific success, should we really give up our views regarding violence, hierarchy and ideological submission, and should we accept an existing relationship of suppression without any opposition? We decided to keep a certain distance to avoid being classified according to one or the other of the genders. In this way, we could choose between the manners of behaviour which were expected from one gender or the other, but at the price of remaining strangers. Without wanting to, we had already decided to remain strangers, by presenting ourselves as two women travelling alone (without a man). Many small breaches of the norms cemented our role. We wore no head-scarfs but frequently trousers, rode to town without a man, hardly worked in their eyes, smoked too much and also in front of persons who had to be respected, went home after dark and went out to drink tea with men who were no relatives of ours. As Europeans, we were forgiven many things, and they even said, 'You are like us. You dress properly and you speak Turkish. You are Turkish women'. How gladly we would have believed them that they really saw us like that.

What could not be surmounted was our disbelief. As the prayer characterizes everyday life and the fear of burning in hell dominates every action, it was unimaginable for the women and men of the village that, even after their efforts to convert us, we still preferred to remain '*gavur*'.[12] But '*gavur*' we remained, without being thus called in the village any more. We continued to be strangers who were integrated as such into a kin group, perhaps being appropriated by our hosts, by their possible hopes and expectations. Yet even this role of 'outsiders' did not save us from frequently having to declare our positions. We took a determined stance against enthusiastic tales of war, and although this sometimes led us to somewhat questionable pacifistic statements, we could define the boundaries between their position and ours regarding war, expansion and nationalism, without triggering any quarrels. Conflicts arose when we could not stand never being alone and consequently urged our neighbours to leave 'our' house on occasion; or when we failed to pay visits frequently enough or to spread our visits equally.

The most difficult part was to be involved in a conflict between the genders. We had lots of contact with the young unmarried women. One of the girls soon attracted our attention. N had no father and a sister had died only a few months earlier. Her second sister had been married off to Samsun shortly before our arrival. One brother worked in a nearby town and another in the south of

Turkey. The necessary shopping was usually done by one of the brothers in town, who then sent the goods to the village by bus or brought them himself fortnightly. Even in times of crisis, mother and daughter did not leave the village. A male relative would take on these tasks. N valued our attention highly and we liked her very much, too. When one day she asked us if we could go to town together, we consented. We left it up to her to decide whether that was possible for her as an unmarried woman. Twice we had to postpone the trip but on the third try we made it. The three of us squeezing into one row of seats, we lurched to the town which was one hour's ride away. We went shopping at the weekly market. N had money of her own which she had earned working for rich farmers as a day labourer during the hazelnut harvest in the lower flatlands.

We paid a visit to her relatives in Trabzon and then wanted to take the first bus back to the village. But since this one was completely crammed we had to wait two hours for the next. The women from the village spent this time in the bus. We decided to have a cup of tea in the family tea-garden, where men without female company usually are not allowed to stay. But in this small provincial town, the garden, which should by rights have been reserved for families, was almost exclusively filled by men. We, as foreigners, could be admitted into the tea-garden; many knew us from narrations, some exchanged a few words with us, others invited us to a cup of tea from time to time. Our friend was not treated with such friendliness; she had to stand stern looks. We started to feel uncomfortable too and tried to relieve the tension through jokes. Some men from the *mahalle* (village quarter), among them N's brother, discovered us. But on this day they did not come and sit at our table as usual; their glances from afar were cool and reproachful. We fled to the bus where the women had already been waiting for some hours. N's aunt and a cousin who had both acted appropriately by staying in the bus looked us up and down. Impatiently we waited for the departure. The long, exhausting journey tires people and takes their mind off things. Shortly after the bus had taken off, N collapsed. She had fainted. We covered up her attack because we feared that her fainting would be regarded as a just punishment and a welcome reason not to let her go to town on her own any more.

Back in the village we disappeared into 'our' house as fast as possible. Over the course of the next days we frequently heard that the girl N was good-for-nothing, lazy and disrespectful. We defended her but that did not influence anybody's judgement. N's *amcaoğlu* (father's brother's son, i.e. cousin) was indignant because it was he who had to pay for her behaviour. He was asked by the men of the village why the women of his *mahalle* behaved so dishonourably. We were left speechless. The older women remained silent like us. What do they think, the mothers whose daughters are under such pressure? We felt guilty. Should we not have broken the standards together with N? Mathieu (1985) is of the opinion that the accusation of unjustified interference with other societies, for example by women doing research, only serves to divide and silence women. To what extent can we interfere in the lives of women, air opinions and then take off again? Where is the border between cowardice and ethnocentrism? Where is the starting point for the necessity to state positions, to intervene and to put up resistance, and where are the limits of contemptuous disdain of another culture and Eurocentric feelings of superiority? And if we consistently defend ourselves, does this leave us any chance to perceive another society in its independence? At the moment, all we can do is reflect on our own behaviour and demonstrate the contradictions which every woman meets within a patriarchal or sexist society.

In her anthology *Toward an Anthropology of Women*, Reiter (1975: 14) stresses that the claim that men are invariably better informants can only be explained by the male bias in research. The perception of men as more easily accessible is one which we transposed from our culture, just like the one that they dominate the central institutions of a society and are therefore better at conveying them. That is why we always turn to men and, by behaving the way we do, make them the better informants.

We share this view, but we still think that for certain reasons it is harder to interview women in patriarchal societies. Men regard themselves as the representatives of the central institutions of their society. Showing an interest in the women, their work and their views, leads to jealously among the men and to fear of men's jealousy among the women. After the wedding, Turkish women move into the husband's household, which may be situated in another village. If we want to interview this year's unmarried women next year, or continue an established relationship, we shall have to visit many villages and towns. It is generally much more complicated to have a conversation with women. Little children, all kinds of work and having to serve the men in the evening, prevent women from leading any extensive talks. Evenings spent with women alone are much more instructive, relaxed and exciting. Men are not the better informants; women are just busier, and it thus takes longer to get coherent information.

FIELDS OF POWER IN THE VILLAGE

Although we were usually not regarded as individuals, but rather as a man-less unity, there nevertheless appeared differences in our reception. These differences had a negative effect both on our relationship with each other, and on that with the villagers. Nevertheless, or maybe just because of that, several approaches and individual ways of access opened up for us. The following points try to sum up the reasons for our differential reception by the villagers and the basic difficulties of our stay. (a) We had studied Turkish for different lengths of time, so that, especially in the beginning, inequalities in the competence of language appeared. (b) In Vienna Sabine had known our contact woman for the second village for several years, a relationship which was characterized by the positions of social-worker/client. Ruth had met her only briefly. The contact woman informed her family of our project and also about her relation to us. Thus Sabine became a sort of 'rescuing angel' for migrants from Turkey. (c) At times we suffered from an inundation of contact, never from any lack of contact. There was no way we could be on our own. (d) We had great problems with the basically conservative, often reactionary attitude of the villagers, and we could not cope too well with their constant attempts at converting us to Islam either. All of that often led us to a vehement distancing from them. (e) One of us appeared as a married woman, the other one as a virgin. On the one hand, this meant that we had different access to the women, and, on the other hand, that the virgin became a potential partner for marriage. She constantly had to fight against being married. In contrast to the married woman, she was not sexually taboo. Naturally, this led to a difference in the way the men dealt with us. (f) The fear of 'social death' was constantly breathing down our necks. There was a constant danger of being rejected because we might have made the conditions of our lives in Austria and our ideological views too transparent or could not explain them sufficiently and might therefore be regarded as whores or communists. (g) The fights of power and rivalry between us were not only a burden for our dealings with each other, but also for our dealings with the others. The women tried – surely unconsciously – to fan the flames of rivalry. (h) The bad conscience regarding the child she had left back in Austria diminished the mother's joy in the project.

This list should give an insight into the difficulties which can appear in a 'field' situation. Certainly the problems are only partly gender-specific. Some of them are equally known to male anthropologists. The difference lies surely in how we treat them. The description of the problems in this essay is a result of this difference.

II The impurity of research and female fertility

Sabine Strasser

PERSONAL RELATIONS

Since the 1988 research and the resulting essay, a lot of things have changed. Ruth did not take part the second time – she had decided on a rather demanding full-time job and a training in analytical psychotherapy. The reason for such an extended excursion into another realm of science can be found in an interest in the different meanings of '*Ohnmacht*' (see note 2). On the one hand it is a product of the conscious, studied by anthropologists, and on the other hand it is a product of the unconscious, being researched by psychoanalysis (fainting-fits are typical symptoms of hysteria (comment by R. K.)). For the past two months, Ruth and I have been working together in the same Association again.[13] Maybe some day we can continue our scientific work together. However, the consequence of Ruth's decision was that, in the spring of 1990, I went to the village on my own. The preparations were easier than the first time, as my conceptions were far clearer. After all, this time I knew what awaited me.

During the one and a half years between my visits, I had corresponded with some of the girls and young women from the village. On the high Islamic holidays, I had afforded the luxury of a telephone call to one or two households – a call from Austria is always a cause for great excitement in the *mahalle* (village quarter). The telephone line was so bad though every time I called that I could only guess at the things that were said. On the other hand, staying in touch through letters was rather strenuous for the girls who do not like to read and find even less pleasure in writing themselves. Therefore, I am all the more pleased with the continuity of these relations on both sides. The girls used to express their wish to keep this contact up with the following threat at the end of a letter

Hayat bir gemi	Life is a ship
Yoktur yelkeni	which has no sails.
Unutursan beni	If you forget me,
Dalgalar boğsun seni!	the waves shall drown You!

A second level of communication with the village had taken the form of the friendship with a young woman from the village here in Austria. The contact to this woman called Asiye was activated in 1988 by our search for a village in Turkey. On the basis of the emotional ties I have with her today, I can admit that at first I was more interested in her village of origin than in herself. Now we both know what we can give to each other. She helps me when my writing has me in confusion, explains certain conceptions to me one more time, and keeps me out of the dead-end street of an anaemic construction of a society. She knows the significance she has for me. When I ask her for explanations she sends away her husband so that we can talk openly.

Asiye is one of approximately 46,000 women from Turkey currently living in Austria.[14] Like me, she has been living in Vienna for about ten years, but she will remain an 'alien' by law, so long as she does not apply for Austrian citizenship. By contrast to her husband, she does not want to change her citizenship. Thus her stay continues to be regulated by the '*Fremdenpolizeigesetz*' (foreign residents' law) and employment depends on a permit from the employment exchange.[15] Problems surrounding her permit, the working hours, place of work, child allowance and many other obstacles for 'aliens' which result from Austrian legislation and language problems, are in part my task.

When Asiye had physical problems, we spoke a lot about the causes for her dizziness, her fear that her soul would try to leave her body. She told me of her frequent fainting-fits, that life sometimes wanted to seep out of her, that her hands would grow *kapkara* (black as coal). An oppressive emotional strain (*canı sıkılmak*) would announce an imminent fainting-fit to her. Since I am not medically trained, her accounts frightened me as well and I accompanied her to all kinds of doctors. But none of them could find anything apart from a somewhat low blood-pressure. The mystery of the crises of the women from the Eastern Black Sea, which we were introduced to through N on the bus, was being continued here. But who in Austria is interested in the causes of an illness which cannot be proved?

The relationship between Asiye and me has become a satisfying one. It is not based on common interests and expectations – as is usually the case in friendships – but on the appeal which the difference between us and our expectations has. By being close to Asiye, I have lost most of my fears of insoluble problems appearing in the village. In the meantime, the people there have accepted the fact that the reason for my interest in Turkey is not that I am looking for a man. But in the village and in Vienna, I still have to face the questions of a husband. 'Your hair is growing white already! How old are you now? Well, you must know.' The women pity me for having to find a husband myself, and they think the odds are against me finding one yet.

Although in 1990 I could not find out, before I left for the village, whether the son of the family which was going to accommodate me – Asiye's brother – was to get a work permit in Austria, after thorough consideration I decided not to enter into a fictitious marriage with him (which would have secured his residence and work permit). I knew that he intended to marry a certain girl from the village later on, so I could never have appeared in the village as his wife. Had we (Asiye, her brother and I) tried to keep it a secret, they would have heard about it in the village as *dedikodu* (gossip) in less than a month's time. Social control works very efficiently even in Vienna. Had I married him in order to help him obtain his work permit, what would his family have expected from me as a daughter-in-law? Maybe they would have put me down as a dishonourable, shameless girl who could be used for fictitious marriages over and over again; maybe I would even have been attacked by some men because of my shamelessness. My honour in the form of shame (*namus*), which without any male control appeared highly dubious, would have been jeopardized further. That, in turn, would have marred the honour of my hosts for whose benefit I thought of taking this step. Were they to accept me as daughter- and sister-in-law, this would require me to conform to social rules and would have meant an expansion of the male rule over 'their' women to include me, too. Even if they had found different forms of interpretation for members of the household (*tayfa*), for relatives (*akraba*), and for strangers (*yabancı*), which would have made my marriage appear as something positive through an adroit application of necessities and standards, I still would have felt uncomfortable. I preferred to fight for their sympathy than buy it by marriage.

When Asiye's brother got his Austrian work permit (while I was staying in the village), nobody could have been happier than I was. I did not have to go on feeling that I was being hosted by people whom I could not even help in matters of vital significance.

A never-ending journey

Two questions raised by the essay written in 1988 have been on my mind to this day: do we have the right to do field research at all, and what dangers are involved by interfering in other cultures?

Women from Arab, African and Asian countries, and especially Black Women from the USA, have accused white feminists of using other societies as the 'raw material' for their scientific discourse and of showing a lack of respect for other cultures. Their criticisms demand a thorough reconsideration of aims and, at the same time, a discussion of any new racist tendencies which might attend this criticism. In many cases which call for a re-evaluation of the contents of our scientific work and of its consequences, we still take refuge in nothing but a guilty conscience.

Women of Colour have been pointing out racist tendencies in white feminism to us for a long time. In German-speaking countries, this criticism has been intensely debated only over the past two years. Women like bell hooks, Hazel Carby, Audre Lorde, Nawal el Saadawi and others, object to being claimed as members by a sisterhood which covers up the differences existing between women, such as racism, ethnic identity and status affiliation. Sisterhood, according to bell hooks (1987: 43), is a revolutionary accomplishment that women have to fight for – not simply the supposition that all women are suppressed in the same way everywhere. This applies equally to the relations between women from Turkey living in Austria and ourselves. Austrian women are not oppressed in the same way, nor is there any cause for that feeling of superiority which keeps tempting us to try and act as the mouth-pieces of other women or, respectively, to use them for our feminist hopes and fears.

Trying to present 'foreign women' in Austria as the victims of their men, being beaten and veiled, is a distraction from the economic and legal situation of the migrants. A woman's dependence on men can largely be attributed to the fact that, by law, women joining their husbands in Austria are not allowed to work during the first three years of their residence. Then there are the dangers of a divorce which, if it comes to the worst, could result in the deportation of the woman. There is the terrible housing shortage which plunges many families into misery. The tightening of the foreign residents' law allows for an inconspicuous deportation of refugees and undesirable 'aliens'. The draft for a new law on political asylum is not in accordance with the Geneva Convention on refugees. To this day, foreigners have not even got a communal right to vote in Austria regardless of how long they have been living here or whether or not they were born here.

So, in fact, there are enough challenges for 'white' Austrian women without having to give ourselves airs and playing 'big sisters' to the women from all kinds of countries. The issue is a struggle for human rights in Austria, a country which pursues a policy of exclusion and which makes no efforts to stop racism.

> White women don't work on racism to do a favour to someone else, solely to benefit Third World women. You have to comprehend how racism distorts and lessens your own lives as white women – that racism affects your chances for survival, too, and that it is very definitely your issue.
>
> (Smith 1982: 49)

The acceptance of differences does not exclude a joint pursuit of common aims.

Black women's criticism of white women's discussion of foreign cutlures takes on quite different forms. While Amadiume (1987) sees no difference between male and female anthropologists, and wants to exclude non-indigenous researchers from all research in her country (Nigeria), female Arab anthropologists (Altorki *et al.* 1988) emphasize the importance and the advantages of indigenous research in their home countries, without wanting to exclude the others. Nawal el-Saadawi's (1980) criticism refers to the concentration of feminists on phenomena such as circumcision of the clitoris, polygamy and repudiation. She warns us against satisfying ourselves by doing reputedly 'good deeds' for others which lead us to forget the essential problems of the struggle for liberation.

> It is Arab women alone who can formulate the theory, the ideas and the modes of struggle needed to liberate themselves from all oppression. It is their effort alone that can create a new Arab Woman, a life with their own originality, capable of choosing

what is more genuine and valuable in her cultural tradition, as well as assimilating the progress of science and modern thought.

(Nawal el Saadawi 1980: XVI)

In a preface to a reader[16] by Turkish feminists (Neusel *et al.* 1990), they, too, emphasize the development of their own scientific work. Discovering the speedy developments of feminism inside Turkey as well as abroad, female social scientists are primarily interested in connecting these works. Their criticism of German (and presumably also of Austrian) feminist research corresponds to critique raised by Black American women against white researchers: the white middle-class woman is taken as a measure for feminist claims. The accusation of Eurocentrism is raised, but they acknowledge the attempt of white women to analyse the differences of nationality, class, and ethnic and religious affiliation. However, their interest still concentrates on the internal exchange of their own works. The differences among the women in Turkish society are already demonstrated by the diversity of the contributions.

I fear that in the near future the question of the justifiability of research by white women 'in' other cultures will not have to be raised any more for a different reason. A new theory of 'ethnic relations' describes racist behaviour as natural. This 'differentialistic racism' (Balibar 1990: 30) – which is fast spreading – says that 'natural distances' should be kept and the 'thresholds of tolerance' be observed. Other cultures should best be kept outside of our 'clean white world' by clear frontiers. With the tightening of its borders around the EC countries, Europe seems to be on the brink of reducing its interests to 'ourselves'. In Austria, the 'multicultural-ity' of our society is verbally recognized, but the legal parity of 'foreigners' as a prerequisite for an equal juxtaposition of cultures is (consciously) neglected. Meanwhile, attacks on refugees and immigrants are increasing.

By using an approach of 'natural distances', we can withdraw from a difficult discussion and restrict ourselves to our own culture, ostensibly without a bad conscience. I hope that the debate on the differences among women is not going to develop in this direction. Europe and feminism both need permeable borders.

Personal relations in the village

Now I was really on my own. Immediately after my arrival in the small town of Y, I was bundled into the bus by my hosts. I was tired from the journey, so I just let it happen, and I was glad to find everything the way I had expected it. Clearly I – on my own – had to be assigned to the women. And the place for women, as soon as they have dealt with their shopping, visits to the dentist, examinations at the public health station, or civil wedding is, in town, the bus.

This bus, the same one which had taken N and us back to the village at that time, was soon bouncing through the hazelnut gardens. One could still see the houses on the steep green slopes, as the hazelnut leaves had not shot yet. Soon those leaves would cover up the whole village life, I thought. They seemed to be the perfect supplement to the veiling of the women by cloth. They protected from the looks of strangers, who would never enter somebody else's garden without being invited and accompanied. I thought of N and her letters, in which she had written about her fits. I was determined to find out what these fainting-fits stood for, what caused them, and why they were not regarded as an illness to be treated by the doctor (*dokturluk*) but by the healer (*cincilik*). What do the girls think of these symptoms, what do the men think, and the youngsters and the old ones? Which period of life is especially dangerous for the women, and why do all the villagers and specialists believe that women are more subject to these symptoms than men?

The women and I had a common interest in certain questions. I wanted to understand the reasons for their greatest problems in the course of their biographies and the ideological backgrounds for their crises. They wanted to be able at last to talk about their problems at length and without the danger of being shut out.

The girls of the *mahalle* had prepared a room for me in an empty house – they already knew my needs, too. This room became a meeting-point for the girls. There they could eat and drink tea during menstruation in the Ramadan; they could smoke an undisturbed cigarette, and hide from work – no man could enter this room without previous announcement. After all, I was an unmarried woman on my own. Unmarried men I only met in other houses. Actually, my host was the only man who entered this room, even when he was alone. Sometimes a man would come in the company of his wife or mother. It felt good to be treated with respect.

But none of this means that the conversations with the girls and women were easy. Because of my topics – the biographies of women that touched on menarche, menstruation, matrimony, sexuality, childbearing, obsessions and death, as well as relations to women and men – most women wanted to speak about them separately. My room became a place of secrets and these are attractive. When I asked a woman for an interview, the others were jealous, envious or simply curious, but they would surely be somewhere close to my room.

As soon as I had settled down comfortably with a woman, lit a fire in the oven, poured the tea and checked the tape-recorder, thus ready to ask the first question, a head would be poked through the door, enquiring how we were. 'Whatever are you doing?', one after the other would ask, as if they did not know. 'When will you come to us for a visit?' they had to ask at this very moment, or suddenly wash the dishes outside my front door. And finally one would hang up her laundry right outside the window of my room so as to be able to follow a part of the conversation. At times, the tension was unbearable. I understood that, in any case, the claim to a confidential talk gave reason for conflict. It was not until the girls and young women wanted to lead these conversations of their own accord that we found a time and place in common which would allow private talks without raising any conflicts. We would carry out some task together; I would be sent off to protect a girl who otherwise would have had to spend a night alone in a house; I abstained from going to festivities so I could talk at length with a woman who had to stay at home. In the end, these conversations even became the basis for friendships with some. After I had done a couple of interviews I became more relaxed, could smile at interruptions, and today these disturbances recorded on the tapes create a strange longing for the women in the village by the Black Sea.

All girls and women are concerned that no gossip (*dedikodu*) should be created by these talks. After the first interview, A said 'I have told you everything, I put the responsibility in your hands. If anybody should hear this tape, you know what would happen here'. I was frightened myself by the prospect that these intimate, personal experiences, thoughts and dreams of girls might fall into the hands of a man. For several days, my chief occupation was to find a suitable hiding place for the tapes. That they would be searched for, I knew. Those tapes containing statements which, in my opinion, presented a danger for the women, I always took with me on my excursions to town and left them with a girl-friend in Istanbul at the earliest opportunity. Some of these statements might have resulted in violence or separation.

I also had to get used to not always being presented with innermost feelings in my interviews. After a broken engagement, the woman will blame the man and vice versa. The girl actually has to deny ever having wanted the man, because otherwise no other man might want her. Her decent behaviour would be questioned. The statement of an 'abandoned' girl says more about the norm than about her true feelings, which I was only rarely told.

Older women especially did not like to talk about their youth and the time after their wedding. Those were the women whose conversation I sought most persistently and it was only later that I realized that these women's behaviour often reminded me of the stubbornness with which my mother had avoided answering my questions about the past. But then these are the women who stand to lose the most. They have an interest in keeping up the existing order now that they have daughters-in-law and grown-up sons and can enjoy their greatest freedom of action. Still, even at this age, their influence on the decisions of the men depends on their individual skills.

When the questions became too embarrassing for them, they would literally try to stuff me by putting things in my mouth – fresh bread, delicious butter, jam, eggs, or whatever was at hand – and would proudly remark that I had gained weight again. Others would show their masterpieces of needlework. Their interest lies with their skills and achievements, not with the memories of a painful past. At this age, many of them have a job on the side which heightens their freedom of action, as midwife (*ebe*), a setter of bones (*kırıkcı*), exceptionally able knitters, or as specialists for injections.

Thus the contents of the conversations depended on the interests and experiences of the women, and they differ according to age group. After menarche, the freedom of movement, love and the limits of education are important. At a marriageable age (usually around 20), the fears of matrimony are combined with those of remaining unmarried. Curiosity regarding sexual intercourse is combined with being afraid of it. These ambivalent feelings continue after the wedding. The fear of pregnancy fights with the fear of childlessness. 'The longing to live on your own in town without being controlled by your in-laws has to fight with the husband's obligation to his parents.

In my conversations with women who were in the middle of a crisis, i.e. having fits of dizziness and fainting, could not have children or attracted attention through their shameless behaviour, I was astonished to notice how clearly they could analyse their problems. Loneliness, being shut out, segregation, the desire to go out, the yearning for a husband and children, the death of a close

relative and the fear of their own death, all that was vividly reported
to me. One day I learned during an interview that all these women
had already been to see a *cinci-hoca* (healer). They are responsible
for the treatement of the crises of the women, as they have power
over the *peri* (demons) and know how to drive them out of the
women's bodies.

FEMALE FAINTING AS A 'SYMPTOM OF SANITY' – THE FEMALE TREATMENT OF MALE DOMINANCE

The crises of women which have no biological causes are described
as *cincilik* (a matter for the healer). They appear mainly in the
fertile periods of life of the women, between menarche and meno-
pause. Men are rarely subject to these crises. The transitions from
one social role to the next are characterized by fertility and
impurity.

Impurity must first and foremost be seen as an infringement of
corporeal limits by liquids such as blood, urine, faeces and perspiration. This impurity requires a ritual cleaning (*aptes*) before praying
or the touching of the Koran. Sexual intercourse equally puts man
and woman in a state of impurity and, like the end of menstruation
and the end of the impure period after childbirth, demands a great
purification (*būyūk aptes*). Because of their reproductive capacity,
women are more affected by impurity. Whereas a man's purity can
immediately be restored at any time, that of women is uncontrol-
lable during menstruation and after childbirth. As a woman
threatens the congregation of believers, so does the blood threaten
the body of a woman. It is the male fear of chaos and impurity
which finally leads to the women being shut off from religious
practice and public life. Blood, the sign of the fertility of women,
becomes a symbol of their impurity and uncontrollability and thus
serves as an explanation for their inferiority.

The most decisive points in a woman's life deal with this ritual
impurity. The menarche, which indicates the girl's childbearing
ability, serves as a cause for being integrated into the world of
grown-up believers and, at the same time, for a first exclusion from
ritual practice and public life for as long as she is fertile. From this
point on, the honour of the family depends on the girl's modest
behaviour.

The wedding is the most exciting event in the lives of the women
and men in this village. The preparations alone bear cause for
dangerous conflicts and great tensions. Matrimony is necessary for

all people in order to stay normal – unmarried persons are regarded as *deli* (mad). But even in matrimony, impurity is caused by sexual intercourse, which seals the marriage, proves the girl's purity through her virginal blood and is essential for the procreation of descendants. In the days after the wedding, the woman must be protected. Now her husband and his family, not her own, are responsible for her honour. Purity is also the prerequisite for getting pregnant. After menstruation, when all impure blood has left her body, a woman is regarded as being especially fertile.

Childbirth brings about impure blood. The woman stays at home for seven days, and for forty days she returns home for the *ikindi* (afternoon prayer). The blood that nurtures the child during pregnancy does not become impure until its issue. The young woman has to be looked after, as she is in extreme danger of being killed or made ill by a demon. She is not left alone. One of her husband's shirts lies next to her on the bed and a pointed object like a knife is used to keep away the *alkarisi* (woman of red), a demon who appears only within forty days after birth. She is not told any bad news, as the fright heightens the danger of becoming possessed by a demon. Her status as a mother raises her standing, but immediately after childbirth she is impure and in grave danger.

If the crises of the women (rarely those of the men) are related to limited periods (transitions to a new social role, such as that of a marriageable girl, a married woman, a mother) and to body (outflow of blood, amniotic fluid, sperm, perspiration), it becomes clear that impurity and infringement of bodily limits during these phases are regarded as causes for these crises. The *peri* (female demons) enter the body of the woman and make her impure, sick, irresponsible, mad. The greatest danger for this entrance of demons is after giving birth, upon the occurrence of a great scare (as it is said of the menarche or the first sexual intercourse), or during loneliness and grief. 'Women have menstruation, childbirth and matrimony, men are only affected by the problems of wedlock', is the explanation one *cinci-hoca* gives for the different grades of being endangered by *cin*.

Shortly before fainting, women often curse, scream, threaten and swear – thereby violating several social limits. They tear off their headscarf, the symbol of sexual purity and decency, and make indecent (*ayıp*) gestures, bringing shame over their families. But as the *cin/peri* are the cause for this behaviour, the unruly woman cannot be blamed for it. Girls and women describe their state after such a fit as pleasant, purified, whereas before they had had the feeling of being unable to rid themselves of an oppressive burden (*canı sıkılmak*).

The concept of purity also plays an important part in healing. The body is sealed with holy symbols, and *surahs* from the Koran are read to provoke the demon and require him to leave the body. Ritual cleaning with holy water is meant to cure the woman and make her *tertemiz* (sparkling clean) again. Although these purification rituals are forbidden by both the Turkish state and orthodox Islam (Eyūboğlu 1978: 8), demons and healers still form an important part of the religious conception of the world and of everyday life in many villages both in Turkey and, through migration, beyond. The *cin* serve to relieve the women, just as the *cinci* are used for the maintenance of order. The belief in demons is more widespread among women than among men and, of the women, it is especially the old ones who are afraid of the *cin/peri*. The young women have other explanations for their crises, too, as we have mentioned above. Because they can find no way out of the contradictions between inner needs and outer conditions, often all that remains is the demonstration of impurity on the outside, a rebellion against all that is pure, and against the social order.

IMPURITY IS A QUESTION OF FRONTIERS AND RESISTANCE

The control of female sexuality and fertility is no peculiarity of Islamic society. What is interesting is the maintenance of this control in a specific social context, and especially the reaction of the women to it. The search for an approach to gender relations brought me to the illnesses and impurities, which in effect contain a fundamental – though unconscious – resistance. It is a form of resistance which bears the symbols of uncontrollability and which most of all signifies the violation of social rules by women. But the byword for this resistance is impurity – impurity which can mean the exclusion from society.

To prove the existence of *cin* and *peri* is not my concern. It is enough that these demons are simply a part of everyday life for the women and men in this village and in many rural areas of Turkey. In the search for explanations of the symptoms which these girls and women manifest, I examined the different interpretations of this behaviour given by both women and men. Three basic structures presented themselves. The picture which the young men have of their society is partly secular. They look for worldly explanations. Since they do not seem to be interested in finding out their part in the women's crises, they think that love is the reason for the problem. The girls are in love, cannot get the man right away and so get sick with yearning. The different view of the young women who, after all, are the actresses of these fits, stems from the fact of being at the receiving end. They see certain problems, which they are partly conscious of, as a cause for their fits. Old women and men are the ones who live with the world of the *peri* the most distinctively. They concede that these conceptions are old woman's talk, but still believe in them. Yet some old women remarked with a sigh that the young women's fits stem from their knowing too much. In former times, such symptoms had rarely existed.

While searching for explanations for these symptoms, I came upon von Braun's analysis of hysteria (1990). It conveys an insight into the history of hysteria – the history of changing female reactions to changing forms of suppression – in occidental culture. Her work describes forms of female resistance, which might be detectable beyond the Western world in all viriarchal societies and may be instructive for the research on the symptoms of the women in the Black Sea region.

> Hysterics, I claim, are anything but patients suffering from a lack of ego. That they suffer from something is certain, but precisely from that which is attributed to them they do *not* suffer. They are rather the expression (maybe the strongest) of a rebellion against the destruction of the ego, which takes place on a collective level. The hysterical production of symptoms is the individual expression of a collective suffering and the attempt to fight the causes of the suffering – and for the very reason that it reveals collective suffering beyond the individual, its bearer, it is always treated only as the disease of the individual. If there is a disease which would offer a chance to speak of collective causes, then it is this one, which has been restricted to the one gender for thousands of years – without anybody ever being able to find a biological cause.
>
> (von Braun 1990: 75, 76)[17]

The application of von Braun's analysis to other cultures must be treated with care. But her statements raise useful questions regarding the fits of dizziness and fainting among women in a Turkish village. Are the *cin* and *peri* the causes for a suffering which has no biological reason, or are the demons nothing but another adroit attempt of a male ideology to cover up the collective causes for individual female resistance? If women understand their symptoms as impurity and obsession for which they cannot be blamed, but from which they have to be cured, they will not be able to recognize the possible qualities of their symptoms – as symptoms of sanity, as a sign of individual resistance against collective oppression.

What surfaces once again is the question of my interference, of my feelings of enlightened superiority in dealing with these conceptions, which contains a division into corporeal and emotional symptoms and, after all, also a certain protection for the women. If the conception of demons were to be destroyed and be replaced by the Western medical system, the women themselves would become responsible for the symptoms and there would be no social institutions to deal with their causes.

We have to draw up our borders anew – and I guess border areas are always fertile and impure. Interference is an infringement of borders which contains both aspects – and the way and the direction of the interference will decide whether it will be fertilizing or polluting.

NOTES

1 This essay was first published by Ruth Kronsteiner and Sabine Strasser as 'Frauen im Feld – überlegungen zu einer nie enden wollenden Reise', in B. Kossek, D. Langer and G. Seiser (eds) *Verkehren der Geschlechter. Reflexionen und Analysen von Ethnologinnen*, Vienna: Wiener Frauenverlag, 1989.

2 In German, *Ohnmacht* has the double meaning of a state of fainting and lack of power (M. G.).

3 The association 'Miteinander lernen – Birlikte öğrenelim' (Learning Together – Educational Activities with Women and Children from Foreign Countries) is an organization of women from Turkey and Austria. The activities of the association consist of German classes, literacy courses, groups for pre-school activities and social work. At the time being, there are thirteen women working for the association, some as employees but some of them also as freelancers or in an honorary capacity.

4 These questions have to be put time and again, even in our society. Christina Thürmer-Rohr's (1987) caring look at the female 'Mittäterschaft' (complicity) in contemporary Western society does this just as much as Mathieu's (1985) unkind revelation of the male short-sightedness of Godelier's (1984) concept of the consent of the dominated ones to their domination.

5 *Frauen und ihre Arbeit erleiden einen Verlust an gesellschaftlicher Präsenz, die sie nicht trotz, sondern aufgrund der Abtrennung der sozialen und ökonomischen Welt der Frauen von der der Männer vorher besaßen*

und deren relative, wenn auch untergeordnete Eigenständigkeit sie nicht trotz, sondern aufgrund des Gleichheitspostulats geknüpft an den abstrakten, vorgeblich geschlechtsneutralen Wertmesser Geld, nun nicht mehr behaupten können.

6 The patriarchal domination clearly defined by social rules is the domination of the fathers over the sons. The rules of authority are known to everyone, the exertion of power against women is men's right, and women experience force directly. Women are not identified with men, i.e. they do not endanger the power of the men. The perpetrators are less anonymous. Sexist domination is the domination of men *qua* sex over the women as a sex. It is determined by the postulate of equality and by the access of women to money as a means of power. In this case, women endanger the power of men. The consequence is haphazard violence and an anonymization of the perpetrators. The protective function of the patriarchal extended family lapses and woman must protect herself on her own (Bennholdt-Thomsen *et al.* 1987: 22*ff*).

7 This term was defined by Maria Mies, Claudia von Werlhof and Veronika Bennholdt-Thomsen referring to proletarianization. The development of this term was elaborated by Mies (1983).

8 *. . . muß, wie in jeder anderen Forschung auch, entschieden werden, welche Forschungsmethoden der jeweiligen Fragestellung angemessen sind. 'Frauenforschung' selbst ist also keine Methode, sondern ein methodologisch bzw. politisch eigenständiger Forschungsansatz. Die tatsächliche Präferenz für qualitative Methoden ist Resultat der politisch-inhaltlichen Positionen und Erkenntnisinteressen, die damit aber nicht zu weiblichen Methoden avancieren.*

9 *. . . daß sie nämlich immer als politisch motivierte Forschung verstanden werden will und verstanden werden kann, in der nicht Beliebigkeit, sondern konkrete Erfahrung, Subjektivität und politisches Interesse zentrale Forschungskategorien sind.*

10 The contact lenses created some problems for the one who wore them and again and again they gave us both a good opportunity to work off our bottled-up aggressions.

11 *Nicht alle Ethnologinnen haben diesen Vorteil (des Zugangs zur Frauenwelt als Frau) zugunsten ihrer Feldforschung bewußt genutzt. Manche sind der Versuchung, eine männliche Rolle in einer männlichen Umgebung zu spielen, erlegen.*

12 *'Gavur'* means unbelieving as well as merciless, cruel.

13 At the moment, we are both working in the Coordination Office of the Educational and Advisory Institutions for Women from Foreign Countries.

14 Currently there are (officially) 413,392 foreigners living in Austria (approximately 6 per cent of the total population), among which 103,800 are from Turkey, 58,000 men and 45,800 women; the percentage of foreigners in Vienna is 11.1 per cent of the total population (from: Österreichisches Statistisches Zentralamt – Bevölkerungsfortschreibung 1990). Unofficial estimates place the percentage far above these numbers.

15 In Austria, all foreigners are subject to the regulations of the 'Ausländerbeschäftigungsgesetz' (law regulating the access of foreigners to the

labour market). Employment is only granted if the situation and development of the labour market allows it. Only after five years of legal employment in the federal territory is it possible for a foreign resident to choose a place of work without direct control of the labour exchange.

16 This anthology *Aufstand im Haus der Frauen. Frauenforschung aus der Türkei* was edited in German by Ayla Neusel, Sirin Tekeli and Meral Akkent, and in Turkish by Sirin Tekeli (Turkish title: *Kadın Bakış Açışdan 1980 'ler Türkiye' sinde Kadinlar*) at the same time. Soon to appear in English and French.

17 *Die Hysteriker, so behaupte ich, sind alles andere als Kranke, die an Ichlosigkeit leiden. Daß sie an etwas leiden, ist gewíß, aber an dem, was ihnen unterstellt wird leiden sie eben nicht. Sie sind viel mehr der (vielleicht stärkste) Ausdruck einer Auflehnung gegen die ich-Vernichtung, die auf kollektiver Ebene stattfindet. Die hysterische Symptombildung ist der individuelle Ausdruck eines kollektiven Leidens und der Versuch, die Ursache des Leidens zu bekämpfen – und eben weil sie über das Individuum, ihren Träger hinaus das kollektive Leiden offenbart, wird sie immer nur als die Krankheit des einzelnen behandelt. Wenn es eine Krankheit gibt, bei der es sich anbieten würde, von kollektiven Ursachen zu sprechen, dann ist es diese, die über Jahrtausende auf das eine Geschlecht beschränkt blieb – ohne daß sich dafür eine biologische Ursache finden ließ.*

7 The differences within and the differences between

Henrietta L. Moore

The anthropological study of gender and gender relations has produced, over the last twenty years, both new ethnography and theoretical illumination. It is a notable feature of the study of gender in
anthropology that new theoretical insights have been sustained by
very detailed ethnographic material. In the initial stages of what
came to be known as the 'anthropology of women', arguments
about the universality of male domination gave rise to a series of
new ethnographic studies of women's lives and their perceptions of
their lives (Rosaldo and Lamphere 1974; Reiter 1975). Explanations
for the universality of male domination were sought through the
investigation of a number of analytical dichotomies which were said
to characterize gender relations in all societies. These dichotomies –
nature/culture, public/private (Ortner 1974; Rosaldo 1974; Ardener
1975a) – were subsequently re-examined by a number of scholars
who challenged both the content of the categories and their universal applicability (MacCormack and Strathern 1980; Rosaldo
1980). Variability in the content of these categories only became
clear as a result of detailed ethnographic work and, through the
new data made available, it became obvious that these categories
were a feature of anthropological discourse rather than of the social
or symbolic systems of the societies studied by anthropologists.

In a recent summary of these developments, Jane Collier and
Sylvia Yanagisako point out the pervasive nature of analytical
dichotomies in general anthropological theorizing, and especially in
explanations of gender and gender relations (Collier and Yanagisako 1987b: 18). They demonstrate that the nature/culture opposition owes much to structuralist theorizing, while the public/
private distinction has strong allegiances with the structural-func-
tionalist tradition (1987b: 18). However, they also argue that such
binary thinking is a notable feature of more recent attempts to

account for gender and gender relations, including Marxist and feminist-Marxist efforts to explain gender relations as the outcome of the specific relationship established between production and reproduction in given contexts. Collier and Yanagisako (1987b: 20–5) maintain that the distinction between production and reproduction is simply part of a Western folk model which distinguishes between the production of people and the production of things. It is, therefore, quite unsurprising to discover, as has been suggested by other scholars, that culture/nature, public/private and production/reproduction are actually transformations of one another, since they are all part of the same Western folk model. They should be understood as features of anthropological discourse rather than as features of other cultural discourses (1987b: 20). They are clearly anthropological imports rather than natural facts.

A further point concerning the analytical dichotomies which inform the anthropological analysis of gender and gender inequality is that they are always hierarchically or inclusively organized. Thus, culture is superior to nature, and the public world of men encompasses the private world of women (Ortner 1974; Strathern 1981; Collier and Yanagisako 1987b: 28). Notions of hierarchy and encompassment, therefore, inform anthropological understandings of gender difference, of the distinction between the categories female and male, of the differences between women's and men's world-views, and of the differences between women's and men's sociological roles. The problem of hierarchy has been recognized in some recent debates, where both Marxist and non-Marxist scholars have suggested that one of the more notable failures of the anthropology of gender has been the inability to think about difference without implying hierarchy (Leacock 1978; Etienne and Leacock 1980; Bell 1983; Strathern 1987). The chapters in this volume make it very clear that the problems of hierarchy and encompassment still shadow discussions of difference and sameness in anthropological theorizing, and that these problems seriously undermine the ability of anthropologists to comprehend gender equalities, as well as inequalities.

SAMENESS AND DIFFERENCE I

Debates about sameness and difference are central to the enterprise of anthropology as the comparative study of human societies, and they are equally important in the study of gender and gender relations. From the earliest stages of the feminist critique within the discipline, researchers emphasized the cross-cultural variability in the categories 'male' and 'female', and in the activities and behaviours of women and men. The result was not only an emphasis on the differences between cultures, but an emphasis on the fact of differences between women and men. Similarities between women and men were rarely, if ever, discussed. This was partly because of the apparent focus on gender difference in indigenous discourses and partly because of an enduring confusion in anthropological theory about whether similarity implies sameness, and about whether sameness implies equality. In Chapter 5, Marianne Gullestad comments perceptively on the anthropological neglect of the similarities between women and men.

Many of the contributors to this volume exhibit considerable unease when it comes to the question of how to handle sameness and difference analytically. This is partly because the whole debate on sameness and difference has received new impetus in feminist anthropology and in feminism in general through the critique of the unitary category 'woman'. One important question to arise out of this critique is whether or not gender difference should be privileged over all other forms of difference. If gender makes a difference, then so too do race, class, sexuality, religion and other forms of difference. The question which follows is how are the intersections between these different forms of difference to be theorized, and how are they to be acted on politically? This is a question addressed by Strasser and Kronsteiner (Chapter 6). However, while the primacy of gender difference is being questioned, and rightly so, several chapters demonstrate that gender difference is not the stable concept that anthropologists had assumed it to be.

Both Stolcke (Chapter 1) and Howell and Melhuus (Chapter 2) begin their discussions of gender difference with the position adopted by Collier and Yanagisako that interrogates the assumption that biological sex differences are the basis for gender differences.

> Although we do not deny that biological differences exist between men and women (just as they do among men and among women), our analytic strategy is to question whether these differences are the universal basis for the cultural categories 'male' and 'female'. In other words, we argue against the notion that cross-cultural variations in gender categories and inequalities are merely diverse elaborations and extensions of the same natural fact.
>
> (Collier and Yanagisako 1987b: 15)

This statement should not seem particularly radical given that feminist anthropology has, from the start, sought to problematize the relationship between sex and gender, and has emphasized that sex differences do not account for variability in gender constructs. However, Collier and Yanagisako are seeking to go a stage further by trying to prise anthropological discourse away from the necessary relationship between sex and gender which it posits. In other words, they want to question the biological basis for gender categories, and they want to undermine the idea that behind culturally determined gender constructs there is a set of biological categories which, while they do not determine gender constructs, provide the basic starting point for them. What is interesting in this regard is how very difficult this project is likely to be. While the chapters begin by endorsing Collier and Yanagisako's position, their authors also express reservations about the prising apart of sex and gender, understandably unwilling to place themselves in the untenable position of suggesting that biological sex differences have nothing to do with gender constructs.

Stolcke offers a way forward in her discussion of the social construction of sex differences as natural facts, and she properly points to the political project involved in discourses which seek to locate social differences or distinctions in natural facts. She emphasizes the point that views of nature, biology and physiology – natural facts – are socio-political conceptualizations. In spite of Stolcke's criticisms of Collier and Yanagisako, this point is very close to one they make themselves, where they stress that the assumption of natural differences between women and men is part of a Western cultural conception, and that we should therefore view difference, including so-called naturally occurring differences, as social constructions (Collier and Yanagisako 1987b: 29).

This kind of debate marks a step forward in the anthropological study of gender because it moves away from the view that variation in gender constructions and roles are merely cultural elaborations of the facts of biological sex difference, toward analysing the ways in which cultures actually construct differences between women and men – as well as other forms of difference – and why they construct those differences in the way that they do. The ground for the analysis of difference has thus shifted. However, there is clearly much more work to be done, and it is possible to interpret Collier and Yanagisako's position as a call for a more radical Foucauldian reading of variable cultural discourses on gender.

There are now a number of very powerful and pertinent feminist critiques of Foucault's work: from the anthropological point of view it clearly presents problems of ethnocentrism (Benhabib and Cornell 1987; Spivak 1987; Fraser 1989, Chapters 1–3; Harstock 1990). However, in the context of the consistent anthropological tendency to posit biological sexual difference underlying cultural constructions, it is worth noting once more Foucault's argument in *The History of Sexuality Vol. I*: 'Sex' is an effect rather than an origin, that far from being a given and essential unity, it is, as a category, the produce of specific discursive practices.

> The notion of 'sex' made it possible to group together, in an artificial unity, anatomical elements, biological functions, conducts, sensations, and pleasures, and it enabled one to make use of this fictitious unity as a causal principle, an omnipresent meaning; sex was thus able to function as a unique signifier and as a universal signified.
>
> (Foucault 1984: 154)

His basic argument is that the notion of 'sex' does not exist prior to its determination within a discourse in which its constellations of meanings are specified, and that therefore bodies have no 'sex' outside discourses in which they are designated as sexed. The construction of fixed binary sexes, with fixed categorical differences, is thus an effect of discourse. If sex is an effect of discourse, then it cannot be seen as a unitary essentialism, and, more importantly, it cannot be seen as invariant or natural. Biomedical discourse, which seeks to establish 'sex' for us, is itself framed by gendered meanings (Hubbard 1990). Two quite radical positions follow from this point.

First, in terms of anthropological discourse, the distinction between sex and gender on which feminist anthropology has rested its case falls away. As Judith Butler points out, in her brilliant reading of the above passage from Foucault, perhaps there is no distinction to be made between sex and gender after all (Butler 1990: 92). The second, which follows from the first, is that we cannot assume that binary biological sex everywhere provides the universal basis for the cultural categories 'male' and 'female'. If gender constructs are culturally variable, then so also are the categories of sexual difference.

The distinction which has to be made in this argument is between the social construction of binary sex categories, which are fixed and discrete, and the existence of physical variations in human populations, which are essential for the sexual reproduction of those populations. In order to argue that we should interrogate the social construction of fixed binary categories of sex, it is not necessary to argue that human populations around the world are unable to recognize differences in male and female genitalia, or that they are unable to recognize the different roles women and men have in sexual reproduction. It is clear that the recognition of such physical differences and capabilities does not automatically produce a discrete, fixed, binary categorization of sex in the manner of Western discourse. Ethnographic material suggests that the differences between women and men which other cultures naturalize and locate in the human body, and in features of the physical and cosmological environment, are not necessarily those which correspond to the constellation of features on which Western discourse bases its categorizations.

It is interesting to consider the ethnographic data on the Khumbo of Nepal provided by Hildegard Diemberger (Chapter 4) in this light. She demonstrates that the social differences between women and men are located in the body as natural differences, but the female and the male, as flesh and bone, are located in all bodies. The sexing of bodies and the constructions of gender in Khumbo discourse appear to collapse the difference established between sex and gender in anthropological discourse. Diemberger pushes her argument still further to demonstrate how the female and the male, flesh and bone, are constructed within Khumbo discourse as necessary features of bodily identity. These are not just procreation theories, which is the discursive disciplinary space to which anthropology normally confines such notions; they seem instead to be theories of social (gender) difference grounded in the physiology of the body, and are therefore also part of the biological facts of sex difference. The apparent collapse of the sex/gender distinction in Khumbo discourse, as we are used to it in anthropology, creates a certain confusion, which is usually resolved by assigning such female/male, flesh/bone notions (defined by Lévi-Strauss as occurring in many Asian societies) to the level of gender symbolism. However, it is clear from a reading of Diemberger's work that these notions are not just about gender (understood in the terms of the anthropological discourse), but that they are also about the categorization of sex difference, which is precisely why anthropology assigns them to the domain of procreation beliefs where the instability of their sex/gender status can be contained.

Diemberger confronts these difficulties in her paper. She demonstrates that bodily identity is part of a set of discursive practices – which she sometimes glosses, mistakenly I think, as linguistic, when they are clearly material, practical and linguistic – in which each 'child is appropriated [at the time of conception] by a socially and historically shaped interpretation of anatomic elements and physiological processes' (p. 106). This is very close to Foucault's own project, which is concerned with how the categories of sex and sexual differences get constructed within discourse as necessary features of bodily identity. The regulatory aspect of discursive practices, through which notions of identity and subjectivity are produced, is apparent from the ethnography. Diemberger tries to convey the effects of discourse on the sexed body when she says that it is a language of the body whose words and gestures appear as natural rules to the ideological background of gender relations.

In this argument there is no suggestion that Khumbo do not recognize the different roles of women and men in sexual reproduction or that they do not recognize the differences between male and female genitalia. The main point is that anthropology has the greatest difficulty in understanding categories of sex and notions of sexual difference which do not correspond neatly to discrete physical bodies already designated as sexually differentiated. Many of the differences which concern the Khumbo seem to be internal to bodies, that is, within them rather than between them.

SAMENESS AND DIFFERENCE II

The question of differences within rather than between is relevant to the way in which many chapters in this volume approach the analysis of gender models and gender meanings. In the early stages of the analysis of gender in anthropology, it was implicitly assumed that each society had a single gender ideology or model, and that such models were based on two discrete categories, the 'female' and the 'male'. It logically followed from this that the social valuations of women and men were equally monolithic, and could be correlated quite straightforwardly with the status of women in any particular society. The picture which has emerged from more recent ethnographic work is much more complex, and suggests that there is no single way of categorizing the female and the male, and no single gender ideology or model within any one society (Reeves Sanday and Goodenough 1990). The emphasis now is on variation within cultures, as well as variation between them.

This point is most clearly evident in Serge Tcherkezoff's chapter on Samoa. His material is particularly interesting because it highlights the fact that in most anthropological analyses of gender, the categories female and male are implicitly premised on the husband/wife dyad. The elision of the husband/wife dyad with the categories male/female, and the concomitant focus on relations between spouses as a gloss for gender relations in general, may explain why it has taken anthropology so long to recognize intracultural variation in gender models, meanings, categorizations and roles. Tcherkezoff's emphasis on the sister/brother pair raises some very interesting questions, including the problem of what gender really is and how to approach it analytically. Tcherkezoff explicitly says that sisters and brothers are not women and men. Sexuality and sexual reproduction are associated with women and men, but social reproduction and social continuity are associated with sisters and brothers. These two ideologies or models clearly affect the self-understandings and the gender identity of all women and men. However, Tcherkezoff makes it clear that questions of gender and the cultural construction of the categories female and male are anthropological questions, and that they confuse rather than illuminate the Samoan material. In his chapter, Tcherkezoff tackles both this and the further question of what the anthropological term gender is supposed to designate. He concludes that sisters are not considered feminine, and they are not representatives of the category woman. Gender, insofar as it designates any category, identity or role in Samoan discourse, appears to apply to women and men who are actively involved in sexual relationships with each other. This would seem to validate the unacknowledged anthropological strategy of glossing gender categories and roles with the husband/wife pair. However, it does leave the problem of what to do with the meanings, beliefs and roles associated with sisters and brothers, and it raises the issue, once again, of the relationship which anthropological discourse establishes between sex and gender.

In terms of the established discourse within anthropology, persons who possess the appropriate physical attributes, notably female genitalia, are held to be members of the category 'woman'. Variation, where it exists, resides in the different meanings given to that category, and in the different beliefs about, and tasks prescribed to, persons who are so characterized. If, however, sisters are not women, then a particular sort of difficulty is raised, because it means that persons with the appropriate physical attributes are not always in the category 'woman' or, at least, not in all contexts. Western discourse, as it informs anthropology, does not find it easy to comprehend how persons can sometimes be in the category woman and sometimes not. This is because of the complex set of links that it establishes between sex, gender identity and person-hood. In Western discourse, sex/gender is at the core of person-hood, so much so, that if someone you know as a man suddenly announces that he is a woman, he literally becomes a different person.

Howell and Melhuus (Chapter 2) discuss the emergence of the investigation of indigenous concepts of personhood as a major domain of study within anthropology. They rightly point to the extraordinary male bias present in this field, and to the consistent tendency to ascribe fixed and singular concepts of personhood to different cultures in a way that takes no account of gender. Pre-sented as gender-neutral, these concepts of personhood are fre-quently male persons in disguise. Howell and Melhuus convincingly identify the problem as arising within Western culture discourse itself. The problem of fixed and singular persons, whose conceptual-ization varies between cultures, but not within them, is analogous to the difficulty which anthropology has had with gender, where an overwhelming concern with inter-cultural variability has obscured the important fact of intra-cultural differences. Howell and Melhuus make the crucial point that concepts of personhood do vary within cultures, according to such factors as gender, age and class. Such variations are frequently linked to differential moral evaluations, and to specific ideas about agency and autonomy (Strathern 1981, 1984). Women and men are very often thought to be different sorts of persons, endowed with different attributes, and possessed of different natures and capabilities. Historians and political scientists, as well as other scholars, have examined notions of this kind in relation to Western cultural ideas (e.g. Riley 1988). Once again, it is clear that differences within are crucial.

The more pressing difficulty with concepts of personhood, how-ever, is whether or not they are always gendered, and thus whether or not gender is always at the core of personhood. Howell and Melhuus question whether it is possible for an idea of personhood which is not gendered to exist. Such a question can be approached through the collection of more empirical data, but what it prompts, more importantly, is an enquiry into the assumptions which underlie the anthropological discourses on personhood and gender identity (e.g. Strathern 1988). Much new research on the gendering of body parts, bodily substances and social acts, makes it clear that there is no one-to-one correspondence between gender identity, under-stood in terms of Western discourse, and notions of personhood. In other words, individual persons, while having recognizable biological features, may not have a singular gender identity in the way that anthropological discourse has conventionally understood this term. This is evident in Strathern's discussion of the partible, multiply-constituted person from whom aspects of identity may be detached (Strathern 1988). Anna Meigs (1990) points out that the Hua of the Eastern Highlands in Papua New Guinea do classify individuals by external genitalia, but that they also classify persons according to whether or not they possess greater or lesser amounts of male and/or female substances. The social categorization of persons is based on the amount of female substances their bodies have been in contact with. These substances are transferable between the genital classes through eating, heterosexual sex and everyday casual contact (1990: 108–19). The result is that a genitally male person may be classified as female, and a genitally female person as male. In such cases, it seems clear that concepts of personhood, including notions of moral worth, agency and autonomy, are gendered, but that they are not gendered in the sense that they correspond to the discrete binary categories female and male when these are premised on the discrete categorization of biological sex differences evidenced by external genitalia.

Howell and Melhuus point to the search for unity which seems to characterize the anthropological enquiry into indigenous concepts of personhood, and are anxious to emphasize the fact that more than one concept of personhood may exist in any particular society and that gender differences are relevant to the concepts of personhood. However, it is clearly necessary to go beyond this position and recognize that the increasing evidence for the instability of the sex/gender distinction, as anthropology has conventionally applied it, complicates the investigation of indigenous concepts of personhood still further. Once more, it becomes crucial to investigate differences within categories and entities, as well as between them, and this applies to the categories woman and man, the categories female and male, and the social entities of cultures, bodies and persons.

SAMENESS AND DIFFERENCE III

Anthropological theorizing is much indebted to post-Enlightenment thought, and to the notion of persons as autonomous, rational and self-determining. These ideas, which have been much criticized in contemporary postmodernist and deconstructionist writing, underpin a notion of the knowing subject which is unitary and which authors its experiences in the world. In spite of ethnographic data to the contrary, much anthropological writing on the person still proceeds on the implicit assumption that the physically discrete nature of the body is somehow evidence for the unity of the person. However much cultural notions of the person may vary, they will still be premised on the existence of discrete physical bodies. This rather strange assumption is a legacy of anthropology's long-running dispute with psychoanalysis, and with the discipline's resistance to Lacanian and post-Lacanian theorizing. Anthropology, while it talks of persons and selves, rarely speaks of subjects. The result of this is an inability to investigate the differences within individual subjects, those very differences which constitute them as subjects.

One important point in this regard is the insistence in contemporary theorizing that the unity of the subject is illusory or fictive, that is, it has to be created. Marianne Gullestad (Chapter 5) provides ethnographic data in her paper to support this point. She shows how Norwegians create the experience of a whole person, and of a unified family, through the processes of externalizing and objectifying the idea of wholeness in the physical arrangements of the house. There is much ethnographic data to support arguments about the constructed nature of the concept of the person and of personal identity itself. However, these arguments have found little support in anthropology in general. This is partly because of the specific ways in which anthropology has engaged with the politics of representation. In the early decades of the twentieth century, the insistence on the unitary, autonomous and rational nature of all human subjects was part of anthropological attempts to counter racist, discriminatory and pathologizing accounts of non-Western peoples. With hindsight, this particular anthropological position does not seem especially radical, but it did profoundly influence the nature of anthropological theorizing. At the present time, and in the context of new theories of ethnographic writing, it has become equally important to assert the validity of informants' interpretations and experiences. The result is that anthropology is still beset with the problem of how or whether to represent 'the other' – and for this reason finds it exceptionally difficult to imagine how it is possible to take on neo-Lacanian ideas of the constitution of subjectivity, without representing the subjects of anthropological enquiry as fragmented, illusory and, possibly, pathological. The point has also been taken up by feminist scholars in other disciplines (e.g. Mascia-Lees *et al.* 1989; Flax 1987). The problem for anthropology is how to acknowledge multiple differences and multiple identities within the subject, without representing the subject as somehow negative or damaged. This problem is acute because if anthropology is to be able to theorize the similarities and differences between people, and if feminist anthropology is to be able to theorize and politically organize in the face of the recognition of differences between women, then we can no longer proceed as if categories of difference were simply attached to persons. We have to begin to recognize how persons are constituted in and through difference. Multiple forms of difference – race, class, gender, sexuality – intersect within individuals, and identity is therefore premised on difference. The pressing task for the anthropology of the future is that we must begin to acknowledge the differences within rather than simply the differences between.

References

Abadan-Unat, N. (ed.) (1985) *Die Frau in der türkischen Gesellschaft*, Frankfurt/Main: Dağyeli.

Aiono, F. (1984a) 'The confessions of a bat', *Savali*, English edition, Apia, Western Samoa, July: 22–9.

—— (1984b) 'Correspondence', *Oceania* 55, 2: 145–6.

—— (1986) 'Western Samoa: the sacred covenant', in *Land Rights of Pacific Women* (coll. eds.), Suva: Institute of Pacific Studies, pp. 103–10.

Allen, N. J. (1976) 'Sherpa kinship terminology in diachronic perspective', *Man*, 11: 569–87.

Allione, T. (1986) *Women of Wisdom*, London: Routledge & Kegan Paul. (First edition 1984.)

Altorki, S. and Fawzi El-Sohl, C. (eds) (1988) *Arab Women in the Field. Studying Your Own Society*, New York: Syracuse University Press.

Amadiume, I. (1987) *Male Daughters, Female Husbands. Gender and Sex in an African Society*, London: Zed Books.

Appadurai, A. (1986) 'Introduction: commodities and the politics of value', in A. Appadurai (ed.) *The Social Life of Things. Commodities in Cultural Perspective*, Cambridge: Cambridge University Press.

Ardener, S. (ed.) (1975a) *Perceiving Women*, London: Dent.

—— (1975b) 'Belief and the problem of women', in S. Ardener (ed.) *Perceiving Women*, London: Dent.

Aziz, B. N. (1978) *Tibetan Frontier Families*, New Delhi: Vikas.

Bacot, J., Thomas, F. W. and Touissant, C. (1940) *Documents de Touenhouang relatifs a l'histoire du Tibet*, Paris: Librairie Orientaliste Paul Geuthner.

Balibar, E. (1990) [1988] 'Gibt es einen "Neo-Rassismus"?', in E. Balibar and I. Wallerstein, *Rasse, Klasse, Nation. Ambivalente Identitäten*, Hamburg: Argument-Verlag, pp. 23–38.

Banton, M. (1988) 'Which relations are racial relations?', Presidential address to the Royal Anthropological Institute, 29 June, London.

—— (1989) 'Science, law and politics in the study of racial relations', Presidential address to the Royal Anthropological Institute, 28 June, London.

Barker, M. (1981) *The New Racism*, London: Junction Books.

Barnes, R., de Coppet, D. and Parkin, L. (eds) (1985) *Contexts and Levels* (Oxford symposium in anthropology, 1983), Oxford: JASO.

Bell, D. (1983) *Daughters of Dreaming*, Melbourne: McPhee Gibble.

bell hooks (1984) *Feminist Theory. From Margin to Center*, Boston: South End Press.

Bender, D. R. (1967) 'A refinement of the concept of household: families, co-residence and domestic functions', *American Anthropologist* 69: 491–504.

Benedict, P. K. (1942) 'Tibetan and Chinese kinship terms', *Harvard Journal of Asiatic Studies* 6, 34: 313–37.

Benhabib, S. and Cornell, D. (1987) *Feminism as Critique: Essays on the Politics of Gender in Late-Capitalist Societies*, Cambridge: Polity Press.

Bennholdt-Thomsen, V., Dokter, A., Firat, G., Holzer, B. and Marciniak, K. (1987) *Frauen aus der Türkei kommen in die Bundesrepublik*, Bremen: Edition CON.

Berghe, van den, P. L. (1986) 'Ethnicity and the sociological debate', in J. Rex and D. Mason (eds) *Theories of Race and Ethnic Relations*, Cambridge: Cambridge University Press.

Biddiss, M. D. (1972) 'Racial ideas and the politics of prejudice, 1850–1914', *The Historical Journal* 15, 3.

Bloch, M. (1986) *From Blessing to Violence*, Cambridge, New York, New Rochelle, Melbourne and Sydney: Cambridge University Press.

Borchgrevink, T. and Melhuus, M. (1985) 'Familie og arbeid. Fokus på sjømannsfamilier, *Report No. 27*, Oslo: Work Research Institute.

—— and Solheim, J. (1989) 'Kjønn og modernitet', Research proposal to Norwegian Council for Scientific Research (NAVF) on 'Basic research on women'.

Borish, S. M. (1991) *The Land of the Living. The Danish Folk High Schools and Denmark's Non-Violent Path to Modernization*, Nevada City, CA: Blue Dolphin Publishing.

Bourdieu, P. (1977a) *Outline of a Theory of Practice*, Cambridge: Cambridge University Press. (First published in French, 1972.)

—— (1977b) 'The Kabyle house or the world reversed', in *Algeria 1960*, Cambridge: Cambridge University Press.

Braun, C. von (1990) [1985] *Nichtich. Logik, Lüge, Libido*, Frankfurt/Main: Neue Kritik.

Bridenthal, R., Grossmann, A. and Kaplan, M. (eds) (1984) *When Biology Became Destiny: Women in Weimar and Nazi Germany*, New York: Monthly Review Press.

Brox, O. (1984) *Nord-Norge. Fra allmenning til koloni*, Oslo: Universitetsforlaget.

Butler, J. (1987) 'Variations on sex and gender: Beauvoir, Wittig and Foucault', in S. Benhabib and D. Cornell (eds) *Feminism as Critique*, Cambridge: Polity Press.

—— (1990) *Gender Trouble: Feminism and the Subversion of Identity*, London: Routledge.

Bynum, C. W. (1986) 'Introduction', in C. W. Bynum, S. Harrell and P. Richman (eds) *Gender and Religion: On the Complexity of Symbols*, Boston: Beacon Press.

—— (1989) 'The female body and religious practice in the later middle ages', in Michel Feher *et al.* (eds) *Fragments for a History of the Human Body*, vol. I, Boston: Zone/MIT Press, pp. 161–219.

Caplan, P. (ed.) (1987) *The Cultural Construction of Sexuality*, London: Routledge.

Carby, H. V. (1985) 'On the threshold of woman's era: lynching, empire and sexuality in black feminist theory', in L. Gates Jr. (ed.) *'Race', Writing and Difference*, Chicago: University of Chicago Press.

Caritas Española (1988) *Situación en España de los immigrantes procedentes de países de mayoría islámica*, La Acción Social, Madrid.

Carrithers, M., Collins, S. and Lukes, S. (eds), (1985) *The Category of the Person: Anthropology, Philosophy, History*, Cambridge: Cambridge University Press.

Cashmore, E. E. (1984) *Dictionary of Race and Ethnic Relations*, London: Routledge.

Centre for Contemporary Cultural Studies, University of Birmingham (1982) *The Empire Strikes Back: Race and Racism in 70s Britain*, London: Hutchinson.

Clarke, G. (1980) 'The temple and kinship among a Buddhist people of the Himalaya', PhD thesis, Oxford: University of Oxford.

Collier, J. and Yanagisako, S. J. (eds) (1987a) *Gender and Kinship: Essays Toward a Unified Analysis*, Stanford: Stanford University Press.

—— (1987b) 'Toward a unified analysis of gender and kinship', in J. F. Collier and S. J. Yanagisako (eds) *Gender and Kinship: Essays Toward a Unified Analysis*, Stanford: Stanford University Press.

Conze, W. 'Rasse', Brunner, O., Conze, W. and Koselleck, R. (eds) (1984) *Geschichtliche Grundbegriffe: Historisches Lexikon zur politisch-sozialen Sprache in Deutschland*, vol. 5, Stuttgart: Klett-Cotta.

Corlin, C. (1978) 'A Tibetan enclave in Yunnan: land, kinship and inheritance in Gyethang', in M. Brauen and P. Kvaerne (eds) *Tibetan Studies, Presented at the Seminar of Young Tibetologists Zurich, June 26th-July 1st 1977*, Zurich: Museum für Völkerkunde der Universität Zürich.

Corominas, J. (1982) *Diccionario Crítico Etimológico Castellano e Hispànico*, Madrid: Editorial Gredos.

Csikszentmihalyi, M. and Rochberg-Halton, E. (1981) *The Meaning of Things. Domestic Symbols and the Self*, Cambridge: Cambridge University Press.

Cunningham, C. E. (1965) 'Order in the Atoni house', in W. A. Lessa and E. Z. Vogt (eds) *Reader in Comparative Religion. An Anthropological Approach*, New York: Harper & Row.

Dahl, H. F. and Vaa, M. (1980) *Norge. Paxleksikon*, vol. 4, Oslo: Pax Forlag.

Daly, M. (1973) *Beyond God the Father. Towards a Philosophy of Women's Liberation*, London: Women's Press.

Danielsen, K. (1984) 'Identitetsforvaltning blant gamle damer på Frogner', in I. Rudie (ed.) *Myk Start – Hard Landing*, Oslo: Universitetsforlaget, pp. 123–35.

del Valle, T. (1989) 'The current status of the anthropology of women: models and paradigms', in W. A. Douglass (ed.) *Essays in Basque Social Anthropology and History*, Reno: Universidad de Nevada-Reno, Basque Studies Program, pp. 129–47.

—— (1991) 'Género y sexualidad: aproximaciòn antropològica', in T. del

Valle and C. Sanz Rueda, *Gènero y Sexualidad*, Madrid: Fundaciòn Universidad Empresa, pp. 13–111.

—— and Sanz Rueda, C. (1991) *Género y Sexualidad*, Madrid: Fundaciòn Universidad Empresa.

——, Apalategi, J., Aretxaga, B., Arregui, B., Babace, I., Diez, M. C., Larrañaga, C., Oiarzabal, A., Pérez, C. and Zuriarrain, I. (1985) *Mujer vasca. Imagen y realidad*, Barcelona: Anthropos.

Delaney, C. (1986) 'The meaning of paternity and the virgin birth debate', *Man* 21, 3: 494–513.

di Coiri, P. (1990) 'Marco teórico-metodológico para la historia de las mujeres y de las relaciones de género', in P. Ballarín and T. Ortiz (eds) *La Mujer en Andalucía, Ier Encuentro Interdisciplinanio de Estudios de la Mujer*, Vol. I, Granada: FEMINAE, Universidad de Granada, Seminario de Estudios de la Mujer, pp. 127–36.

Diemberger, H. (1991) '*Lhakama* [*lha-bka'-ma*] and *Khandroma* [*mkha'-'gro-ma*]: The sacred ladies of Beyul Khenbalung [*sbas-yul mkhan-pa-lung*]', in E. Steinkellner (ed.) *Tibetan History and Language*, Vienna: Arbeitskreis für tibetische und buddhistische Studien Universität Wien.

—— (1992) '*Lovanga* (*Lo 'bangs pa?*) *Lama* and *Lhaven* (*Lha bon*): historical background, syncretism and social relevance of religious traditions among the Khumbo (East Nepal)', in S. Ihara and Z. Yamaguchi, *Proceedings of the 5th Seminar of the International Association of Tibetan Studies Narita (Japan) 1989*, Narita: Naritasan Shinshoj.

—— (forthcoming) '*Gangla* (*Gangs-la*), *Tsche chu* (*Tshe-chu*), *Beyul Khenbalung* (*sBas-yul mkhan-pa lung*) – Pilgrimage to hidden valleys, sacred mountains and springs of life water in southern Tibet', Contribution to International seminar 'Anthropology of Tibet and the Himalayas', September 21–28, 1990, Zurich, to be published in the proceedings.

—— and Schicklgruber, C. (forthcoming a) 'Pholha and Yullha among the Khumbo, North-eastern Nepal. The contradiction between residence and descent and its expression in religion', in A. Gingrich, S. Haas, S. Haas and G. Paleeczek, *Kinship, Social Change and Evolution*, Proceedings of the Symposium held on the Occasion of the 69th Birthday of Walter Dostal in Vienna, 7th and 8th April 1988, Vienna: Verlag Ferdinand Berger & Söhne.

—— and —— (forthcoming b) 'Beyul Khenbalung [*sBas-yul mkhan-pa-lung*], the hidden valley of the Artemisia – on Himalayan communities and their sacred landscape', in A. W. Macdonald (ed.) *Mandala and Landscape* (in press).

——, Hazod, G. and Schicklgruber, C. (1989) 'Mutterwort und Vaterfolge: Frauen und Mutter machen Gesellschaft – Das Beispiel der Khumbo', in *Von Fremden Frauen*, Frankfurt/Main: Suhrkamp.

Douglas, M. (1970) *Natural Symbols: Explorations in Cosmology*, New York: Pantheon Books.

Dowman, K. (1980) *The Divine Madman*, Clearlake (USA): The Dawn Horse Press.

—— (1984) *Sky Dancer – The Secret Life and Songs of the Lady Yeshe Tsogyel*, London: Routledge & Kegan Paul.

Dumont, L. (1966) *Homo Hierarchicus*, Paris: Gallimard. (English translation, 1970, Chicago: University of Chicago Press.)

—— (1979) 'Postface' to *Homo hierarchicus*, Paris: Gallimard (coll. 'Tel').

—— (1983) *Essais sur l'Individualisme*, Paris: Le Seuil.

—— (1986) *Essays on Individualism*, Chicago: University of Chicago Press.

Durkheim, E. (1964) *The Division of Labour in Society*, New York: The Free Press.

Erdheim, M. (1988) *Die gesellschaftliche Produktion von Unbewußtheit*, Frankfurt/Main: Suhrkamp.

Eriksen, T. H. (1991) 'A community of European Social Anthropologists', *Current Anthropology*, 32, 1 (February): 75–8.

Etienne, M. and Leacock, E. (eds) (1980) *Women and Colonisation*, New York: Praeger.

Europäisches Parlament (1990) *Bericht im Namen des Untersuchungsausschusses Rassimus und Ausländerfeindlichkeit*, Sitzungsdokumente Serie A-B – 195/90, Brussels.

Eyüboğlu, I. (1978) *Zeki: Cinci Büyüleri ve Yıldızname*, Istanbul: Seçme Kıtaplar.

Fatum, L. (1989) 'Women, symbolic universe and structures of silence. Challenges and possibilities in androcentric texts', *Studia Theologica* 43: 61–80.

Fernández Viguera, B. (1990) 'Pobreza femenina: una violencia desde la división sexual del trabajo', in V. Maquieira D'Angelo and C. Sánchez (eds) *Violencia y Sociedad Patriarcal*, Madrid: Editorial Pablo Iglesias, pp. 105–25.

Fiorenza, E. S. (1988) *In Memory of Her . . . a Feminist Theological Reconstruction of Christian Origins*, New York: Crossroads.

—— (1989) 'Text and reality – reality as text: the problem of a feminist historical and social reconstruction based on texts', *Studia Theologica* 43: 19–34.

Flax, J. (1987) 'Postmodernism and gender relations in feminist theory', *Signs* 12, 4: 621–43.

Fortes, M. (1953) 'The structure of unilineal descent groups', *American Anthropologist* 55: 17–41.

—— (1987) 'The concept of the person', in *Religion, Morality and the Person*, Cambridge: Cambridge University Press.

Foucault, M. (1984) *History of Sexuality, An Introduction*, Vol. I, Harmondsworth: Penguin.

Fox, R. (1967) *Kinship and Marriage*, Harmondsworth: Penguin Books.

Fraser, N. (1989) *Unruly Practices: Power Discourse and Gender in Contemporary Social Theory*, Cambridge: Polity Press.

Freeman, D. (1984) 'The Burthen of a Mystery', *Oceania* 54, 3: 247–54.

—— (1985) 'Reply to Shore', *Oceania* 55, 3: 214–18.

Freemantle, F. and Trungpa, C. (1975) (trans.) *The Tibetan Book of the Dead*, Berkeley: Shambala.

Gaenszle, M. (1989) 'Verwandtschaft und mythologie bei den Mewahang Rai in Ostnepal: studie zum problem der "ethnischen identität" ', PhD thesis, Heidelberg: University of Heidelberg.

Geertz, C. (1984) 'From the native's point of view', in R. Shweder and R. Levine (eds) *Culture Theory: Essays on Mind, Self and Emotion*, Cambridge: Cambridge University Press.

Glazer, N. and Moynihan, D. P. (eds) (1975) *Ethnicity: Theory and Experience*, Cambridge, MA: Harvard University Press.

Godelier, M. (1982) *La Production des Grands Hommes*, Paris: Fayard.

—— (1984) *L'idéel et le matériel. Pensée, économies, sociétés*, Paris: Fayard.

—— (1989) 'Sexualite, parente, pouvoir', in *Recherche* (numero special 'La Sexualité'), September, 213: 1141–55.

—— (1990) 'Inceste, parente, pourvoir', in *Psychanalystes* (numero special 'Le Sexuel Aujourd'hui'), September, 36: 33–51.

Goldstein, M. C. (1986) *English Tibetan Dictionary of Modern Tibetan*, Dharamsala (India): Library of Tibetan Works and Archives. (First edition, Berkeley, 1984.)

Gordon, L. (1977) *Woman's Body, Woman's Right*, Harmondsworth: Penguin.

Gould, S. J. (1991) 'The birth of the two-sex world', *The New York Review of Books*, June 13.

Griaule, M. and Dieterlen, G. (1954) 'The Dogon', in D. Forde (ed.) *African Worlds. Studies in the Cosmological Ideas and Social Values of African Peoples*, London: Oxford University Press.

Grønhaug, R. (1974) 'Micro-macro relations', Part II, *Bergen Occasional Papers in Social Anthropology*, 7, Bergen: University of Bergen.

Guidieri, R., Pellizi, F. and Tambiah, S. J. (eds) (1988) *Ethnicities and Nations: Processes of Interethnic Relations in Latin America, Southeast Asia, and the Pacific*, Rothko Chapel Book, Austin: University of Texas Press.

Guigo, D. (1986) 'Le systeme de parente tibetain', *L'Ethnographie*, LXXXII, 98–9: 71–117.

Gullestad, M. (1978) 'Arbeidsdeling, forvaltning av lønnsinntekter og makt i familien', *Tidsskrift for Samfunnsforskning*, Bind, 19: 415–30.

—— (1979) *Livet i en gammel bydel*, Oslo: Aschehoug.

—— (1984a) 'Sosialantropologiske perspektiver på familie og hushold', in I. Rudie (ed.) *Myk start – hard landing*, Oslo: Universitetsforlaget.

—— (1984b) *Kitchen-table Society*, Oslo: Universitetsforlaget; Oxford: Oxford University Press.

—— (1985) *Livsstil og likhet*, Oslo: Universitetsforlaget.

—— (1986a) 'Symbolic fences in urban Norwegian neighbourhoods', *Ethnos* 51: 102, 52–69.

—— (1986b) 'Equality and marital love. The Norwegian case as an illustration of a general Western dilemma', *Social Analysis* August, 19: 40–53.

—— (1989a) *Kultur og hverdagsliv*, Oslo: Universitetsforlaget.

—— (1989b) 'Small facts and large issues: the anthropology of contemporary Scandinavian society', *Annual Review of Anthropology* 18: 71–93.

—— (1989c) 'The meaning of nature in contemporary Norwegian everyday life. Preliminary considerations', *Folk* 31: 171–81.

—— (1990) 'Doing interpretive analysis in a modern large-scale society. The meaning of "peace and quiet" in Norway', *Social Analysis* 29: 38–61.

—— (1991) 'The transformation of the Norwegian notion of everyday life', *American Ethnologist* 18, 3: 480–97.

—— (1992) *The Art of Social Relations. Essays on Culture, Social Action and Everyday Life in Modern Norway*, Oslo Universitetsforlaget; Oxford: Oxford University Press.

Gunson, N. (1987) 'Sacred women chiefs and female "headmen" in Polynesian history', *Journal of Pacific History* 22, 3–4: 138–73.

Haavind, H. (1985) 'Power and love in marriage', in M. Holter (ed.) *Patriarchy in a Welfare Society*, Oslo: Universitetsforlaget.

Hall, E. T. (1973) *The Silent Language*, New York: Anchor Press/Doubleday. (First published by Doubleday & Co. in 1959.)

Haraway, D. (1989) *Primate Visions: Gender, Race and Nature in the World of Modern Science*, New York: Routledge.

Harding, S. (1986) *The Science Question in Feminism*, Milton Keynes: Open University Press, and Ithica: Cornell University Press.

Hartsock, N. (1990) 'Foucault on power: a theory for women?', in L. Nicholson (ed.) *Feminism/Postmodernism*, London: Routledge.

Hauser-Schäublin, B. (1985) 'Frau mit Frauen – Untersuchungen bei den Iatmul und Abelan, Papua Neuguinea', in H. Fischer (ed.) *Feldforschungen – Berichte zur Einführung in Probleme und Methoden*, Berlin: Dietrich Reimer Verlag, pp. 179–201.

Hazod, G. (1991) 'Die "Herkunft" und die "Ankunft" des tibetischen Königs', in E. Steinkellner (ed.) *Tibetan History and Language. Studies in Honour of Geza Uray*, Vienna: Arbeitskreis für Tibetische und Buddhistische Studien.

Heelas, P. and Lock, A. (1981) *Indigenous Psychology: Towards an Anthropology of the Self*, London: Academic Press.

Hirschon, R. (ed.) (1984) *Women and Property – Women as Property*, London: Croom Helm.

Hobsbawm, E. (1975) *The Age of Capital*, London: Weidenfeld and Nicolson.

Hofstadter, R. (1955) *Social Darwinism in American Thought*, Boston: Beacon Press.

Højrup, T. (1983a) *Det glemte folk*, Copenhagen: Institut for europeisk folkelivsforskning. (Statens byggeforskningsinstitut i Danmark.)

—— (1983b) 'The concept of life-mode. A form-specifying mode of analysis applied to contemporary Western Europe', *Ethnologia Scandinavica*: 15–20.

Holtedahl, L. (1986) *Hva mutter gjør er alltid viktig*, Oslo: Universitetsforlaget.

Howard, A. (1970) *Learning to be Rotuman*, New York: Teachers College Press, Columbia University.

Howell, S. (1984) 'Equality and hierarchy in Chewong classification', in R. H. Barnes, D. de Coppet and R. Parkin (eds) *Contexts and Levels*, Occasional Paper No. 5, Oxford: JASO.

Hubbard, R. (1990) *The Politics of Women's Biology*, Rutgers: Rutgers University Press.

Husband, C. (ed.) (1982) *'Race' in Britain: Continuity and Change*, London: Hutchinson.

Jacobsen-Widding, A. (ed.) (1983) *Identity: Personal and Socio-Cultural*, Uppsala: Acta Universitatis Upsaliensis.

Jaggar, A. M. (1983) *Feminist Politics and Human Nature*, Sussex: Harvester Press.

Jäschke, H. A. (1975) *A Tibetan English Dictionary*, Delhi: Motilal Banarsidass. (First edition, London, 1881.)

Jenkins, R. and Solomos, J. (1987) *Racism and Equal Opportunity Policies in the 1980s*, Cambridge: Cambridge University Press.

Jensen, A. R. (1969) 'How much can we boost IQ and scholastic achievement?', *Harvard Educational Review*, 39: 1–123.

Jordan, W. D. (1968) *White over Black: American Attitudes Toward the Negro 1550–1812*, Harmondsworth: Penguin.

Just, R. (1989) 'Triumph of ethnos', in E. Tonkin, M. McDonald and M. Chapman (eds) *History and Ethnicity*, London: Routledge.

Kamen, H. (1988) *La Inquisición Española*, Barcelona: Editorial Critica.

Kamu, L. (1988) Interview in *Matai Samoa* (film video), G. Milner (real. and prod.), Chr. Toren (interviewing), London: University of London Studio, K. Brooks (ed.), Royal Anthropological Institute, London, and Media Support and Development Centre, University of Manchester (distrib.).

Karmay, S. (1975) 'A general introduction to the history and doctrines of Bon', in *Memoirs of the Research*, Department of the Tokyo Bunko, 33: 171–218.

—— (1987) 'L'âme et la tourquoise', in *L'Ethnographie* XXXIII: 97–130.

Keesing, R. M. (1975) *Kin Groups and Social Structure*, New York: Holt, Rinehart & Winston.

Kirkpatrick, J. and White, G. M. (1985) 'Exploring ethnopsychologies', Introduction to J. Kirkpatrick and G. M. White (eds) *Person, Self and Experience. Exploring Pacific Ethnopsychologies*, Berkeley: University of California Press, pp. 3–34.

Krämer, A. (1902) *Die Samoa Inseln*, Stuttgart: E. Naegele.

Kvaerne, P. (1975) 'On the concept of Sahaja in Indian Buddhist Tantric literature', *Temenos*, II: 88–135.

Lalou, M. (1959) 'Fiefs, poisons et guerisseurs', *Journal Asiatique*, T.CCXLV, 1–2: 157–201.

Lamphere, L. (1977) 'Anthropology: a review essay', *Signs* 2, 3: 612–27.

Laqueur, T. (1991) *Making Sex: Body and Gender from the Greeks to Freud*, Cambridge, MA: Harvard University Press.

Lawrence, E. (1982) 'Just plain common sense: the "roots" of racism', in Centre for Contemporary Cultural Studies, University of Birmingham, *The Empire Strikes Back: Race and Racism in 70s Britain*, London: Hutchinson.

Leach, E. R. (1966) 'Virgin birth', *Proceedings of the Royal Anthropological Institute*: 39–50.

Leacock, E. (1978) 'Women's status in egalitarian society: implications for social evolution', *Current Anthropology*, 19, 2: 247–75.

Leeds, A. (1972) 'Darwinism and "Darwinian" evolutionism in the study of society and culture', in T. F. Glick (ed.) *The Comparative Reception of Darwinism*, Austin: University of Texas Press.

Lévi-Strauss, C. (1958) *Anthropologie Structurale*, Paris: Plon.

—— (1962) *La Pensée Sauvage*, Paris: Plon.

—— (1969) *The Elementary Structures of Kinship*, Boston: Beacon Press.

—— (1985) *The View from Afar*, New York: Basic Books.

Levine, N. (1988) *The Dynamics of Poverty*, Chicago and London: University of Chicago Press.

Love, J. W. (1983) 'Review of *Salailua: A Samoan Mystery* by Bradd Shore', *Pacific Studies* 7, 1: 122–45.

MacCormack, C. and Strathern, M. (eds) (1980) *Nature, Culture and Gender*, Cambridge: Cambridge University Press.

MacDonald, A. (1971) 'Une lecture des Pelliot tibetain 1286, 1287, 1038, 1047, et 1290 – essay sur le formation et l'emploi des mythes politiques dans la religion royale de Srong-bcan sgam-po', in *Etudes tibetaines dediées à la mémoire de Marcelle Lalou*, Paris: Adrien Maisonneuve.

McDonald, M. (1989) *We Are Not French! Language, Culture and Identity in Brittany*, London: Routledge.

—— (1990) 'Constructing genders. Panel report from the 1st EASA conference, Coimbra', *EASA Newletter* 3: 11–12.

McDougal, C. (1979) *The Kulunge Rai*, Katmandu: Ratna Pustak Books.

Mageo, J. M (Danaan) (1989) 'Aga, Amio and Loto: perspectives on the structure of the self in Samoa', *Oceania* 59, 3: 181–201.

March, K. S. (1987) 'Hospitality, women, and the efficacy of beer', in *Food and Foodways* 1: 351–87, London: Harwood Academic.

Marcu, J. (1987) 'Equal rites (?) and women in Turkey', *Mankind* 17, 2: 120–9.

Martin, E. (1987) *The Woman in the Body: A Cultural Analysis of Reproduction*, Boston: Beacon Press.

Martinez-Alier, V. (1989) *Marriage, Class and Colour in Nineteenth Century Cuba: A Study of Racial Attitudes and Sexual Values in a Slave Society*, 2nd edn, Ann Arbor: University of Michigan Press.

Mascia-Lees, F., Sharpe, P. and Ballerina-Cohen, C. (1989) 'The postmodernist turn in anthropology: cautions from a feminist perspective', *Signs* 15, 1: 7–33.

Mathieu, N-C. (1985) 'Quand ceder n'est pas consentir', in N-C. Mathieu (ed.) L'arraisonnement des femmes. Essais en anthropologie des sexes. Cahiers de l'homme, nouvelle série XXIV, Paris: EHESS, pp. 169–254.

Mauss, M. (1979) *Psychology and Sociology*, London: Routledge.

Mayr, E. (1982) *The Growth of Biological Thought: Diversity, Evolution and Inheritance*, Cambridge, MA: Harvard University Press.

Meigs, A. (1990) 'Multiple gender ideologies and statuses', in P. Reeves Sanday and R. Goodenough (eds) *Beyond the Second Sex*, Philadelphia: University of Pennsylvania Press.

Melhuus, M. (1990a) 'A shame to honour – a shame to suffer', *Ethnos* 1–2: 5–25.

Melhuus, M. (1990b) 'Gender and the problem of hierarchy', *Ethnos* 3–4.

—— (forthcoming) ' "I want to buy me a baby". Some reflections on gender and change in modern society', in T. Bleie, V. Broch-Due and I. Rudie (eds) *Symbols and Social Practices*, Oxford: Berg.

Meyer, F. (1988) *Gso-ba rig-paö*, Paris: Presses du CNRS.

Mies, M. (1983) 'Subsistenzproduktion, Hausfrauisierung, Kolonialisierung', in *Beiträge zur Feministischen Theorie und Praxis* 9–10: 115–24.

Miller, D. (1987) *Material Culture and Mass Consumption*, Oxford: Blackwell.

—— (1988) 'Appropriating the state on the council estate', *Man* 23: 353–72.

Moore, H. L. (1986) *Space, Text and Gender. An Anthropological Study of the Marakwet of Kenya*, Cambridge: Cambridge University Press.

—— (1988) *Feminism and Anthropology*, Cambridge: Polity Press.

Morgen, S. (1989) 'Gender and anthropology: introductory essay', in S. Morgen (ed.) *Gender and Anthropology. Critical Reviews for Research and Teaching*, Washington, DC: American Anthropological Association, pp. 1–20.

Morin, F. (1980) 'Identité ethnique et ethnicité. Analyse critique des travaux anglosaxons', in P. Tapp (ed.), *Identités collectives et changements sociaux*, Toulouse: Ed. Privat.

Nader. L. (1989) 'Orientalism, occidentalism and the control of women', *Cultural Dynamics* 2–3: 323–55.

Nash, J. (1989) 'Gender studies in Latin America', in S. Morgen (ed.) *Gender and Anthropology. Critical Reviews for Research and Teaching*, Washington DC: American Anthropological Association, pp. 228–45.

Nash, M. (1989) *The Cauldron of Ethnicity in the Modern World*, Chicago: University of Chicago Press.

Nawal el-Saadawi (1980) *The Hidden Face of Eve. Women in the Arab World*, London: Zed Press.

Needham, R. (1960) 'The Left Hand of the Mugwe', *Africa*, 30, 1: 20–33.

—— (1971) *Rethinking Kinship and Marriage*, ASA Monograph 11, London: Tavistock.

—— (ed.) (1973) *Right Hand, Left Hand: Essays on Dual Symbolic Classification*, Oxford: Oxford University Press.

—— (1980) *Reconnaissances*, Toronto: University of Toronto Press.

—— (1987) *Counterpoints*, Berkeley: University of California Press.

Neusel, A., Firin, J. and Meral, A. (eds) (1991) *Aufstand im Haus der Frauen. Frauenforschung aus der Türkei*, Berlin: Orlanda Frauenverlag.

Oppiz, M. (1968) *Geschichte und Sozialordnung der Sherpa*, Innsbruck and München: Universitätsverlag Wagner Ges.m.b.H.

—— (1988) *Frau für Fron*, Frankfurt/Main: Suhrkamp.

Ortner, S. B. (1974) 'Is female to male as nature is to culture?', in M. Rosaldo and L. Lamphere (eds) *Woman, Culture and Society*, Stanford: Stanford University Press.

—— (1981) 'Gender and sexuality in hierarchical societies: the case of Polynesia and some comparative implications', in S. Ortner and H. Whitehead (eds) *Sexual Meanings. The Cultural Construction of Gender and Sexuality*, Cambridge: Cambridge University Press, pp. 359–409.

—— and Whitehead, Harriet (eds) (1981) *Sexual Meanings. The Cultural Construction of Gender and Sexuality*, Cambridge: Cambridge University Press.

Paul, Diane Y. (1979) *Women in Buddhism. Images of the Feminine in Mahayana Tradition*, Berkeley: Asian Humanities Press.

Pelliot, P. (1963) *Notes on Marco Polo*, Vol. II, Paris: Librairie Adrien-Maisonneuve.

Peter, Prince of Greece and Denmark (1963) *A Study of Polyandry*, The Hague: Mouton.

Petersen, A. (1985) *Ehre und Scham. Das Verhältnis der Geschlechter in der Türkei*, Berlin: Express-Edition.

Poovey, M. (1986) 'Scenes of an indelicate character: the medical "treatment" of Victorian women', *Representations* 14: 137–68.

Potash, B. (1989) 'Gender relations in sub-Saharan Africa', in S. Morgen (ed.) *Gender and Anthropology. Critical Reviews for Research and Teaching*, Washington DC: American Anthropological Association, pp. 189–227.

Quinn, N. (1977) 'Anthropological studies of women's status', *Annual Review of Anthropology* 6: 181–225.

Reeves Sanday, P. and Goodenough, R. (eds) (1990) *Beyond the Second Sex: New Directions in the Anthropology of Gender*, Philadelphia: University of Pennsylvania Press.

Reiter, R. R. (ed.) (1975) *Toward an Anthropology of Women*, New York: Monthly Review Press.

Reme, E. (1988) 'Bilder av virkeligheten. Bilder som uttrykk for livserfaring og virkelighetsopfatning', unpublished hovedfag thesis, Bergen: University of Bergen, Department of European Ethnology.

Rex, J. (1973) *Race, Colonialism and the City*, London: Routledge.

—— (1986) *Race and Ethnicity*, Milton Keynes: Open University Press.

—— and Mason D. (eds) (1986) *Theories of Race and Ethnic Relations*, Cambridge: Cambridge University Press.

Rich, P. B. (1984) 'The long Victorian sunset: anthropology, eugenics and race in Britain, 1900–48', *Patterns of Prejudice* 18, 3.

—— (1986) *Race and Empires in British Politics*, Cambridge: Cambridge University Press.

Riley, D. (1988) *'Am I That Name?': Feminism and the Category of 'Women' in History*, London: Macmillan.

Rona-tas, A. (1955) 'Social terms in the list of grants of the Tibetan Tun-huang Chronicle', *Acta Orientalia Hungarica* V, 3: 249–70.

Rosaldo, M. (1974) 'Woman, culture and society: a theoretical overview', in M. Rosaldo and L. Lamphere (eds) *Woman, Culture and Society*, Stanford: Stanford University Press.

—— (1980) 'The use and abuse of anthropology: reflections on feminism and cross-cultural understanding', *Signs* 5, 3: 389–417.

—— and Louise Lamphere (eds) (1974) *Woman, Culture and Society*, Stanford: Stanford University Press.

Rose, E. J. B. (1969) *Colour and Citizenship: A Report on British Race Relations*, Oxford: Oxford University Press.

Rubin, G. (1975) 'The traffic in women: notes on the political economy of sex', in R. R. Reiter (ed.) *Towards an Anthropology of Women*, New York: Monthly Review Press.

Rudie, I. (1969/70) 'Household organization: adaptive process and restrictive form. A viewpoint on economic change', *Folk* 11–12: 185–200.

Sagant, P. (1985) 'With the head held high. The house, ritual and politics in eastern Nepal', *Kailash* XII, 3–4: 161–217.

Schicklgruber, C. (1992) 'Grib: on the significance of the term in a socio-religious context', in S. Ihara and Z. Yamaguchi, *Proceedings of the 5th Seminar of the International Association of Tibetan Studies Narita (Japan) 1989*, Narita: Naritasan Shinshoji.

—— (forthcoming) 'Who marries whom and why among the Khumbo', contribution to the International Seminar 'Anthropology of Tibet and the Himalayas', September 21st–28th, Zurich, to be published in the proceedings.

Schmitz, L. (1985) *Frauen und Sexualität in der Türkei*, Frankfurt/Main: Haag und Herchen.

Schneider, D. M. (1985) *A Critique of the Study of Kinship*, Ann Arbor: University of Michigan Press.

Schoeffel, P. (1978) 'Gender, status and power in Samoa', *Canberra Anthropology* 1, 2: 69–81.

—— (1979) 'Daughters of Sina: a study of gender, status and power in Samoa', PhD, Canberra, Australian National University.

—— (1985) 'Review of *Sala'ilua. A Samoan Mystery*' (by Bradd Shore, 1982), *Mankind* 15, 3: 257.

—— (1987) 'Rank, gender and politics in ancient Samoa: the genealogy of Salamasina O le Tafa'ifa', *Journal of Pacific History* 22, 3–4: 174–94.

Schultz, E. (1911) 'The most important principles of Samoan family law', *Journal of Polynesian Society* 20: 43–53.

Seyfort Ruegg, D. (1988) 'A Karma Bka' brGyud work on the lineages and traditions of the Indo-Tibetan dBu ma (Madhyamaka)', in G. Gnoli and L. Lanciotti *Orientalia Iosephi Tucci Memoriae Dicata*, Roma: Istituto Italiano per il Medio ed Estremo Oriente.

Shore, B. (1976) 'Incest prohibitions, brother–sister avoidance and the logic of power in Samoa', *Journal of Polynesian Society* 85, 2: 275–96.

—— (1981) 'Sexuality and gender in Samoa: conceptions and missed conceptions', in S. Ortner and H. Whitehead (eds) *Sexual Meanings. The Cultural Construction of Gender and Sexuality*, Cambridge: Cambridge University Press, pp. 192–215.

—— (1982) *Salailua. A Samoan Mystery*, New York: Columbia University Press.

—— (1983) 'A response to the Book Review forum', *Pacific Studies* 7, 1: 145–56.

—— (1984) 'Reply to Derek Freeman's review of *Salailua . . .* ', *Oceania* 54, 3: 254–60.

—— (1985) 'Response to Freeman', *Oceania* 55, 3: 218–23.

Showalter, E. (ed.) (1989) *Speaking of Gender*, New York: Routledge.

Shweder, R. and Levine, R. (1984) *Culture Theory: Essays on Self and Emotions*, Cambridge: Cambridge University Press.

Signs Editorial (1987) 'Within and without: women, gender, and theory', *Signs* 12.

Smith, B. (1982) 'Racism and women's studies', in G. T. Hull, P. Bell Scott and B. Smith (eds) *But Some of Us Are Brave*, Old Westburg, New York: The Feminist Press, pp. 48–50.

Smith M. G. (1986) 'Pluralism, race and ethnicity in selected African countries', in J. Rex and D. Mason (eds) *Theories of Race and Ethnic Relations*, Cambridge: Cambridge University Press.

Snellgrove, D. (1987) *Indo-Tibetan Buddhism*, Boston: Shambala.

—— and Richardson, H. (1980) *A Cultural History of Tibet*, Boulder: Prajna Press. (First edition, New York, 1968.)

Solheim, J., Heen, H. and Holter, Ø. G. (1986) 'Nordsjøliv og hjemmeliv', *Work Research Institute*, Report No. 35, Oslo.

Solomos, J. (1988) *Black Youth, Racism and the State: The Politics of Ideology and Policy*, Cambridge: Cambridge University Press.

Spelman, E. V. (1988) *Inessential Woman. Problems of Exclusion in Feminist Thought*, Boston: Beacon Press.

Spivak, G. (1987) *In Other Worlds: Essays in Cultural Politics*, London: Routledge.

Stein, R. A. (1972) *Tibetan Civilization*, London: Faber and Faber. (First edition in French, Paris, 1962.)

Stepan, N. (1982) *The Idea of Race in Science*, Oxford: St Antony's College/Macmillan Press.

Stolcke, V. (1981) 'Women's labours: the naturalisation of social inequality and women's subordination', in K. Young, C. Wolkowitz and R. McCullagh (eds) *Of Marriage and the Market. Women's Subordination Internationally and Its Lessons*, London: Routledge, pp. 159–77.

—— (1988) 'New reproductive technologies: the old quest for fatherhood', *Reproductive and Genetic Engineering* 1, 1: 5–19.

Strathern, M. (1981) 'Self-interest and the social good: some implications of Hagen gender imagery', in S. Ortner and H. Whitehead (eds) *Sexual Meanings. The Cultural Construction of Gender and Sexuality*, Cambridge: Cambridge University Press.

—— (1984) 'Domesticity and the denigration of women', in D. O'Brien and S. Tiffany (eds) *Rethinking Women's Roles: Perspectives from the Pacific*, Berkeley: University of California Press.

—— (1987) 'An awkward relationship: the case of feminism and anthropology', *Signs* 12, 2: 276–92.

—— (1988) *The Gender of the Gift*, Berkeley: University of California Press.

Szerb-Mantl, B. (forthcoming) 'Household in Lhasa', contribution to the International Seminar 'Anthropology of Tibet and the Himalayas', September 21st–28th 1990, to be published in the proceedings.

Tambiah, S. J. (1985) *Culture, Thought and Social Action. An Anthropological Perspective*, Cambridge, MA: Harvard University Press.

—— (1989) 'Ethnic conflict in the world today', *American Ethnologist* 16, 2.

Tcherkezoff, S. (1983) *Le roi Nyamwezi, le droite et la gauche. Revision comparative des classifications dualistes*, Paris: Maison des Sciences de l'Homme and Cambridge University Press. (English translation *Dual Classification Reconsidered*, Cambridge: Cambridge University Press, 1987.)

—— (1985) 'Black and white in Nyamwezi ideology', in R. Barnes, D. de Coppet and L. Parkin (eds) *Contexts and Levels* (Oxford symposium in anthropology, 1983), Oxford: JASO.

—— (1986a) 'Les amendes au roi en pays nyamwezi. La continuation du sacrifice par d'autres moyens', *Droits et cultures* 11: 89–110.

—— (1986b) 'Le prix de la vengeance ou la continuation du sacrifice', *Droits et Cultures* 10.

—— (1986c) 'Logique rituelle, logique du tout', *L'Homme* 100, 26, 4: 91–117.

—— (1989) 'Rituel et royauté sacrée. La double figure du Père', in A. Muxel and J. M. Rennes (eds) *Le Pere*, Paris: Denoel.

—— (forthcoming a) 'La question du "genre" à Samoa. D' l'illusion dualiste à la hiérarchie des niveaux', *Anthropologie et Sociétés* 16, 2 (in press).

—— (forthcoming b) 'Les enfants-de-la-terre à Samoa. La Terre et le sang, la maison-mère et le village exogame', *Etudes Rurales*, special issue 'La terre en Océanie', J. F. Baré (ed.) (in press).

—— (forthcoming c) 'Hierarchical reversal, ten years later. R. Needham's queries, India, Samoa, and the problem of ideology', *Journal of Anthropological Society of Oxford* (in press).

—— (forthcoming d) 'Une hypothèse sur la valeur du "prix de la fiancée" nyamwezi', in F. Heritier-Auge and E. Copet-Rougier (eds) *Les Complexities de l'alliance. Economie, politique et fondements symboliques de l'alliance, Volume 3: Afrique*, Paris: Editions des Archives Contemporaines ('ordres sociaux') (in press).

—— (1991) 'Temas de nuestra epoca', *El Pais* v, 210 (November): 1–8.

Thorsen, L. E. (1989) 'Det fleksible kjønn. Mentalitetsendringer i tre generasjoner bondekvinner, 1920–1985', unpublished doctoral dissertation, Oslo: University of Oslo, Department of European Ethnology.

Thürmer-Rohr, C. (1987) *Vagabundinnen. Feministische Essays*, Berlin: Orlanda Frauenverlag.

Tonkin, E., McDonald, M. and Chapman, M. (eds) (1989) *History and Ethnicity*, London: Routledge.

Tsuda, S. (1978) 'A Critical Tantrism', *The Memoirs of the Tokyo Bunko* 36: 167–231.

Tucci, G. (1966) *Tibetan Folk Songs from Gyantse and Western Tibet*, Ascona: Artibus Asiae.

—— and Heissig, W. (1970) *Die Religionen Tibets und der Mongolei*, Stuttgart, Berlin, Köln and Mainz: Kohlhammer.

Uebach, H. (1980) 'Notes on the Tibetan kinship term Dbon', in M. Aris and A. Kyi (eds) *Tibetan Studies in Honour of Hugh Richardson*, Warminster (England): Aris and Phillips.

Uray, G. (1960) 'The four horns of Tibet according to the royal annals', *Acta Orientalia Hungarica* X, 1: 31–57.

—— (1978) 'The Annals of the "A-za Principality" ', in L. Ligeti (ed.) *Proceedings of the Csoma de Koros Memorial Symposium*, Budapest: Akademiai Kiado.

—— (1982) 'Notes on the thousand-districts of the Tibetan empire in the first half of the ninth century', *Acta Orientalia Hungarica*, XXXVI, 1–3: 545–8.

—— (forthcoming) 'The personal names in the 7th–8th century Tibetan sources and the study of Tibetan history', paper read at the 2nd Hungarian Conference of Onomastics, Budapest, 1969, and published in Hungarian (Budapest: Akademiai Kiado 1970); to be published in English in a collection in honour of Burmiok Athing Densapa of Sikkim, Dharamsala (India): Library of Tibetan Works & Archives (in press).

Valcárcel, A. (1991) *Sexo y filosofía. Sobre 'mujer y poder'*, Barcelona: Anthropos.

Walsh, E. H. (1906) 'An old form of elective government in the Chumbi Valley', *Journal of the Asiatic Society of Bengal* July: 303–8.

Warren, C. A. B. (1988) 'Gender issues in field research', *Qualitative Research Methods* 9.

Warren, K. B. and Bourque, S. C. (1989) 'Women, technology, and development ideologies: frameworks and findings', in S. Morgen (ed.) *Gender and Anthropology. Critical Reviews for Research and Teaching*, Washington, DC: American Anthropological Association, pp. 382–410.

Weiner, A. (1976) *Women of Value, Men of Renown*, Austin: University of Texas Press.

—— (1985) 'Inalienable wealth', *American Ethnologist* 12, 2: 210–27.

—— (1987) 'Towards a theory of gender power: an evolutionary perspective', in M. Leyenaar *et al.* (eds) *The Gender of Power: A Symposium*, Leiden: Vakgroep Vrouwenstudies FSW, pp. 41–77.

—— (1989) 'Why Cloth? Wealth, gender and power in Oceania', in J. Schneider and A. Weiner (eds) *Cloth and Human Experience*, Washington: Smithsonian Institute Press, pp. 37–72.

White, G. M. (1984) 'Images of violence in a gentle society. Santa Isabel, Solomon Islands', conference paper to Symposium 'Gentleness and Violence in the Pacific' at the meeting of the American Anthropological Association, Denver, November 15–18.

—— (1985) 'Suicide and culture: island views', in F. X. Hezel, D. H. Rubinstein and G. M. White (eds) *Culture, Youth and Suicide in the Pacific*, Conference of the East–West Center, Working Papers of the Center for Pacific Islands Studies, Manoa: University of Hawaii, in collaboration with East–West Center, Honolulu.

Wiethold, B. (1981) *Kadınlarımız. Frauen in der Türkei*, Hamburg: ebr Rissen.

Wildt, C. (1987) 'Frauenforschung und feministiche Forschung', in A. Bell (ed.) *Furien in Uniform? Dritte österreichische Frauensommeruniversität*, Innsbruck: Vor-ort, pp. 141–57.

Wolpe, H. (1986) 'Class concepts, class struggle and racism', in J. Rex and D. Mason (eds) *Theories of Race and Ethnic Relations*, Cambridge: Cambridge University Press.

Wright, G. (1980) *Moralism and the Model Home. Domestic Architecture and Cultural Conflict in Chicago 1873–1913*, Chicago: University of Chicago Press.

Young, R. (1973) 'The historiographic and ideological contexts of the nineteenth century debate on man's place in nature', in M. Teich and R. Young (eds) *Changing Perspectives in the History of Science*, Boston: Kluwer.

Name index

Subject index